Media and Gender Adaptation

Media and Gender Adaptation

Regendering, Critical Creation and the Fans

Lucy Irene Baker

BLOOMSBURY ACADEMIC
NEW YORK • LONDON • OXFORD • NEW DELHI • SYDNEY

BLOOMSBURY ACADEMIC
Bloomsbury Publishing Inc
1385 Broadway, New York, NY 10018, USA
50 Bedford Square, London, WC1B 3DP, UK
29 Earlsfort Terrace, Dublin 2, Ireland

BLOOMSBURY, BLOOMSBURY ACADEMIC and the Diana logo are
trademarks of Bloomsbury Publishing Plc

First published in the United States of America 2023
Paperback edition published 2024

For legal purposes the Acknowledgements on p. viii constitute
an extension of this copyright page.

Cover image: *Elementary* TV Series, Season 2, 2013, Jonny Lee Miller, Lucy Liu,
Aidan Quinn, Jon Michael Hill © Hill of productions / Timberman Beverly productions /
CBS Television Studios / Collection Christophel / ArenaPAL www.arenapal.com

Bloomsbury Publishing Inc does not have any control over, or responsibility for,
any third-party websites referred to or in this book. All internet addresses given in this
book were correct at the time of going to press. The author and publisher regret any
inconvenience caused if addresses have changed or sites have ceased to exist,
but can accept no responsibility for any such changes.

A catalog record for this book is available from the Library of Congress.

ISBN: HB: 978-1-5013-7011-3
          PB: 978-1-5013-7010-6
          ePDF: 978-1-5013-7008-3
          eBook: 978-1-5013-7009-0

Typeset by Integra Software Services Pvt. Ltd.

To find out more about our authors and books visit www.bloomsbury.com
and sign up for our newsletters.

*My child, Fallon, for all your waking years this is what mama
has been doing and you have been an inspiration.
Thank you to my friends and family for all the help and support,
Ma for the love of reading and Da for the work ethic.
For all those who walked with me, thank you.*

Contents

Acknowledgements

I want to acknowledge the rightful custodians of the lands I was born on, wrote on, lived on; the Jagera, Turrabul, Quandamooka, the Kulin nations, the Arakwal and Bundjalung people, and others who I do not know. I am grateful to be here on your land.

Always was, always will be.

I want to thank Professors Belinda McKay and Pat Buckridge for seeing something in me all those years ago and supporting me in starting this journey. Dr David Ellison, Dr Margaret Gibson for the innumerable advice and revisions and assistance during the research for this. A very special thanks to Dr Amanda Howell for co-writing a different book with me during this time too, and for all the help along the way – who would have thought Godzilla would end up here? Dr Emily Hurren-Paterson for always being there too.

This research owes so much to so many in different fields. Dr Rukmini Pande was a beacon both at conferences and as a scholar, J. S. A Lowe was the right person at the right time, and Dr Kristina Busse helped shape this. Vale Kathy Larsen for an acafandom welcome extraordinaire. Any errors that remain are mine.

I am indebted to the authors whose works I embedded myself in: having been breathed out, branwyn and etothepii – your works have meant so much and are so freely given.

Introduction

Suppose, for instance, that men were only represented in literature as the lovers of women, and were never the friends of men, soldiers, thinkers, dreamers; how few parts in the plays of Shakespeare could be allotted to them; how literature would suffer! We might perhaps have most of Othello; and a good deal of Antony; but no Caesar, no Brutus, no Hamlet, no Lear, no Jaques–literature would be incredibly impoverished, as indeed literature is impoverished beyond our counting by the doors that have been shut upon women.

(Woolf 1996, 71–2)

Adaptations of existing works are becoming increasingly prevalent in mass media and popular culture and offer a fertile ground for examination and research. This book threads together a variety of disciplines: sociology, literature, media studies, gender theory and cultural studies, in order to analyse how and why fans adapt works through regendering. Regendering is the process by which a creator – writer, director, illustrator – changes the gender of an existing character while adapting an original work. This technique of changing the gender of one or more characters also offers creative political and social praxis, gender identity exploration and communication, in addition to illustrating a different point of view for a text. In order to do this, the book not only covers the theoretical models that can be applied to regendering as a process, and demographic research combining qualitative and quantitative explorations of fans and creators, it also includes analysis of selected regendered works to ascertain what processes are used.

The sociological data work of this book centres on how fans approach regendered works. Surveys and interviews were used to collate data which was then analysed. This data suggested a number of theoretical positions, which I outline as a result of the combined sociological and cultural drive of fans but also the creative models they use that draw from a variety of backgrounds. Feminist theory, queer theory and trans theory underlie much of the cultural draw to regendering as creator or audience, but also influence literary creativity for creators. Suzanne Black, Abigail Derecho and other theorists have applied the Derridean concept of the archive to fan studies and fanwork revealing '… a complex web of interdependency, one that can be extended to describe the functions and relations of all texts, not just those that claim explicit inter-relations' (S. Black 2012, 1) and a '… tendency to toward enlargement and accretion …' (Derecho 2006, 64). Regendered adaptations are firmly situated within that wider archontic character. However, they force a confrontation with the meaning of gender more broadly, and for some audiences this disrupts the familiar that makes adaptation attractive; the 'feminized' changes to character or narrative undermine the affective connection with the original or present a problem for suspension of disbelief for that narrative or genre.

Moi states that 'literature is the archive of a culture' and adaptations are an archive of a culture that situates itself within an archontic vision of itself and are also part of a community and culture bound to the media that has been given to them as a complete archive of its own (Moi 2008, 268). The archontic situates the adaptation and fanwork not within a hierarchy but as an archive of materials sharing a common ideal and thread, unable to be 'closed' to new works (Derecho 2006, 64). To elaborate 'the way that archontic literature – the array of continuations, sequels, spinoffs, remediations, fan fictions – use the play of similitude and difference to explore "potentialities within the originary texts" (74). These "potentialities" within source texts produce the series' characteristic play of proximity and distance, the familiar and strange' (Derecho 2006; in Howell and Baker 2017). Fanworks and adaptations, professional or not, situate themselves within that archive, and play with potentialities to create a unique reading of the original canon, while maintaining the familiar enough to be culturally relevant to both existing fans and newcomers.

Why study fans and fanworks?

Given that professional regendered adaptation exists – from the straightforwardly gender changes of *Elementary* to the new versions of *Doctor Who* and *Ghostbusters*, the study of fans who do the same in their fanworks (with comparatively small audiences) may seem an odd choice. When looking at adaptations the tendency to look purely at professional works, and those that engage in transmedia adaptation, is understandable; fanworks are explicitly amateur, in the sense of both unpaid and untrained creators, unacknowledged and often subject to legal questions. However, regendering is an extremely popular fannish technique, one that existed within fanworks with a much longer and deeper history than within professional adaptations. As such, my survey and analysis of regendering focuses on fans and fanworks as much as the more obvious and notorious examples of regendering.

Within fandom, the implied and expected reader of regendered narratives exists not only as a close, and trained, reader but also in a state of flow (Van Steenhuyse 2011). They are a knowing reader of the fanwork but also as an audience of that new regendered adaptation. Aspects of characterization do not need to be explained, the author can expect the reader will understand that Sherlock is Sherlock Holmes, with all the archontic iterations stretching out fore and aft and bolstering the representations and the critiques woven into the work. In that state of flow, where the audience is enmeshed within the narrative due to their familiarity with the canon, and the archontic variations, they can integrate the unfamiliar elements of the narrative – not simply the change in gender, but the way that regendering affects the narrator and the themes of the text itself. The converse of this is true as well, where the audience's sense of flow is disrupted by the seeming presence of gender, relying on the narrative default of maleness-masculinity to obscure the canonical presence of gender. This makes the politico-social elements of the text integral to the reading of the work and not simply as a kind of creative feminist praxis, but as a narrative tool aimed at the reader and the audience itself, critiquing the metanarratives of genre.

Modern fandom, historically as framed within fan studies at least, owes its inception to a kind of capitalist version of storytelling and subversion; however, there is also a longer history outside the field of media fandom as it was conceptualized, born from the loins of television and zines (Jenkins 2012). Castle refers to the groups of women who entered into lively conversation with authors during the 1800s, writing to them to plead for changes in the narratives, and rewriting those texts for their friends and circulating their corrections to narratives they imagined as incorrect, or 'filling in' the negatives spaces of the stories with romantic and sexual entanglements (2013). In this way, fanfic authors join with a long literary history of women reacting to and criticizing texts through rewriting the focus of the work, by revisioning and reworking the narratives to their own ends; either by changing the narrative to satisfy their own desires for justice, for romance, or to illustrate the blithe ignorance and imbalances of the original. Fans become part of this history with their work, and even though those narratives are often long gone, hidden in archives or lost entirely, the spirit of that interaction lives on in modern fandom.

Fandom very specifically has shifted to allow for this social-media-constructed affectual discourse and creates systems to collate it through comments, kudos, and social rituals around that feedback (Fiesler, Morrison, and Bruckman 2016). Accordingly, writers and creators are often engaged in greater levels of intimacy with their audience, and the unstable state of creator/audience binaries breaks repetitively. This instability enforces a higher vulnerability on those involved due to the immediacy and affective nature of feedback and critique within shifting ideas of what the relationship is between the author and the reader (Bennett and Chin 2014). The effects of social media on people in general have been researched and key to the influence is the underlying structure – algorithms – as 'not simply a means of interpreting culture, they are also productive of culture, understood in terms of the practices they engender' (Bucher 2018, 150). This is most evident in the ways feedback and responses have shifted with new technologies, and Boyd has examined this in greater detail in terms of teenagers and social media, and also the results of the flawed and unethical 'emotional contagion' research experiment Facebook engaged in for one week in January 2012 (Kramer, Guillory, and Hancock 2014; Shaw 2016). More germane to this research is Post-Object Fandom, which is specifically the fandom that exists for finished television series' and otherwise 'finalized' works, and the detailed analysis Williams has done regarding the ways fans (and anti-fans) express their affective states to each other, and how this creates a sense of community and changes viewing practices (2015). It follows that affect changes viewing, therefore it must also have an effect on fans as simultaneously viewers and creators. The way affect, as well as its performance in fandom, intersects with creativity is becoming a focus for research but there are multitudes of personal anecdotes about the ways in which these affective displays – positive and negative – feed into creative works.

Researcher analysis of selected fanworks is increasingly taking place at an academic level in both the classroom and within journals (Bartlett 2009; Reid 2009). This analysis and attention paid towards fanwork realize their potential both as a literary artefact but also as a social form of community engagement. The foregrounding of gender within the work, particularly that of the presumed female writer, gives rise to numerous methods for analysing and interpreting her work, as Moi suggests in the wider realm of literary criticism (2008). Fanwork, particularly, engages the audience with the author not just the text, in relationships that can prove to be intimate beyond both conventional boundaries of friendship (Lackner, Lucas, and Reid 2006) but also in highly embodied ways of relating reading enjoyment through expressions of physical effects of the works, or expressions of intense emotionality (Baheri 2013; Oeming 2021).

As the vast majority of regendered work is undertaken by fans, for fans, I have included analysis of selected fan texts alongside analysis of three major examples where regendering occurs within professional or commercial works. The focus on professional fans alongside the non-commercially supported fans may seem a strange choice for a media or fan studies text; however, the prevalence of 'fannishness' – a dedication and devotion to adored works – by professionals has long been evident. Similarly, the focus on non-commercial fanworks may seem a strange choice for media studies. The long-held canard that Dante wrote bible fanfic has an element of truth to it, in that creators often seek to adapt works that they find meaningful in some way. By focusing on several well-known adaptations (*Elementary* and *Ghostbusters: Answer the Call*), alongside a novel length and well-reviewed fanfic (*how the mouth changes its shape*) with selected smaller fanfic texts (*Compatible Damage* and *Seems So Easy for Everybody Else*) and the not strictly adaptational but adaptationally resonant *Doctor Who*, this text is able to focus on the audiences and their reactions, as much as the creators themselves.

This intersects in complex ways with the corporate and commercial creator who needs the fan but only within a controlled and supportive space, because it necessarily needs to address the fanfic or adaptation as critique and as creative work – even when it is a commercial adaptation. Fanwork particularly is created to both fulfil a creative need and to comment or expand upon the canonical work (Jenkins 2012). In addition to this is the multiple intersection of privilege and disadvantage within media, which can result in works that subvert gender, sex and racial issues at the same moment they reinscribe them, often while being aware of the 'problematic' nature of the work, and deliberately invoking political nuance to excuse and rationalize creative endeavours (Scodari 2003). This is the backdrop against which these stories appear and construct themselves; not simply the canon, or the archontic version, or fandom, but centuries of history, and specifically women's history and the sub-altern experiences of those outside the gender binary. The 'ongoing desire for and investment in cultivating queer histories' Coccia describes combines with a mythic resonance with fanwork as folklore and communal storytelling as identified by Willis to illustrate the intertextual and community knowledge of the participants (2022; 2016). A combination that intensifies the affective discourse and meaning of the text (2016; Wilson 2016). These regendered adaptations and fanworks link all of these elements together with their own reinterpretation of the canonical or genre narrative.

Gender and sexuality intersect with original media forms and inspire uses of regendering to adapt various canons, to reveal a gap in current and past media in terms of gender and sexuality. Within this book I engage with a number of theoretical positions to illustrate the audience and creator approaches to regendering; I also give space to expand upon the reasons why this technique has inspired significant levels of affect in positive and negative forms. I focus on the affect inspired by the works and that inspires the works, allowing for not just a demographic prediction of popularity/use, but a greater understanding of the emotional and sociological labour those works perform, and the ways this is experienced positively and negatively by the audience.

Regendered works are a form of feminist praxis and/or creative praxis; either a conscious reworking of the original to be more feminist and inclusive, a 'simple' (practical rather than theoretical) desire to see more women in media, or a curiosity as to what that would be like within a narrative to have female characters featured prominently. The works form a kind of emotional or sociological correction to the initial narratives and media in general, born from a desire to see oneself or one's politics made pseudoflesh in the media. This forms a space for the fans – creators and non-creators – to examine the practical embodied elements of gender alongside the narrative structures that alter our perception of the original works and gender itself. Even professional adaptations align with that apparently simple desire to put more women on screen, in narratives. The 'simplicity' of the shift in gender is belied by the conflicts between fans, creators, readers and philosophies of gender and gender expression.

For these professional adaptations, regendering expands the diversity of the work, and differentiates their product from other adaptations while maintaining the familiarity that is increasingly being demanded of media. The importance of regendering as a transformative process in adaptations cannot be underestimated within a culture of adaptational and sequential media dominating the screen, but also as a political manifestation of the dissatisfaction felt by sections of the audience who 'shouldn't have to trend' in order to be recognized as parts of the audience, as Navar-Gill and Stanfill phrase it (2018). These similarities to fanworks, bolstered by the way many professionals showcase their fannishness towards the adaptive material – the Russo brothers are comic book fans who went on to direct several Marvel adaptations, Peter Capaldi notoriously wrote a letter to a *Doctor Who* fanzine as a child and later portrayed the Twelfth Doctor (Hills 2018; Swann 2021). These complicated lines of engagement are the result not of community, but of a counterpublic which contains its own subcultures, metanarratives and forms of 'other'. The professionals and amateurs who adapt and reimagine fictional universes to reflect their fannishness and what they imagine fiction could be create a counterpublic as 'in producing for such a community, they call one into existence' (Stanfill 2013).

The leverage fandom can exert on the market can also be found in the successful transitions individual fans have made to professional publishing, such as E. L. James, Cassandra Clare, numerous authorized adaptation writers and what Hills calls the 'uneasy position between the "official" knowledge of showrunner fans and unofficial fan practices of re-narrating/archiving' in Doctor Who fandom (Hills 2015b). Or the influences described by Navar-Gill and Stanfill as 'trending' in their social network mediated queer critiques of *The 100* and *Orange Is the New Black* (2018). The controlling and commodifying elements of mainstream media are filtered primarily through marketing the ideal fan; J. K. Rowling has always suggested she was comfortable with fanworks, albeit those that 'affirm her own vision, and align with her own politics' as she, and Warner Brothers, seek to 'maintain control over fandom' (Duggan 2022). Similarly, the use of social media by content creators can cause conflicts between the corporate elements, and the fans themselves, where 'fans actively resist the ways their engagement is utilized by media companies' in their critiques and 'actively challenges industry efforts to use fan labor as free series promotion and audience research' (Arcy and Johnson 2018).

In Part One I ground this research in the theory and data I collected during research. Chapter 1 focuses on the question 'why regendering' as a topic for research, and what it reveals as a process of creativity, consumption and social critique. I illustrate the rationale for my work, the focus on fans and fanworks alongside professional adaptation, and also why it is important in this context to combine the traditionally sociological qualitative and quantitative research with the humanities influenced analysis of the media object themselves. As is tradition, I also include here an autoethnography to explore that nexus of gender, sexuality and fandom as someone who could be termed an acafan. My focus on the fans, and fanworks alongside professional adaptations, is driven by the shift in fan studies itself, such as the research from Reid, and Scodari, and *The Fanfiction Reader: Folk Tales for a Digital Age* (Coppa 2017) which collects together fanworks and essays in the fashion of *The Canterbury Tales*. However, the way gender is reworked in fanworks particularly is an under-examined area of fan studies and feminist media and cultural theory. McClellan has recently published work examining genderswap fanfic in Sherlock Holmes fandom (2014), the interplay between gender and cosplay in crossplay (Leng 2013; Tompkins 2019), or Omegaverse fanfic as troubling and contesting gender binaries alongside sexual morality (Busse 2013a; Popova 2018; Weisser 2019).

In Chapter 2 I explore how my method of research, affected as it is by the autoethnographic drive within much of sociology, encompasses questions of gender in research in the contemporary space. Gender identity and nomenclature have gone through significant shifts over the past decade, with even more changes to come. I outline my own position within fandom (and gender) in this section and explain how different approaches to this data affect not only how it is collected but also the results for the analysis. For the ethnographer, fandom represents an excruciatingly self-aware community that can respond poorly to both assumptions of intent, and to research that has not 'emphasized fannish community standards over traditional humanities conventions' where the 'academic has to give way' as described by Busse (2018). This audience, however, can also provide a high standard of introspection and reflection to the researcher.

In Chapter 3 I explore a framework for understanding regendering as a creative process that works with the male default of mainstream media and simultaneously requires it for the process to work. The audience is othered by the dominant male narratives on screen and through regendering those narratives occupies the assumed neutral spaces of many media objects or narratives. That occupation, the push into the assumed narrative blank of the white male character, is performed not simply by changing the gender, but by changing the structural assumptions of the original media. Regendering performs a critique of the original work, to varying degrees, but also reinforces that focus on the male narrative, and male character by devoting the fannish energy into those media objects. The focus on otherness, and othering, is inextricably linked within fandom to intersectionality and questions of representation, and the professional adaptation negotiates these questions too. Regendered fanworks are explicit not only in their representation of othered identities, but also in rejecting wider expectations of a gendered audience and experience of the world.

In Chapter 4 I go deeper into the ways fans use playfulness to explore gender, violence, sex and media. I contextualize the rationale for including case studies that analyse adaptations and fanwork in the traditions of media analysis through this more data-driven work. As regendered narratives illustrate not only the creativity of adaptation when dealing with gender (which extends far beyond simply changing a character's gender) but also the level of nuance and reflection, fans are able to bring to these works because of their deep affective engagement with the work and the audience which reveals the way 'play' becomes serious. There is a significant difference between commercial and non-commercial fanwork; however, in that the emotive efforts of fandom generate another kind of economy where the 'the affective discourse of fandom (that is, excited conversations and expressions of love) is inextricable from the production of fan fiction' (Wilson 2016).

In Part Two I use five case studies to explore how these ideas of play, othering, male defaults, homosociality and identity influence fanworks and adaptation. Fanwork, including professional adaptations, must necessarily choose which canonical signifiers to elaborate upon or investigate; what is chosen is a function of genre, medium, format and in commercial media, the influence of studios and showrunners, but also how they perceive the influence of canonical gender on the canonical narrative.

In Chapters 5, 6 and 7 I analyse selected Sherlock Holmes adaptations – *Elementary* alongside fanworks – in order to explore the ways in which fans, responding to other adaptations, regender famous characters. For Sherlock Holmes adaptations, and BBC's Sherlock particularly, Hills describes an 'epistemological economy' at work where the central character is 'diegetically invoking the validity of fan knowledge' where 'knowingness resides in how it intertextually reworks Conan Doyle's tests and hence hails Sherlockians' (Stein, Busse, and Hills 2014). These choices, the epistemological economy they work within, elaborate on what elements they find central and unique to the original work – choices that increasingly question the assumed fundamental role of gender in media. Fanwork is, at its heart, a repudiation of canon and a privileging of affective reaction to media where the object and fanwork can be seen as 'affect seeking content from the world of things' (Lowe 2020). When this is combined with the often explicitly gendered expectations of creators, mainstream media and the fans, it becomes a gendered exercise, one that can be examined as a feminist act (Bury 2005; Fang 2021; Hannell 2020). In Chapter 5 I analyse the novel-length fanwork how the mouth changes its shape by havingbeenbreathedout as an example of fanfic that uses regendering and lesbianism to shift the focus from the rational workings of the detective genre and expand it in ways that are familiar to the genre but deepened by the use of alternative viewpoints. This is a version of what Walker terms 'narrative extraction' where Black fans dig 'through the narrative to claim what can be claimed … claiming and owning the individual elements of a story that feel most identifiable and true … (that) become our point of access' (Walker 2019). The alternative viewpoint is explicitly lesbian, and explicitly historical, using the genre and the archontic expectations of Sherlock Holmes to problematize not just the misogyny of the original, but also the adaptations.

In Chapter 6 I use two fanworks, *Compatible Damage* by branwyn and *Seems So Easy for Everybody Else*, by etothepii to analyse how regendering can approach gender diversity in ways beyond the binary expectations of mainstream media. In *Seems So Easy* the familiar Sherlock Holmes is rewritten as a trans man, whose position within the detective genre we are familiar with, and the modern habitus established by another adaptation (BBC's *Sherlock*) reveals the inherent imbalances, assumptions and defaults of the original works. Similarly *Compatible Damage* takes the familiar – John Watson the troubled veteran, with shellshock or PTSD depending on era – but regenders it. Joanna Watson is a veteran, whose pursuit for adrenaline involves her in not only the detective genre, but into situations where her gender exposes her to danger and allows her a degree of understanding beyond the male default. Fanwork reimagines and recodes gender and intimacy, particularly regendered work. Regendering is one of the 'extreme forms of refocalization' that Jenkins identified, where fans change the moral alignment of the universe. The repudiation is intentionally critical; it is a moral alignment, and undermining or critiquing the structural forms of the universe (2012, 168). Within these the fanwork is meant to criticize to the canon or the contemporary culture in some fashion, revealing its flaws or discrediting it, sometimes specifically delegitimizing the work and claiming some form of catharsis. Other fanworks – less antagonistic – are still viewed as perpetrating this violence against the body of work that inspired it simply through the act of refocalization. This is particularly evident in audience reactions to adaptations, remakes and reboots, as well as fanworks themselves. This violence, when performed by regendering, is one that uses against the canon, and the social capital of default maleness and masculinity. It uses the new language of fanworks to delegitimize the primacy of canon, and canonical maleness, and destabilizes the perception of gender.

Transformative works rewrite the existing narrative for a multitude of reasons, examined by scholars such as Henry Jenkins within the realm of fan studies and the influential concept of textual poaching from the creative commons of a commercial takeover of folklore and storytelling, or Terry Castle in queer theory where the drive to rewrite is linked to the apparitional and haunted palimpsest underneath a canon that erases lesbians (2012; 1993). The drive to see one's own self in narrative as a minority, or as the subaltern, is only matched by the recognizance of one's own otherness in the narrative where one must 'dig' as Walker identified, in order to find a reflective characterization within the dominant white narratives (2019). The transformative process of fanwork sutures fragments of recognition from the narrative into the reimagined new space of the adaptation.

In Chapter 7 I focus on *Elementary*, a professional adaptation taking inspiration from other adaptations and is 'earmarked by deliberate references to it – for instance, at a not entirely serious level, *Elementary* refers to *The Great Mouse Detective* in its opening credits by mimicking in live action the Rube-Goldenberg-like contraptions from the cartoon … also references canon in titles, in the cases themselves' (Baker 2015, 148). Originally it was conceived as a US 'version' of the BBC's *Sherlock*, but the showrunners' plans were rejected. Given the out-of-copyright status of the original Conan Doyle works (as much as this was a point of contention for the later stories and for his estate) the CBS network elected to create their own modernized version. This both allowed, and demanded, a greater distance from the BBC version. Beyond location changes (*Elementary* locates itself within New York and occasionally the wider United States or internationally, with brief moments in London in Season 7, *Sherlock* is in London and the UK primarily), *Elementary* made one large, and contentious, change – Dr John Watson became Dr Joan Watson. Smaller changes proved to be less contentious, including the nemesis Moriarty being combined with Irene Adler into Jamie Moriarty, or Mrs Hudson becoming Ms Hudson, a part-time muse, part-time housekeeper. Regendering Watson is a choice that has been explored within multiple essays and papers (Farghaly 2015; Stagg 2012; Valentine 2013). As a regendered villain, whose attraction to Sherlock is a manifestation of their shared 'complicated' status as superior to others, Moriarty transfers that attraction, or expands it, to include Joan in 'a lesbian homosocial triangle' (Baker 2015, 153). However, she also maintains her world-spanning violence alongside interpersonal violence. Jamie Moriarty provides a specific intervention in the 'problem' of regendering – her violent tendencies and fatal entanglement with

Sherlock Holmes. This chapter explores how Moriarty regenders violence and reveals the limits to which audiences accept or legitimize violence.

In the final chapters I explore the professional works that have regendered characters: *Ghostbusters: Answer the Call* and the Thirteenth Doctor in *Doctor Who*, and I have focused on these as examples of regendering with different foci, results and responses from the audience. One of the primary, enduring criticisms of regendering is: it isn't *really* an adaptation, it merely uses the name with no real connection to the original. This critique privileges the fan's preferred adaptation (or original) and often links that preference to their identity alongside more media-focused critique, in what Proctor terms 'totemic nostalgia' (2017). It is unsurprising then that a change in gender is perceived by many fans as to be so foundationally shattering as to render any work flawed but also suspect, due to its co-optation of those canonical signifiers, in a kind of trademark infringement or misrepresentation.

In Chapter 8 I focus on one of the more notorious examples of regendering where the backlash from fans would be seen again, but with greater vitriol and aggression than seen previously, even for more historical regendered characters like Starbuck in *Battlestar Galactica*: *Ghostbusters: Answer the Call*. Unlike *Elementary* where complaints became muffled once the series began (particularly those regarding the 'heterosexualizing' of a narrative many see as in some way queer,[1] and the 'damaging' of the canon or the characters) the anger about the female Ghostbusters continued beyond the release of the media, and have become semiotic indicators for cultural conflicts about gender itself. The prevalence of persistent rumours and assumptions about the creators, and reactive positive fannishness, often does not engage with the ways Feig regendered the work. As a result this chapter analyses the film itself as an adaptation of the original, the industrial elements, alongside the fannish responses. Included in this are the ways in which fan studies itself, and media studies, engage in fannish behaviour around media objects. Many of the criticisms of *Ghostbusters: Answer the Call* occurred prior to release, and it is this possessive fannishness over the 'original' works that underlies this chapter, and the following.

In Chapter 9 I analyse the response to the thirteenth season of *Doctor Who* where the eponymous Doctor is played by Jodie Whittaker. The first female Doctor (who wasn't a sex comedy interlude on a variety show that was albeit

---

[1] The question of queerness and Holmes/Watson requires its own thesis to elucidate upon, so I hesitate to make any claim for or against it within the canon.

written by showrunner Moffat prior to his run on the show) was heralded as ground-breaking, but also provoked significant backlash. For *Doctor Who* the ongoing structure of the series and the sheer longevity of it, along with the nostalgic devotion to it, contribute to the way fans and creators responded to the regendering. While less violent and abusive than the *Ghostbusters* response, the fannish practices around the series built on new actors playing the central role reveal the ways in which regendering incurs a critical audience whose negativity is more aligned with external concerns about gender, sexuality and media, than the specific iteration (Hills 2021).

My ultimate conclusion may seem defeatist – that all of the creative ways in which fans approach these ideas and experiments in othering and otherness expose the underlying reality where the default *and* the exceptional remain male and masculine. While on the surface this may seem to undermine the actions of these works, I aim to show that the method matters as much, if not more, than the result. As more fans become the professionals behind the media, the affective properties of the works they created will become more obvious, as will their understanding of the fanbase and fannish techniques of adaptation – creative and contentious as they may be.

Part One

Data and theories

This section includes the data I collected during the research project, including the theoretical grounding for regendering as an adaptational technique. Using theories of otherness, deep play, gendered representations, the formation of counterpublics within fans and audiences, and how those ideas create a default representation in mainstream media that is reworked in adaptations and fanwork. Use of play creates an adaptational frame that simultaneously is ephemeral yet serious, engaging with social and political ideas of the public and counterpublic that inform personal practices as fans and creators. Regendering pushes back into the absent and othered space, occupying the male default, and revealing the "neutral" masculine narrative and as a result goes further than simply the story and universe they inhabit, as fanworks necessarily engage with the media culture as a whole. The narrative, weighted with both archontic/canonical expectations and media saturation, bends both the character and the gender role they inhabit, to reinterpret the female and the feminine. However, this occupation is only possible using the imbalance of representation in wider media sources used as the basis for fanworks. By adapting existing works, regendering exists as a critique of the original narrative, including adaptations, reviews, critiques and other work, but it ultimately relies on the existence of the masculinized male default to exist. In fandom this is an attention economy discrepancy where the prevalence of the masculine extending to the regendered and fanworks means that even though they are by definition transformative, they remain dominated by those representations (Baker 2016, 33–4).

1

Regendering research

One of the major difficulties for media studies is the management of scope and data, alongside the concerns about ethics and identity. My method for engaging with this information overload is through mixed methods; paradoxically, I also expand my textual analysis to include professional/commercial adaptations and fannish ones. This inclusion of professional and commercial works the case studies/media analysis sidesteps much of those concerns about ethics and identity in fan studies research and creates a specific line of enquiry in terms of the audience itself. The increasing shift from creators as a separate pipeline of experience to fandom as fertile grounds for new creators is one founded in the prevalence of remakes, reboots, sequels and the rise of creators such as Jordan Peele and Melissa Hunter whose fannishness around a genre becomes a signifier of quality in professional work. The filmic practices of auteurs who pay homage and bolster their own fannishness with creative praxis have also shifted the adaptation from prioritizing fidelity to the original to understanding that 'where a transgression or change from the original reality is most pronounced, there will be generated the highest level of cultural interest' (Harmes 2014, xvi). The professionals behind media objects like *Ghostbusters: Answer the Call* and *Elementary* are fans – professional ones who have become the canonical creators for works they admire.

How I researched regendering, due to that 'cultural interest' intersecting with tensions about gender, media and society, was a complex issue to navigate. Additionally, regendered works are also examples of an existing canon where they are not simply the work of a fan, but are professional and commercial. The three professional adaptations I focus on in later chapters are heirs to decades-long franchises, or indeed over a century, forming not just a body of work but a complicated intertextual transmedia network or archive of materials. The literary ancestors of fanwork – commercialized, or legitimized, or neither – demand engagement in the form of close reading the works themselves, literary or other forms and genres of media. The linguistic elements of fandom and audiences, the counterpublic it creates, are ill-suited to surface analysis, or heavily quantitative measurements. Similarly, the competing needs of quantitative and qualitative research flatten gender experience. To encompass this my research uses ethnography and autoethnography alongside textual/cinematic analysis, and audience 'netnography' with associated news or essay materials, as 'they triangulate well and offer insight into the layered logic of gender definitions and the resistance against changing this' (Hermes and Kopitz 2021, 83).

The focus on fans, and my own autoethnographic experience, allows for a selection of audiences who find something of worth in that work, or as Russ describes it regarding slash fiction:

> Only those for whom a sexual fantasy "works," that is, those who are aroused by it, have a chance of telling us to what particular set of conditions that fantasy speaks, and can analyse how and why it works and for whom … Sexual fantasy that doesn't arouse is boring, funny, or repellent, and unsympathetic outsiders trying to decode these fantasies (or any others) will make all sorts of mistakes.
>
> (Russ 1985, 89)

This is due to the way that regendering 'doesn't work' for some audiences for whom the fantasy is interpreted from a position about the canon and their personal close reading practices. Those who find it boring often discuss the creative issues about adaptation as unoriginal, or regendering as a commercial tactic. Those who find it funny respond to regendering as less about funniness than using humour to highlight and police gender roles and performances, using the spectre of an incorrectly gendered character to undermine the adaptation but also to reinscribe the 'correctly' gendered roles. For those who find regendering repellent however, these tactics are used alongside media critique, appeals to authority in terms of fidelity to the original, but also aligning the creative process of regendering with political and social movements about gender, race and sexuality.

Thus, it is important to note several ongoing concerns during my research period around the deployment of bots, astroturfing and trolling as means of controlling a media narrative for commercial/political purposes where digital communications often facilitate a lack of truthfulness. Even within a field as niche as fan studies it is important to be aware of how narratives are manipulated through technological means, particularly those that rely on a kind of quantified approach (Bay 2018). This is not to say my respondents were untruthful, but that the static nature of surveys and interviews locks understanding into a singular moment, a mechanism that the majority of my survey respondents went on to deconstruct in their autobiographical 'journeys' through fandom. Online research is also vulnerable to bad actors skewing results and falsifying results in a number of ways (Stella, Ferrara, and De Domenico 2018). The prevalence of Russian political bots on Twitter, Gamergate, review-bombing, harassment campaigns and associated technological 'movements' bolstered by blackhat and automated trolling, and the more garden-variety impersonators and con artists using the web, are all indicators for researchers to be wary of the results of online research that does not include deeply qualitative research alongside quantitative measures.

The theoretical conclusion from my research aligns with those other academics within fan studies such as Busse, Hellekson, Reid, Pande and Stanfill, and the divisions within fandom identified by Scodari (2010, 2010, 2009, 2018, 2020). My focus on the identity of the fans as a part of their praxis is indebted to *Cunning Linguists* particularly, and Reid's analysis of 'dark' fanwork was the precursor to the close reading of fan fiction, and my own autoethnographic work (Lackner, Lucas, and Reid 2006; 2009). As what Russ would call 'one for whom the sexual fantasy works' in terms of the fantasy of this re-othered world of the regendered characters, the impact of regendering is one that required vulnerability to research.

Obligatory autoethnography

The nature of fan studies and media studies necessitates a transition between the perspectives of the academic as the watcher and the observer, and of the audience member as the consumer and the receiver. This transitional space has definite appeal – even non-fannish researchers like Bacon-Smith have tried their hand at fan fiction as part of an ethnographic initiation ceremony of sorts (Bacon-Smith 1992). As such, it is habitual within the academic fanworks to make confession, as it were, to one's fannish sins; confession being absolution, to distance oneself from the abject affective fan behaviour. 'The scholar-fan must still conform to the regulative ideal of the rational academic subject, being careful not to present too much of their enthusiasm while tailoring their accounts of fan interest and investment to the norms of "confessional" (but not overly confessional) academic writing' (Hills 2013a, 11–12) so who am I to break tradition?

The status of fannishness as a feminist act underlies much of my own interests in fandom, which have ranged from the pleasure-based desires often expounded in fan studies, to the explicit creative praxis of fanwork as an area of feminist knowledge and meaning-making that takes place in and around the communities and cultures I already inhabit. My own understanding of my fannishness underwent something of a revelation during the research period, as my interviews often included a kind of demarcation process, a vetting of my intent and my ability to prove a kind of fannishness, and more rarely, my gender, queerness or feminist intent[1]. An instrumental example would be the moment in one interview where the still unsure respondent quizzed me on my own fannishness by asking about my 'first fandom'; after some back and forth establishing which version of *Stargate* I was talking about, and revealing it was *Stargate SG1* the respondent exclaimed 'oh you are very old school!'. More often these conversational provocations were in the form of outreach, openings for my responses to indicate that I was a safe respondent to talk to about fannishness, queerness or gender identity. My openness, and responsiveness, to the participants resulted in a deep and rich data set that also informs the theories I develop through this work, and my analyses of narratives. This social meaning-making inspired me into significant levels of self-reflection in terms of fannishness, queerness and gender, in order to better understand the positions of my respondents, and to be able to answer questions they had posed only to themselves as they told their stories. My 'journey to fannishness' is idiosyncratic, linked with my queerness and my experience of those communities and creators, as much as any specific fandom itself. It is also deeply influenced by the warning offered by Raw, that there is a 'potential to obscure personal motivations influences the research' (2020).

The autoethnographic impulse is a simultaneous revealing of the self while constructing an appropriate narrative for the research project itself. Within fan studies, even in the earliest projects, the drive to participate or claim experience was present. Bacon-Smith was curious enough to write hurt/comfort fiction under a pseudonym, and this resulted in a backlash from the community she was engaged in researching for her presumption and exposure of the community to risk in terms of the subcultural ideals of anonymity (1992, 214–16). Similarly, in the bigger failures in the research, we see those insider/outsider identities becoming methods of gatekeeping in order to retain a sense of safety. The autoethnography as a personal practice forces the writer to identify with those risks, and as a public practice, exposes one to the field and to judgement. So even in the reflectiveness,

---

[1] This is possibly due to the majority of in-person interviews taking place while I sported a close buzzcut; not exactly a pledge of feminist allegiance but a fairly good indicator of feminist/queer leanings.

the desire to protect and to present oneself as a worthy interlocutor affects the narrative created within the autoethnography. The majority of fan studies ethnographic works locate themselves within media properties, or specific fannish activities – writer, collector, artist – but my own focus on gender and regendering, has meant it is more in line with the autoethnographic practices of queer studies, where the confessional aspects are a method of locating risk and safety. My experience as a researcher was highly moderated by the ways in which my own gender presentation shifted during the research period, and other political happenings during the time period (the election of Donald Trump in America, the plebiscite for gay marriage in Australia, the resumption of state-sanctioned homophobia, incarceration, torture and murder of gay men in Ukraine and Russia, the list continues).

Community counterpublics

Kozinets, in his heuristic of online activities, terms a low level of creation/ interaction and silent observation as somewhere between a lurker, mingler or newbie, positioned with a low level of community strength and with a low centrality of consumption activity (Kozinets 2009, 33). I find this delineation lacking, as my position as a consumer of fanworks did cement a significant number of important personal relationships, even if the 'centrality' of that consumption was limited to a specific social group. This experience is common, particularly when examined in the context of fan histories where media fandom occurred across zines, through snail mail and offline groups and conventions. Even within the highly centralized era of Livejournal those 'small community' links did not preclude a higher identification with or connection to a community. The lurker model of Kozinets implies the low level of creation or interaction as one that implies a low connection, when fans themselves do form high levels of connection around the fandom object. I witnessed this disconnect echoed in a panel at *Continuum 9* (a generalist genre nerd convention in Melbourne, Australia) where lurkers spoke about their experiences as non-'active' fans, whose concerns about activity and what is 'enough' to count are common even in those who are far more active. This complexity and tension around who is enough of a fan drive conflict around who is worthy enough, and what kinds of challenges an individual can make towards that fannish object. The performance of fannishness is part of the way fans create communities and it is not easily layered into more quantitative measures of connection, and from there how academics and researchers can envision and portray those connections. Fans develop complex relationships around the performance of fannishness within multi-layered cultures with differing meanings assigned to that activity as a 'hybridity of opposing culture' (Massey 2019). Gunnels and Cole's examination of fans as 'ethnodramaturgs' observes this layering of identity 'simultaneously functions as a producer and a consumer of the culture and its fragments, without necessarily delineating a difference between those experiences' (Gunnels and Cole 2010, para. 5).

Like many fans, I primarily consumed fanfic, fanart and so on for years before engaging in my own creative practices as a fan, and what I created was buried under layers of pseudonyms and identities separate not only to real life, but to my fannish identity as well. Lucy the librarian, Lucy the lurker and Lucy the fanwork producer were my three separate identities online – very different hats, so to speak, with disembodied identities attached. With the addition of Lucy the academic, these three disembodied identities, 'opposing cultures' were coalesced into one uncomfortable space (Massey 2019). Monaco's reflections on memory work and ethnography in fan studies depict 'the scholar-fan's vulnerabilities that are often silenced in published accounts of fandom, autoethnographic writing complicates realist conventions of representation and the ways in which textual strategies construct the authorial voice in relation to the "other"' (Monaco 2010, 102). From this 'sutured identity' (Morrison 2016, 249) of mine, where my identities and activities as a fan and as a scholar were kept separate, came a kind of forced relocation of self through the autoethnographic process and reflection on 'how they may affect our fan engagement' (Busse 2018). My discomfort extends to my autoethnographic practice and the way that 'self-reflexivity demands that we reflect on past events that informed our subjectivities. It means also looking back critically at the "past" of the ethnographic or qualitative research encounter' (Monaco 2010, 104). This self-reflexivity is vital in order to be able to both approach those ethnographic encounters, and to reflect on them.

Changing representations

My self-reflexive account of my fannishness has very few specific memories, unlike many of my counterparts in either fan studies or media studies. Recently, however, with the way fandom is inserting itself into everyday life (via either the home-based technological practices or larger-scale breaks in the fourth wall) (Pink 2008) my scattered consumption of media and fanwork began taking on some pointed commentary about gender, and media structures. My own experiences, trying to understand why I would identify more with a male character over the obvious female-version-of-myself[2], took on a wider scope as more and more research filtered down from academia into the fannish world, and my undergraduate foci on journalism, literature and gender gave me a frame for what I was reading and seeing. I read more and more of the research, and more and more of the meta, and the fannish works about gender, and began to hypothesize about what fandom was achieving when it played with gender – sex being well covered by the generations of aca-fans who have focused on slash, hurt/comfort and pornography. Where even the gender-creative subgenres of Omegaverse and mpreg are primarily viewed through the lens that the fantasy of sex breaks the boundaries and binaries of gender.

The juxtaposition of fannish regendered versions of characters with those that follow the exploitatively objectified models that pre-exist in mainstream media, particularly evident in comics, drew me in. Comparing regendered fanwork and cosplay where it mirrors the original with minor changes accommodating a specific body type to others that echo the 'boob window', painted-on spandex, revealing and hyper-feminized depiction of women that is endemic in much of comics/visual media revealed *something*, I just wasn't sure what. I began to collect, haphazardly, regendered cosplay and fanart and fancasting and meta and fanfic, and eventually a proposition grew from that collection.

Regendered works use the increasing visibility, popularity and acceptability of adaptive works and the familiar newness of those works and their ability to integrate the mutability of the work into audience reception. This takes place within the media and pop culture environment where women's participation is considered irrelevant and representation is disproportionately low as a reflection of the existing world and the market power wielded by women. This environment is changing, as a result of both marketing and demographic research, but also the increasing focus on the attention economy, fan markets and 'influencer' based economies. Regendered works use those concepts to disruptively occupy that absence and the male form.

To excuse a female character's existence and to accept her based on her conformation to masculine ideals while still maintaining the absence of the

---

[2] Severus Snape vs Hermione Granger, for the curious.

female, as identified by Butler in *Bodies that Matter* as a requirement of the performance and reiteration of masculinity, is to both make the female/feminine invisible and to act as a correction to the female/masculine (Butler 2011, 89–95). Or, to quote Bradley herself (possibly, this is something of an oral history), to make a kind of 'man with breasts' as a sop to female absence does not represent women as a group nor provide reasonable access. Primorac and critics like Genevieve Valentine and Sophia Macdougall have identified this representation without depth within Sherlock Holmes remakes specifically (2013; 2013; 2013). There are other theorists who link the lack of agency for women to the Hays Code, and the sudden reduction of women to approved kinds of feminine roles, with appropriate punishments for transgressive behaviours (Zeisler 2008). This is the background against which fans adapt existing works, and female characters are developed; it is also the background that regendering springs from.

This 'freedom' of negative and 'unappealing' representation seemed to be key to my nascent ideas about representation and were crystallized at numerous points throughout the research process. The expectation that a character or media identity must perform appealingly within her narrow frame of expertise was found in a number of diverse areas: she cannot simply have short hair and be muscular unless that is a presentation of sexuality as in the backlash against the straight-yet-butch depiction of Cassandra in *Dragon Age II*, she cannot be elderly and scholarly on television where anyone might see her regardless of her level of education as in the reactions to Mary Beard's work as a historian. And even if one is performing humour as a woman, one must also be cute or at least sexually appealing or fight against it as detailed by Tina Fey; 'she wasn't there to be cute. She wasn't there to play wives and girlfriends in the boys' scenes. She was there to do what she wanted to do and she did not fucking care if you like it' (Fey 2011). Regendering, as an adaptive technique, draws attention as it is 'the moment in which gender is hypervisible in its complex intersectional entanglement with class, race and sexuality' where the default masculinity of the original is unremarkable even though it too is gendered, raced, classed and sexualized (Hermes and Kopitz 2021, 73). Within fictional frameworks this becomes concerns about agency, and appeal and wish fulfilment.

This expansion of the roles and abilities in the representation of women offered by the practice of regendering became very clear as I continued this research. It is not simply a matter of rewriting a character to correspond to heterosexual narratives, or to make it 'easier' to identify with – indeed, the practice of identifying with men often seems to be an unspoken skill of female creators and my research with fans showed this. Instead, regendering is a way of insisting on a much deeper representation of women without the limitations of attractiveness, 'specialness' or the other benign acts of misogyny that result in the imbalance of gender roles in media. However, this imbalance extends beyond the media object, and becomes resonant, or reflective, of 'resistance against the overturning of female-male difference' (Hermes and Kopitz 2021, 77).

The corollary to expanded female representation is that the resultant media representation of women as a universal class – usually slim, white, middle-class and heterosexual – precludes any ambiguity of gender, or gender presentation. It provides only the slightest titillating ambiguity to sexuality and gender presentation, with no real representation of women's complex identities – particularly those who are marginalized. The presence of anyone who may not be a woman but is gendered that way by society – forced to join the 'class' of womanhood and suffer the marginalization regardless of gender – is interrogated through gender-creative fanworks such as Omegaverse, BDSM-verse or mpreg narratives. These representations exist not as a reflection of the demographic populations, nor audience reality, nor any form of reality other than the imaginary construct that allows for endless masculinity and defaults, to the point it shapes our own perceptions around its reality warping field where even diversity is limited to male representation. This concern about those limitations shifted the parameters and construction of my initial research, particularly finding that there *was* a dominant regendering narrative where male characters were regendered more than female ones, but also that there were common approaches to the shifts in both fanwork and professional adaptation. These shifting limitations, and the ways in which fanworks interrogate and play with gender, made the narrow professional regendering obvious.

Psychological dominance

The 'psychological dominance' of the male-masculine default of media narratives extended into fanworks while also affecting the perception of those media narratives and our approaches to them academically or creatively. This dominance occurs even where quantitative research illustrates there is parity, or even more focus on marginalized views. In my research I requested fans to use a short-answer box for gender identity (survey and interview questions appear in Appendices 1 and 2). This illustrated that there was a wide range of ways fans approached the class of womanhood, and that it was both playful ('penguin') and more precise ('cisgender female').

The spectres of embodiment and essentialism haunt the way feminism speaks of itself, and of women. Particular to this are the ways the male as the neutral and default identity erases the feminine, as explained by Gatens, but also the way the feminine is essentially the Other, as expounded on by Irigaray (1996; 1991). The seeming absence aided by the liquid mutability of the female experience in literature, particularly that of lesbians, is evident in the works of numerous theorists including Castle and Spender (2013; 1985). The intersectional demands of femininity according to other axes of oppression such as race, ethnicity, disability, class, familial status and so on can be erased by using 'women' as a placeholder to encompass the entire gender. Crenshaw's work foregrounds those intersections as not only important sites of political action and oppression, but as sites where activism itself acts against those it seeks to support (Cho, Crenshaw, and McCall 2013). The male as neutral, and default, significantly affects the reception, perception and practice of regendering.

As in Spender's research into speech and gender, where the perception of women's language is given more space than it takes up because it is a diversion from the expected default (1985) (which itself links to the ways Moira Gatens (1996) identifies the male default at the basis of more benign kinds of bigotry), unexpected elements in a work differentiate it enough to make it seem it has greater weight in the literature than it technically has. The term is used within psychological and sociological fields to encompass the emotional and mental effects of dysfunctional relationships that do not have a physical basis, where control is exerted through attention, approval and the withdrawal of social support when 'rules' are transgressed (Burgoon, Johnson, and Koch 1998, 253). This well suits the ways in which the literary and media expectation of the male and masculine undermines the presence of the female fan, who still operates within that hierarchy for her own works and practices as a fan. Stanfill explains that subcultures split, and this acts as a way to inscribe beliefs and reinstate cultural relevance (2013), and this is particularly evident in two seemingly disparate concerns about regendering: the supposed misandrist impulse to destroy men (particularly straight, white men) and the heterosexualizing effect of regendering.

Regendering has its basis and creative model in the experience of adaptation and exploration, a relationship with a media object that does not prioritize fidelity as much as recognition, and affective connections with that object. I have identified several theoretical positions for what that recognition is founded in: otherness, violence, fandom as community, sexual processes and psychological dominance. The otherness of the regendered work can be seen in both absence and presence of that as a thematic concern; the lack of women in many popular narratives leaves both a gendered absence in the work, but also fills the role of the other with a male character, and regendering draws out this sense of otherness within that work. Similarly, violence relies on a gender binary and imbalance in mainstream narratives, where the real experiences of gendered violence are read into a male-dominated narrative through regendering; it is also a metanarrative in the way that these forms of adaptation are considered violent towards the canon, towards the 'normal' fan's enjoyment. The community of fandom is more accurately a counterpublic where subcultures exist, including those that expand and explore narratives, or critique them, through adaptation and reimagining. This community is also one that practises sex through text, through desire, and in ways that are often perceived as transgressive. Finally, my psychological dominance theory encompasses much of the way critics, audiences and academics approach regendering. Where quantitative research reveals that there is no support for a belief or concern, the issue does not stop being important to those who express or hold it. That oversized importance lies in a number of areas, primarily the expectations of normativity that have been disrupted; or within the counterpublic, an expectation from the public that is to be defended against.

It is relatively simple to see the matrix of subversion and transgression in adaptation and fanwork applied to gender, or race, or other intersections of privilege, in terms of the very much alive author practising their politics in reading against the original work. This does not, however, address the ways in which their work can, and indeed does, reinscribe those hegemonies and perceptual boundaries. Recent years have also seen the focus of fan studies shift to focus on markets and tools, on the use of fanwork to industry and education. This has resulted in an almost binary split between a feminized audience in terms of transformative media fandoms, but one that retains a default male identity for the creators of the media products. Such a split allows for transgressions of the capitalist culture of media conglomerates to be delegitimized as 'women's hobbies' at the same time those actions on the behalf of male creators earn titles like 'pastiche' and 'homage' and 'reboot'. The feminine is receptive in the binary construction/representation of gender, and thus the audience is feminine for their reception of the work, in a reasonably circular feat of logic. The fan who then becomes productive transgresses more than her gender role, she also transgresses the perspectives she is given by the media. Jenkins, along with Sandvoss and Grey, has written at length about the ways this transgressiveness is received and hypothesized multiple originating events and emotions for why fans process their dissatisfaction into forms of production (2012; 2005; 2007). Other theorists have rejected ideas about the roles of audience and creator and instead have hypothesized the events and emotions around fanwork creation are about wider ideas of gender and narrative, and the community of fandom as a place and space, not simply as a manifestation of adoration (Hellekson and Busse 2014; 2006).

This replication and transgression of male dominance are echoed in regendering by the relative imbalance of male characters being reimagined as women, and it is within the works themselves that fans tackle these tensions. It also obscures the way in which fans and fandom envision a more expansive model of womanhood, where it exists as a class of identity that encompasses more than narrow definitions.

2

Fans and regendering

As adaptations become more and more integral to creative industries and the practices within the professional realm echo and draw from fandom the commonalities between the fannish and professional creators coalesce. Particularly since the audience who grew up with widespread media and film, alongside fandom and the internet, are now part of that industry, what Hadas terms 'a geek echo of 1960s Hollywood' (Hadas 2014). Using the audience and their fanworks as a creative practice ground for professional uptake by the industry has had a long history and is very obvious when looking at the longer-running franchises like *Doctor Who* (Moffat being a lifelong fan who originally regendered the Doctor as a woman in a comedy sketch) (Hadas 2014), *Star Trek*, *Star Wars*, almost all comic book-based adaptation. Even outside the film industry, fans become creators within the franchise they adore with some regularity within games and comic books. While industry professionals may assume adaptation shows a 'lack or originality, authenticity and is, moreover, highly commercially driven' the hyperspecific elements of 'localization' are considered 'essential' (Cuelenaere 2021). By looking at a specific form of adaptation – regendering – the hyperspecific localization aspects of gender, media and adaptation can be discerned in terms of both the quantitative qualities, alongside more theoretical and philosophical ideas.

Who does regendering?

The social profile of professional creators is necessarily constrained by the industry they are in, and to a certain extent, qualitative work about that population is going to be affected by the public relations control of information, and the editing and polishing of any responses. In addition to this that population is extremely small as the production aspect for professional works is marked by increasing focus on the safe, which does prioritize ongoing cycles of reboots, remakes and sequels but within a marketing paradigm that avoids risk (Cuelenaere 2021). In order to explore *who* regenders characters in adaptation I specifically looked at fanworks and audiences in addition to analysis of popular work as fan production is less constrained by the market-driven production contexts of film and television, or the PR-moderated communication with others. As the cycles of franchises and long-running series continue to grow, there are an increasing number of professionals working on intellectual property and franchises that they are (or were) fans of. Moffat's fandom around Sherlock Holmes and Doctor Who for example, or even Ryan Reynold's and Deadpool, where the fannishness of the professional is linked not only to the production of the adaptation, but also to how appropriate they are to create or work on that adaptation. Looking at the fans is increasingly a space that observes the creators prior to the work becoming professional.

It is important to note that the fannishness may not be solely linked to a media object, instead it may be a form, a genre or format; romance fans becoming romance authors, horror fans becoming directors, writers and producers, comic fans becoming comic book writers or artists. As such, fans of regendering exist, who enjoy the process of regendering as creator and as audience. The respondents to my survey were primarily fans (although some professionals participated), who identified as fans of transformative works such as fanfic, fanart and other forms; they were recruited via open Twitter and Tumblr posts and shared via emails amongst transformative works fans. My research did not select for participation in regendering; however, the overt focus on that did result in a bias towards creators and audiences with at least an interest in regendering (one that may also be a negative interest). These fans broadly belonged 'to a class that could broadly be described as female' but 'one-fifth of all women and women-adjacent respondents described their gender in a way that separated them from the category "female" or particularized it in some fashion' (Baker 2017). In Table 1 I collate the breadth of this answer to illustrate not only the range but also the playfulness of the answers that show an approach to gender identity mirrored in their work and reading habits. The survey respondents provide data that reveal the creative processes and receptive techniques for regendering separated from the need for corporate backing and funding. As such they are not directly attributable to professionals and adaptations; however, those affective and creatives practices are likely to overlap in some ways.

Table 1 Answers to 'What Gender Do You Identify As?'

Agender

Androgynous

bigender (female and nb/masculine)

Cis female

cis lady

Cis woman

cisgender female

Demigirl

Deminonbinary

Female

Female (demigirl/genderqueer)

female (with a strong streak of genderqueer)

Female, more or less

female/genderless

Female/Genderqueer

Fluid

Genderfluid

Genderfluid (biologically female)

Genderfluid; mostly female right now

Genderqueer

Genderqueer afab

girl/penguin/?? (sorry I can)

I am anti-gender

I reject gender as a concept, but society deems me female.

lady, i guess.

Male

Male/Agender

Masculine Genderqueer

Neutrois

Nonbinary

Non-binary – demigirl

Nonbinary (agender)

Non-binary/Androgynous

non-binary/butch

None

None (agender)

Primarily female

Queer

queer femme

Questioning

Trangender

transgender/agender (they/their pronouns)

Transmasculine

Woman

woman I suppose (not tomsehting I'm paying much attention to on internel level)

The depth of the responses generated allowed for significant analysis of how and why these fans engaged with regendering and adaptations that regender characters. The 'visceral appeal' of fannish work uses the existing emotional bond with a work alongside kinks, fetishes and sexual content that appeals to a reader (Kristina Busse and Farley 2013). This 'Id Vortex', as named by Ellen Fremedon, is inextricably linked to shame, as much as to fulfilment (Gray et al. 2017, 55). In turn, the shame-fulfilment cycle fuels divisions in terms not only of taste and class, but when viewed in conjunction with the activism of media, a judgemental function is performed upon an emotional engagement. So, while no emotional response is mandatory, or 'logical', and fandom as a whole is a space where many fans exercise their 'id', or their instinct and impulse, over rational or even socially appropriate engagement, those aspects inform reactions to works. The ways fans separate out emotional affect, rational engagement and recombine them are important to understand when looking at the specific tropes common in adaptations and in the media that is adapted.

The obvious reading of regendering as a quantitative 'fix' for the male-dominated media it adapts is only a small part of what regendering means to creators and audiences. The space available to women characters who are a regendered version goes beyond the tropes and stereotypes common to mainstream media due to their reflection and reworking of that existing character. In addition to this the regendered character can function as a commentary on the original, or genre, or media more widely, and on society itself.

Why regendering?

Several interviewees highlighted variant paths to consuming or creating regendered work. Often this was due to a parasocial relationship, such as a favoured writer who wrote pieces in a 'different' fandom to the one they originally inhabited, or writers who would write in favoured fandoms or pairings but using tropes, themes and methodologies new to the fan:

> … didn't think genderswap fanworks would be something I would be into, but have loved a particular writer's work and so I've delved in.
>
> (AS252)

> My first genderbent fic was How the Mouth Changes Its Shape, by breathedout. I love her work, and read it because it was her. I wasn't seeking genderbent fic. And it was glorious! I now gobble it up. Reading complex female characters is very satisfying.
>
> (AS214)

The experimental elements of fanwork alongside the community focus lead to the 'transformational' exposure which led the fan to be interested in regendering, as well as other fandoms. The memetic spread of motifs, pairings, ideologies, genres and formats is swift within fandom, and is evident in fanwork as much as fandoms. This is key to analysing the works themselves, understanding the networks through which those ideas become part of an archontic whole, rather than more isolated imaginings; it is not limited to the media object itself, or even to transformative fandom online, rather it draws from complex personal archives of interest, interpretation and consumption across transmedia works, disparate interests and the counterpublic of fandom itself.

Sex and gender

The presence of sex within fandom has led to investigations where the sheer presence of female-led sexual desire is an anomaly to be sociologically corrected, or at least rationalized. The status of fans as sexually suspect has been a perpetual concern, even when it was thought to result from an imbalance of humours; it was the excitable female brain whose attachment to works (fictional, or biblical) became sexualized and erotically charged. Or in more modern terms, how women are 'hardwired' to pursue certain kinds of erotic or sexual material due to the evolutionary effects of brain development (Ogas and Gaddam 2012; Salmon and Symons 2004; 2001). Byron's work inciting a 'potentially hysterical mass readership of women', the excitable tears of The Beatles' fans who 'peed, fainted, or simply collapsed from the emotional strain', the presumed 'overly vulnerable female audience' devoted to Justin Beiber; all are examples of the emotional lability of the fan*girl* and her over-attachment to her object of desire[1] (Duffett 2017, 2; Ehrenrich, Hess, and Jacobs 1992, 86; Throsby 2010, 228). For the female fans interviewed and surveyed, sexual or romantic desires were not sublimated into inappropriately gendered attachments (Salmon and Symons 2004, 98) but were instead openly delineated as part of their fannish approach. The desire for Watson, played by Lucy Liu, is influenced by her appeal as an actress; the desire for *Elementary* is positioned as both affective enjoyment of the police procedural, or of Sherlock Holmes archontic iterations, moderated by the stylistic choices of the show runners in their casting. Catbus (interviewee pseudonym) explained their fannish desire for regendering as entwined with their own gender identity and their fannish praxis specifically as a kind of outreach to others facing similar issues:

Lucy: Do you create any genderbent fanwork?

Catbus: Yes! Primarily stuff with um characters not changing their assigned sex at birth but um changing the gender they're presented as in the text. I tend not to write fanfic unless I end up doing that so it's in there every time. Um, I haven't written a great deal of fanfic in the past few years but everything I've written in the past few years has involved playing with characters as they are set up in the narrative and turning them into trans characters.

  …

  one, it's really fun, two, a lot of … as a trans reader who very very rarely gets anything but the short end of the stick in my media, um, it's really really wonderful to be able to sit down and actually work on this and go well no, I headcanon these particular characters as trans for these particular reasons, and writing stories where that's addressed a little more, where that's just there in the text, in my version of the text. One, helps me feel a little (pause) helps me clarify my ideas about why I think these particular characters are trans even with the in the canon narratives where its often, eventually, rejected as a possibility for them.

---

[1] The tears, violence and occasionally murderous rage of sport fans are sufficiently masculine as to not be suspected of latent sexual desires as presumably those can be expressed normally, unlike feminine and female desires.

Um, and also because it just, it gives me a chance to present something to other fans, especially younger fans because I remember growing up without any of this sort of stuff and be able to present to younger fans these options that are accessible in the way all other fic is accessible now.

I did not specifically enquire about sexual identity; however, 14.05 per cent of survey respondents mentioned queerness specifically, and 100 per cent of interviewees. This was coded based on explicit references to sexual acts, sexuality or romantic preference. An interest in sexuality in general was also present in the answers from many survey respondents about how they approach regendered fanworks as creators and as consumers:

Catbus: And it gives a whole lot, a new dynamic to it because that's really interesting because there is that – as much as I hate to say it, in that case I much prefer a het to the weird hateful dudeslash that usually goes on.

Because hatesexy dudeslash is starting to wear thin for me. Hatesexy het with Natalie Dormer? I can roll with it. And more importantly, *Elementary* gives us the other option, hatesexy lesbianism, because Joan and Moriarty have way better chemistry than Joan and Sherlock.

[both laugh]

Lucy: for context, there is an onlooker giving thumbs up at this point as well

***

Mariel: There's a whole lot of stealth genderbending going on in slash, both of the turn-a-male-into-a-female variety (mpreg, anyone?) and the let's-deal-with-uncomfortable-sexist-stereotypes-by-erasing-females-from-existence variety.

…

Playing around with other aspects of sex and sexual orientation hasn't earned any special opprobrium thus far, as long as it still appears to be vaguely slash (in *Almost Human*).

***

Artoria: I think it's also a challenge because readers are often sexually attracted to canon characters because of the actors playing them, so when that changes (I can't think what a female version of Clark Gregg, for example, would actually look like), the character intrinsically becomes less interesting. For me, the most successful genderbent fic does not involve my OTP characters, because I am better able to appreciate the fic on its own terms. (As an aside, are you familiar with that old *Saturday Night Live* sketch, about the porn film reviewer? 'I started watching this film with some interest … and then more attention … and then a great deal of attention … and then, suddenly, I lost interest.')

The majority of openly non-straight respondents (78 per cent, making up 11 per cent of total respondents) were supportive or demanding of seeing their sexuality within their media or their fanworks. Similarly, 67.27 per cent of gender non-conforming respondents actively created or consumed regendered works, 10.91 per cent rejecting them. This trend was similar to respondents who identified as female/woman/cisfemale, with 78.63 per cent consuming or creating those works, with only 11.97 per cent actively rejecting those works. This is a more tentative correlation, but echoes much of the qualitative responses from participants, who identify their own experiences of gender and queerness as the reason behind their fannish works that explore those themes.

Themes and tropes

The metanarrative of fandom, particularly adaptational and transformational fandom, is: fanwork is activist work. This metanarrative – an overarching ideal held by fandom – is occasionally a contentious one (Brough and Shresthova 2012; Stanfill 2019). The proposition is that there is no negative effect associated with consumption or creation, but that simultaneously there is a positive one. In this respect the literature is fairly clear – 'bad' media does not make an individual a bad person, by whatever standards being used, but exposure to media that reiterates and supports objectification, or bigotry, can have the effect of increasing that within the viewer/reader due to '… mass media's role in socialization that supports violence against women' (Dill, Brown, and Collins 2008). At the same time, exposure to literature, specifically reading widely, is correlated with a greater sense of empathy, and that '… exposure to fiction was positively correlated with social support' (Mar, Oatley, and Peterson 2009). A similar argument about fanwork as activism is that the pleasure of the works, as primarily female and primarily queer in audience or creation, makes it subversive, transformative and radical. This does not address the way fanwork reinscribes and supports existing hierarchy, where the 'fandom killjoy' is responsible for pointing out and critiquing the structural inequities, thus marking them troublesome (Pande 2018).

Fandom itself reimagines these arguments within fanworks, specifically around intersections of gender, violence, sexuality and race. The intersectionality of activism in general is increasing in attention but has been the subject of academic inquiry since the 1970s and Crenshaw's work. This increasing visibility of intersectionality, and the shift of focus from singular points of oppression to multiple facets have affected the way this metanarrative is idealized and discussed within fandom and fan studies. Wanzo's examination of the whiteness that dominates scholarly practice within fan studies (2015) and Pande's work regarding decolonizing the academic position where 'defenses of media fandom communities based on a progressive view of them as interest in social justice issues do not encapsulate the full complexity of the matter' due to 'multiple power dynamics' at play (Pande 2018, 322). There have been shifts in both the position of fandom in terms of activism, and in how gender and queerness are revealed/experienced due to concurrent political shifts within media and world politics. There has also been a change in the ways audiences respond, the backlash against *Elementary* seems to hardly rate when compared to the abuse and vitriol aimed at *Ghostbusters: Answer the Call* for example; and indeed the regendering within *Hannibal* barely garnered a mention. This can be explained by form (television vs film) or by the protagonist (the characters regendered in *Hannibal* were support characters, Watson is traditionally a secondary character who was more central in *Elementary* but in *Answer the Call* all four protagonists were regendered). Race particularly has become a vector for abuse around media, and adaptation (particularly those that involve regendering) with the intersectional nature of misogyny and racism made obvious in the mistreatment of Leslie Jones in *Answer the Call* for example, or even much of the commentary about Lucy Liu in *Elementary*.

The narratives my participants created around activism and regendered fanwork were primarily situated in the ideas of authenticity and representation; the inability to find these in mainstream narratives was corrected by their fannish involvement. This included the act of consumption as creation, and the primary criticism of regendered narratives was either a morally suspicious motive for correction (primarily the implied or imputed motive of hetereosexualizing a homosexual pairing) or a failure in the authenticity of that regendered character:

> A lot of the genderbends in general I've found to be excuses to turn one half of a popular slash ship into a "straight" ship, with the character that was genderbent becoming a glorified mary sue. I don't engage with those either, because I do not find those engaging. … Often, from other writers, it's not that good and will mess up genders, etc – if a guy has suddenly been graced with a temporarily female body, he's not going to stop thinking of himself as a he! – so I don't do this often, either.
>
> (AS127)

***

Mostly because I don't see the point. Then because I find it annoying that the reader or writer doesn't enjoy the character enough to the point that they feel the need to change their gender. Gender is unimportant and inconsequential. So why bother, unless you do not appreciate the character as they are. If that is the case, why write about that character?

(AT111)

Jenkins states 'correction' as one of the methods of fanwork creation in his list of the ten types of fanfic and regendering is no different to other genres of fanwork in this respect (Jenkins 2012). The corrective motive does differ in how and why it seeks to correct the original work. In many cases it is a motivation to correct *media* not the original media product; the question is not 'why did Watson do that?' or 'why did they kill Moriarty like that?' but 'why did they make Sherlock male?'. This is only a question prompted by both creative praxis and exposure to this as an adaptive choice. Regendering is not simply a modern conceit, but it is one gaining traction and popularity particularly as more professional works use it as a way to differentiate their adaptations within an oversaturated space. The correction of a media imbalance is one that views media holistically, and as a political space, rather than simply an affective concern about media choices. By correcting the media they consume, fans can create more representation of themselves and of the world they see.

Motives

The paracosm of fandom holds slash as a form of corrective reworking where the male-male relationship, slash, is a queer reparative action 'resistant and subversive in their exploration of queer identities' but nonetheless mirrors existing hegemonic structures around race (Pande 2018, 13). This leads to a defensive position within fandom about regendering when engaged in by professionals in particular although occasionally within the community, where regendering is decried as a form of correctional heterosexuality relies on the counterpublic norm of male-male pairings and slash. This is often associated with highly popular slash pairings like Watson and Sherlock, and most often levelled at mainstream creators like those behind *Elementary*. The more 'palatable' heterosexual pairing is seen to erase the queer subtext of the original and the archontic, rather than as an iteration of its own expanding the representation of women. This was expressed by a number of respondents where regendering is suspicious, particularly when engaged in by professionals who may 'add a het love story' or 'as a cheap love interest' but even fanfic may be 'lazy and uncomfortably sexist or homophobic'.

The motivation for creating or consuming regendering is an element to the perceived authenticity and success of the work. Some fans identified any regendering as a creative failure even if the results were pleasurable, others only viewed certain kinds of regendering as creative failures. Depictive failures evoked a much more personal result, an affective disgust with the work that transgressed a gender value. A failure of authenticity however could be across two axes – creative or depictive. A creative failure of regendering was one that either moved too far from the original character or one that changed too much of the original material. This could take a number of forms, where femininity is overemphasized, often to the point of offensive tropes or stereotypes.

The motives towards production illustrate the defensiveness where regendering is fraught, susceptible to being warped into something misogynistic, or transphobic. Avoiding those possibilities functioned as a creative praxis for many fans, but also for professionals. One of the respondents to the interviews was Tansy Rayner Roberts, a fantasy author from Australia who had recently finalized a regendered version of *The Three Musketeers* as an online serial funded through Patreon. She engaged with this corrective trend as one that resulted from both widespread gender imbalances, but particularly those within genres and at a creative level:

> **Tansy:** I get more excited about them (professional regendered works), because fandom has always done that as a subversive transgressive thing and I like the subversive transgressive thing, but when it's on the screen and there's millions of dollars behind the production, like the choice they made to make Starbuck female? That was really interesting, especially with because they announced it early and there was this whole backlash, up until the point that she walked onto the screen. At which point you're like '... yeah, I can see that'. And I think that probably helped a lot of later genderbent things. And now I'm trying to think, actually, the most – it's doesn't relate to the question but the most, we've mainly been talking about when the male character gets turned into the female because you know traditionally there's been so many more interesting and varied roles for men so that's something we do. But the hardest thing I found for me to do was I love the

female characters in the three musketeers they have very different roles but I love them all, changing them into men was far harder work. Like it's really easy for me to write funny flirtatious really competent female!Aramis. that's easy. But doing, turning Milady into a male character, turning Constance and Queen Anne in particular into male characters was difficult, especially because the musketeers spend a lot of time effectively apologising and hiding for Queen Anne's you know very dodgy behaviour and when you genderswap everything, you've got a group of women running around protecting a man who's been having it off on the side, you know? Milady is one of the best and most interesting female characters ever written writing her as a man, I liked writing her as a man I liked the fact that having a male villain whose primary method is seduction is very rare, so that's interesting. But at the same time having watched all these amazing screen Milady's and wanting to embrace that character ... I really love the BBC Tv series of Musketeers and their interpretations of these women, so yeah, I found that was almost like taking a step backwards.

She also identified the creative puzzle solving of regendering as an attractive proposition for her as a fan, and as a history scholar (she has a PhD in Classics and studied English at university). The position of women in the narrative and in society, past, present and future, is mediated through her regendering praxis as an author and as a reader.

Regendering as a fannish praxis reveals 'corrective' possibilities of their texts; education, dissemination, reworking history or the failures reiterating existing power structures and ignorance. They do not simply serve as reflections of specific fan interests – or not only as that – but as a way of communicating with the dominant and default groups of masculinity, maleness, whiteness, neurotypical status, heterosexuality and broadening it to be inclusive. The power of the representation is not only to empower the other, but to forcibly shift the narrative and expose the default for the shallow narrative it is.

Politics

The narrowed audience for fannish works and the weight of the expectations that politicize the creative praxis of regendering contribute to the niche state of these works as activist entities. They provide spaces for individuals to explore their own identities, and to communicate identity formation with others, but their relevance to the wider spaces of fandom is often reliant on adherence to other expectations, to the gift and attention economy and to conformation with other expectations. Fandom has a number of archives, spaces public and private, standards of etiquette and behaviour, and expectations of audience, all of which create a counterpublic that is often inaccessible to the public in a meaningful way (Bury 2005). Regendering relies on a familiarity with the canon narrative (and often with other archontic variations), and it only manifests as activism due to the default masculine focus of media as a whole. Regendering female characters to male ones is easily read as removing the female focus and putting it onto an imagined masculine, particularly when it occurs within the counterpublic metanarrative of slash. However, when regendering male characters to female, or male characters to non-binary ones, or cis male characters to trans male ones, this still focuses fannish narratives onto male characters even when changing the gender to reveal the inherent and underlying focus or marginalizations within the canon.

Similarly, the counterpoint to the idea of fanwork as political praxis is the defence of it as an act of desire, unanswerable to anything other than the id, or to enjoyment/pleasure. This desire for pleasure is explained by several respondents, as is the othering effect those works have on the object of those desires: 'I believe that a lot of slash is actually about women's engagement with their own imaginaries, their own desires, and their marked bodies' (AS15). Pande suggested that 'fandom is framed around perceptions of pleasure for its community' (2018, 13) and this frame is often presented as a transgressive process, which foregrounds women's pleasure (be it sexual, romantic, violent or selfish, or any combination of those). However, what those pleasures entail remains evident in broad strokes only – the 'four categories' Massey identifies for slash fans where queer women identify with visual/textual imagery of male pleasure and reconfigure or reconsider gendered behaviour, distance from the ethical issues of objectification, simple enjoyment of 'depictions of male pleasure' or exploration of existing relationship dynamics in canon (2019). The particulars of those pleasures are where identification happens, or othering. An examination of those specific particulars shows that fannish capacity for pleasure is matched by their capacity to recreate hegemonic power structures, where 'seemingly subversive fan fiction that depicts same-sex couplings can reinforce heteronormativity' even when dealing with explicitly queer canon (Hunting 2012). Even when those structures are disavowed – the ideological position of slash as gay activism – other structures are instead reasserted: 'the body horror aspect of a sex swap is hot' or 'truthfully I've found most genderswapping fics to be terrible and end up reinforcing the very gender stereotypes they are attempting to criticize (maybe? or is it just a kink for some?)' (AS275; AS9).

The intersectional axes of oppression make it difficult to claim activism from the mere existence of a creative work, or practice. However, fans often reject this concept for their own works – they may talk about fandom in aggregate, or other ways of being a fan, but the concept of fannishness as activism is one most often tied to representation, to wider trends within fandom, and to non-fanwork activities like fundraising and political essays that nonetheless still reinscribe marginalization. This conflict between the deeply personal axes of pleasure and desire with what are delineated as political axes of representation and identity is given voice in regendered works, even as they may not speak to all forms of representation or identity. Similarly, while the individual works are where fans exercise and explore identity formation, particularly for gender and sexuality, these works must be placed within a wider view of fanworks where they necessarily form a subset, a subaltern to the already subaltern.

Just as the works I examine are a counterpublic, transgressing multiple boundaries of taste and quality and expected performances of femininity and fannishness, this research deliberately privileges those narratives over the more widespread ones of non-regendered work. It is by examining these works as sites of activism, of pleasure and desire, representation and identity, that a view of the default narratives of fandom and media can be uncovered and revealed. Regendering functions within the counterpublic as a way of reinterpreting the othered feminine, and the other as a space of connection with peers. By changing the gender in adaptation, the specific forms of gendering that take place seemingly unnoticed in the media are highlighted.

The way fans and creators subvert the 'default' into the unclaimed through regendering characters is also applicable to other kinds of reworkings. It is also important to the ways in which creative counterpublics create metatextual ideologies, and what position the works take within those environments. The othering is a natural progression of community formation and by studying the ways in which creators signify that process within regendering, I have established the importance of play and desire within gender construction, both affective states integral to fannish praxis. This can be expanded to other gender-creative fanworks, but also to work processes, like the translation of classics by women (Anne Carson is an obvious choice, but also Wilson's translation of Homer's *Odyssey* is a recent work that deals with the gendered nature of the original and the world of Classic Literature). The process of translation is one that requires a translation of cultural context, and Farley comments that 'from the point of view of reader-centered literary theory, there is little difference between the interpretive activity of translating and the interpretive activity of writing fan fiction' (2013). The result of regendering is also evident in mainstream works that are not adaptations, but examples of gender-blind casting, as they engage with how a creator thinks of their work within the communal effort of a film script.

Clashes between fans and the 'ivory tower' have been illuminating in terms of how fans perceive themselves, and research into their works where acafandom is critiqued 'for attempting to generalise singular or limited experiences to the broader fandom community or develop a truth that applies to all of fandom' (Raw 2020). These conflicts have provoked high levels of negative affective displays and defensiveness from fans who prefer to understand their fanwork as a politically neutral act situated in pleasure and personal identification rather than as a literary form open to critique where 'fans were troubled by the work of academia opening up what they was as the closed fan community to outsider critique' in a number of instances (Raw 2020). This is most clearly represented in contemporary fan studies projects that are delving deeply into the ways in which fans, fandom and fan studies itself, replicate the structures of oppression even as they disavow them, questions of monetization, race, class, gender, sexuality, ability that provoke conflict within fandom and in academia. This may seem like a rather negative view of fandom, or my own research, but there are ways that the replication of those structures within fandom serves to further explore ways to undermine and rework them into something better. Without those structures, and the ethos of fannish assemblage and reimagining, fanworks would not exist as a means for those fans to communicate aspects of themselves through their work, or to create ways of interacting with the structural inequalities that make it clear that survival is possible, and that those inequalities exist, and that there is hope for changing them.

Recognition of the socially charged nature of otherness, and the way it is deployed within fanwork, and adaptation relies on understanding the subcultural elements of the counterpublic formation. This theory of re-othering allows for the presence of those subcultural elements that reinscribe some aspects of mainstream hegemony while subverting others, and that these works rely on the dominance of the mainstream to perform that work. Adaptations, even for audiences unaware of the original work, are in conversation with that original and with other adaptations, other works within the genre, the criticism and reviews of the work, alongside the creator's personal response – the Archive is manifest within the adaptation, even without conscious or deliberate inclusions.

3

Theories

The art of the 'crossover', combining two seemingly unrelated media products into a whole, is an honoured pastime of fandom, and the media genres it reifies. Guerrero-Pico and Scolari link it with interdisciplinarity within academia and describe it as '… the semantic link of crossover with other hybrid species, as the mashup and remix …' (Guerrero-Pico and Scolari 2016, 184). As such my work here exists in a nexus of gender theory, fan studies, literary criticism and sociology[1]. These are the domains that work together to support my analysis of media that changes the gender of one or more characters, and also the fans of those works. This culture of fannishness is impossible to quantify, or even qualify. It is not a subculture in sociological terms, with concrete social roles and rules, it is instead something more like a counterpublic, where the variations and fractures of the mainstream are echoed and replicated within the fannish 'version'. This includes the marginalizations evident in wider media and culture, like racism, sexism, classist and homophobic elements and ableism among others. Autoethnographic observations of fans have identified this not only in tropes and characterizations – fondly referred to as 'fanon' – but in textual 'tics' seemingly common to and springing from fandom. So, while my focus is definitively on regendering, it must also include space for racial intersections alongside other axes such as neurotypicality, transgender identity and cultural situations.

Within regendering the 'question of intersectional identity' connects very clearly with some aspects, as the regendered character may also be 'racebent' (as in *Elementary* with John Watson becoming Joan a Chinese American woman), or the response to regendering may include racial abuse (as in the experience of

---

[1] Much like my only fanfic attached to my academic name being a crossover between Terry Pratchett's *Discworld* series and the *Star Wars* universe, prompted by a Tumblr post, in turn prompted the exasperation many female fans felt watching science fiction replicate the same tedious emotional mistakes of any other type of fiction.

Leslie Jones after appearing in *Ghostbusters: Answer the Call*), thus revealing the way those gendered elements and expectations are also racialized. The effects of this are, as Crenshaw argues in non-media contexts (1991), intersectional and the experiences of the character Watson and the audience reception of the character are compounded by the racial and gender difference. Pande terms this a 'failing to engage with axes of identity apart from gender and sexuality' (2018, 16). The work of scholars in race studies as it intersects with fandom and media such as Rukmini Pande and Poe Johnson provides an inspiration for my work and makes clear that singular lenses for analysis are too narrow, to the detriment of not only the analysis but also the people involved as the audience, the creators and the wider society around that media (2018; 2019).

Wanzo's work regarding Blackness, specifically within an American context of research into popular culture, addresses some of these specific intersections as complicating 'the portrayal of the fan as embracing alterity by choice' as opposed to the hypervisible alterity of the black fan, the queer fan and one can also presume the gender non-conforming fan too (2015, para. 2.1). Her work also identifies that this 'romanticization of fan exceptionalness has perhaps produced resistance to emphasizing the normativity of some fandoms' (Wanzo 2015, para. 2.2). This is important to note in respect to gender as well, where the normativity of the white, male default is suppressed in order to valorize the queerness of slash as transgressive within fannish counterpublics. Additionally, the theoretical positioning of fandom as a space of female and/or queer joy in the way it produces slash or regenders characters actively suppresses and erases the overwhelming whiteness of those works and the racialized elements within them and the audience response as it creates a 'fandom killjoy (whose) pleasure threatens the invocation of a broadly inclusive, woman-centric, and queer-coded community' (Pande 2018, 13).

Race and fandom are areas that are vastly under-researched in English outside specific areas like Japanese fandoms, music subculture and to a certain extent sport, where participation in fandom is often visibly racialized by either the fandom object, or by the fan. This is not to say that work about fans and race is non-existent, but as Wanzo notes 'many claims in fan scholarship about alterity, fan interpellation, ambivalent spectatorship, and antifandom become more nuanced if we look at particular traditions of African American fandom and black cultural criticism' (2015, para. 1.6).

There are researchers addressing this in terms of race and fandom, rather than simply race in the media that spawns fandoms. There are similar findings between race studies and gender studies when applied to fandom, wherein a default identity position can be identified as nominally rejected by the fans but then replicated in their works and the focus of their works, such as Pande's *Squee from the Margins* (2018). The particulars of the default identities are different, as are the specific mechanisms for its enforcement at a subcultural level. In terms of race we see very clearly the way expectations of whiteness, or the 'structures of whiteness' affect the 'fandom algorithm' and go on to structure 'fandom interactions' (Pande 2018, 16). Those structures have particularly negative effects on non-white audiences and recreate themselves within the minds of the white audience (Johnson 2020; Walker 2019). The interactions and effects mean that 'the problems that have historically been faced by nonwhite fans in these spaces are seen to be reflective of larger societal trends that fandom spaces merely mirror' (Pande 2018, 16). The refusal to acknowledge fandom as a space that reinforces and reinscribes those trends undermines the positivity associated with the idea of fandom as that broadly inclusive space, or one of activism.

My conclusion may seem overly negative – that all of the creative ways in which fans approach these ideas and experiments in othering and otherness expose the underlying reality that in spite of the ways fandom innovates it replicates existing hegemony. While on the surface this may seem to undermine the actions of these fans, and their works, the method matters as much, if not more, than the result, as fanwork is inherently explorative and deeply personalized. This is also why it has remained important to look at the fannish creations alongside commercial adaptations; the methods are important to the audiences as much as they are evident in the works.

Representation and otherness

Regendering is a complex adaptational technique that is not limited to fans and, if one counts pre-filming regendering where a character is written as one gender then played by a performer of another, it has happened repeatedly at every level of filmmaking. A female or feminine presence is read into the works through transgressing the perceived roles of audience and creator, rather than through active presence within the narrative; regendering makes this 'reading' explicit through the shift from audience to creator, and from subtextual assumptions of crossgender identification to explicit representation. This transgressiveness is often experienced both as a boundary violation for the original content creator – see here any number of authorial essays about the sanctity of their work and the illegitimacy of fanworks that aren't contractual professional works such as those written by Diana Gabaldon calling it 'immoral', George R.R Martin who is 'against it' and Annie Proulx saying that 'These are not their characters. The characters belong to me by law' (Gilbey 2014; Martin 2010; Nepveu 2010) – but also of feminine roles as the purely receptive audience. Regendering sits at a nexus between traditional ways of approaching fannish practices of rewriting, and performances of gender.

Regendering occurs due to an existing imbalance of gender within media, but also the imbalance in representation is emblematic of an imbalance in creative practice; fans occupy that imbalance and recreate not only the worlds and universes of the media, but their own experiences. Fanwork is, at its heart, a repudiation of canon and a privileging of affective reaction to that work. When this is combined with the often explicitly gendered expectations of creators, mainstream media and the fans, it becomes a gendered exercise, one that can be examined as a feminist act. Transformative works rewrite the existing narrative for a multitude of reasons, examined by scholars such as Jenkins within the realm of fan studies, or even Castle in queer theory (2012; 2013). The drive to see one's own self in narrative as a minority, or as the subaltern, is only matched by the recognizance of one's own otherness in the narrative.

The focus on otherness, and othering, is inextricably linked within fandom to intersectionality and questions of representation. Ideas of identity and representation, and the importance of recognizing one's self within works, or revealing that through fictional works, are integral to both fans as audience members who create, and the fans who become professional and adapt their fannish objects. However, the power differentials and hierarchies within this split between fandom and adaptation need to be addressed. In the case of the fans, these regendered adaptations that they create are explicit not only in their representation of othered identities, but also in rejecting wider expectations of a gendered audience and experience of the world. The basis of this version of otherness is vague within fandom – unlike Butler's gender theories, or even intersectionality with the often-mislaid attribution to Crenshaw – it is linked more with the psychological positions of otherness, or the social feeling, the affect associated with being not-male, not-white, not-'normal'.

In addition to the rather straightforward concerns about women and gender in heterocentric conceptualizations of society, there are the questions of gender that are provoked by the works. This includes the way regendering is used to depict gender uncertainties and transitions – not that they are the same, but the way in which the stories chosen investigate gender points to a kind of instability for women specifically. Maleness remains unchanged, un-mined, while femininity, femaleness and masculinity are worked with and around by the creators. The absence of masculine uncertainties, and the central experience of femininity and femaleness, or masculinity and femaleness, reverting to a de Beauvoir-accented sense of manufactured womanhood, or Gaten's 'default' (2014; 1996). This questioning of gender roles is reflected upon within fannish engagement with the canon, or with media; regendering is a method of centralizing this imbalance in perception and social response. It rarely accepts the male, or the masculine, as the default experience, or a neutral identity, but insists that works about masculinity are already prevalent and suffocate those about women, and femininity, and that it is a political act to focus on women. That it is also one which replicates women as Other, as uncertain, remains a site of contention and complexity for the works and for the fans.

This explicit othering, and the naming and rejection of the male gaze, is woven into the experiences of being women and the expected performances of femininity within the text. Authorities loom large, with expectations of gender policing manifest in both actions and inaction within the texts and also in negative responses to these works. Even commercial regendering works play with the audience expectations of regendered characters, and how that reflects on the original works as well as how it changes the narratives available for female characters.

Violent tendencies

Men are afraid that women will laugh at them. Women are afraid that men will kill them.

(Attributed to Margaret Atwood)

Feminist activism around domestic violence, reproductive justice, rape culture, intersectional elements of racial and ethnic violence, all reveal the personal landscape of love and romance as one fraught with incredible risk and danger for women. The explosive resumption of the #MeToo movement from the earlier work done by Tarana Burke on Myspace in 2006 (Guerra 2017), and revelations about long-term sexual predation by powerful men in Hollywood, politics and almost every other workforce, was nascent during my research and much of the examples of regendering, but these works show the foundations for it. Alongside these social movements was the backlash against two major examples of commercial regendering: *Ghostbusters: Answer the Call* and the Thirteenth Doctor in *Doctor Who*. The response to these commercial works included threats of violence, multiple essays and opinion pieces about the damage done to 'childhood' media objects and the active use of technology and the internet to situate regendering as a cultural war against men (Hills 2021). These responses are explored further in this book, focusing on the critical rhetoric about *Ghostbusters: Answer the Call* and the Thirteenth Doctor of *Doctor Who* alongside the treatment of the women who played these roles.

The way these interactions within the narrative work and towards it echo the way in which real women's lives and experiences are policed, but also how in media, fandom and other discourses female characterization is policed for those transgressions. The well-worn objections to the 'bossy woman' alongside admiration for the 'leader' who is presumed male – and drilling down through those objections to layers and layers of intersecting axes of oppression – are critiqued within these regendered narratives by taking those admirable masculine-male characters and laying them at the foundation of the female character. Scodari's comments about the ways in which female characters are judged by fans who otherwise claim to want more powerful women are the counterpublic against which the regendering presents the recontextualized characters (Scodari 2003). The regendering also recontextualizes what is meant by strength, by leadership, by violence; the ability to endure, to continue, to swallow anger and hurt and act, is how the canonical aspects of the characters are regendered.

The characterization of regendering as violence, in the way it changes an original work so thoroughly, gives rise to a response that characterizes itself as a defence, as a reaction to aggression. This is most evident in the reactions to commercial and highly publicized examples of regendering, such as *Ghostbusters: Answer the Call*. When it was announced the lead actresses and director were all targeted for abuse, none as much or as violently as Leslie Jones. However, as the response of the fan is characterized as a reaction to provocation, their actions can be minimized. For example, Proctor claims that the negative response to the film was a 'minority cluster of misogynist comments' (2017, 1112) but this is belied by the significant issues faced by Jones for example, who had revenge porn released online and her private site hacked to feature pictures and video of Harambe (Lawson 2018). Even this misogynist and racist attack on her livelihood and personality is dismissed by Proctor in a single paragraph description with a coda that 'some Tweeters challenged Jones' character in GB '16 because they felt that the representation therein was nothing less than racial stereotyping, a form of toxicity in itself' (2017, 1132). This may seem like an example where a problematic or violent sector of the audience is a small number of fans and their actions only relevant to individual situations; however, similar events have occurred in multiple fandoms, with violence against not only directors, actors and other professionals, but also other fans. Regendering, and other forms of critical fandom and creation, is perceived as a provocation or act of violence due to the way the media object is integrated into the sense of self some fans create from media. This sense of self also extends to media as political activism and action.

Even when considering the mainstream media that grounds fandom, race is a prevalent form of hegemonic replication within fannish works and research. Regendering specifically is about gender but the intersection of race and gender for media objects like *Elementary* and *Ghostbusters: Answer the Call* cannot be ignored. It is important to acknowledge that the racial element particularly is often not subverted and is instead reinscribed by fans and audiences in their reaction and fanworks. Pande's research into race and fandom centres post-colonialist theory and reveals that 'media fandom spaces, theorized as inclusive and liberating, are not immune to hierarchies structured by privilege accruing due to income, class, racial, ethnic, and cultural identity, disability, etc. Ironically this lags behind actual fan practice' (2016, 210).

While Wanzo complicates the optimist bent of fan studies genealogies that focus on potential subversion and transgression, or gendered community support, with her work illustrating that race, in the context of fan studies, are '... frequently treated as an add-on or as something that should be addressed somewhere later ...' (Wanzo 2015). This is particularly relevant in the context of Jenkins's reference to women 'colonizing' masculine media via fandom (2012, 114) which ignores white women as a colonizing force of their own, complicit with the existing hegemony even as they are subjugated by it. This is a form of racial violence that exists within media, and fandom, and will exist within regendering too. The tendency to elide that element of bigotry in favour of the socially aware gendered or queered reading is attractive, but in the scope of regendering it is impossible to ignore the intersectional violence faced by Lucy Liu as Joan in *Elementary*, or Leslie Jones as Patty Jenkins in *Ghostbusters*. This intersectional aspect to their regendered performances is explored more in the following chapters, but this reconsideration of 'colonization' as a metaphor for fanwork and fan consumption/production is relevant even without the obvious forms of racism in critique or harassment.

Fans as creators

What does colonization of media mean when it is performed by subjects of a 'permanently contested site of meaning' (Elam 1994, 32)? The properties which inspire fanwork, however, as well as the works themselves, often exhibit the same hegemonies and hierarchies as the canon. The effects of the fanbase's 'transgressive' desires for better and more representation have been felt and changed several properties over the past few years, where fan campaigns, or fannish professionals, led to situations where characters were regendered or changed racial categories *(Hannibal, Elementary)*, romantic connections *(Hannibal, She-ra and the Princesses of Power)* or campaigned against the deaths of queer characters as in *The 100* which resulted in an apology from the showrunner Jason Rothenberg (McNutt 2017). Shifting generations have begun to dominate creative industries, with new showrunners, directors and creators having grown up with media objects they now are professionally a part of. As these fans become the professionals behind the media, the affective properties of the works they created will become more obvious, as will their understanding of the fan base. These works illustrate the ways in which the domain of the 'other' is beginning to be considered as more than simply a 'niche' for media to market to.

The theoretical engagement with gender of the creator has dominated the intellectual understanding of fanwork but has not extended to the works they create *except* in the creation of slash, and to a smaller extent the creation of the 'Mary Sue' (Frey 2009). Regendering allows for the assumption of the male role by a female character, including the narrative-bending focus that would otherwise be critiqued as a 'Mary-Sue'; Willis notes this as a particularly fertile landscape for queer and transgender fans (2006). The adaptation of the fannish critique of fanworks into a wider literary critique is one that echoes how regendering has shifted in its use within fandom to its use within mainstream media; there are very significant differences in the application that necessarily change the audience reaction and can delegitimize gender-creative works.

Critiques and criticisms of the Mary Sue – a character introduced as something of a wish fulfilment or insertion of a semi-biographical character into the work, the name springing from the critical fanwork *A Trekkie's Tale* by Paula Smith in a fanzine from 1973 – have been rightfully identified as a source of discomfort with both the way women write about themselves and the presence of a female character who transgresses expected characterization and economies of attention and affect which place her as a secondary narrative focus (Willis 2006). Much of that work around the discomfort of the term has been done by fans themselves and by professional authors. Seanan McGuire, Sarah Rees Brennan, Holly Black and Zoe Marriott all posted essays on their own sites deconstructing the ways they had seen the term applied to their own original works and how they perceived that to be motivated by a discomfort with female characters who maintain agency and identity (2011; 2011; 2011; 2011). In particular they critique the application of 'Mary Sue' to their original works as a way of further reinforcing the lack of space for female characters with agency:

> The problem with using this term outside of fanfiction is simple: the world of a novel has always configured around main characters ... We can't hold female characters to totally different standards than the ones we hold male characters to, or we ladies are going to back be in the kitchen making jello surprise before long ... We need to criticize female characters and female writers, sure, so long as we're not criticizing them first and foremost for being women.
>
> (Black 2011)

***

> I'm sick of it, Dear Readers. I'm sick of seeing people condemn any female character with a significant role in a book as a Mary-Sue. I'm sick of people talking about how the female characters were too perfect or not perfect enough, too passive or too badass, too talented or too useless, when what they really mean – but don't even KNOW they mean – is that the characters were too much in possession of lady parts.
>
> (Marriott 2011)

The relationship between women and fannish feminist praxis has a long history. Castle refers to the practices of fans in the early novel reading period, their rewrites and reinterpretations, and interactions with the creators to modify the works, as feminist literary critique, and as a kind of homosocial if not homoerotic relationship practice between women (2013, 11–12). This has continued through the centuries into modern fandom. While the presence of the queer female as author has been interpreted as therefore being a presence in the works they create, this does not change the continued dominance of the male narrative within media (Lackner, Lucas, and Reid 2006; Levi, McHarry, and Pagliassotti 2008; Russ 1985).

Sexual processes

The actual work of fanfiction tends towards the character-oriented affectual set pieces. Coppa theorizes, in discussion with a fanfic author Brancher about her work in *The Fan Fiction Reader: Folk Tales for the Digital Age*, that fanfic inserts this affectual load into the works 'because they're looking for stories where sex is profound and meaningful' not because the stories lack sex, but that sexual works lack 'friendship' (2017, 95). This simultaneous delineation of sexual activity and friendship, which also insists on the layering of the latter into the former, echoes in some ways Castle's disbelief that some aspects of queer theory neglect to delineate between the homosocial woman and the homosexual woman (1993). Practising sexual affect, textually and socially, is part of fannish culture and underlies significant aspects of regendered work specifically, particularly examinations of the ways in which gendered experience changes affectual response and projection (Narai 2017; Turner 2016). Gender non-conformity or creativity can be represented as kink or fetish, exploration or affirmation, or any combination of the three (Ellison 2013; Nagaike and Yoshida 2011; Rose 2020).

The prevalence of slash as a method of understanding and sampling fanworks has a long history. It is not difficult to perceive a thread of prurience, or concern about that imbalance, in the focus researchers place on slash; something researchers have identified and push back against (Oak and Ashley 2011). The interpretations of slash that remove the transgressiveness, such as in 'Normal Female Interest in Men Bonking', devalue how fans perceive their work but also the way in which their manifestations of their sexuality, the creativity, their feminism and activism, is unacceptable at mainstream social levels (Green, Jenkins, and Jenkins 1998). Added to this is the transnational research into fandom that is situated within highly homophobic social contexts such as China, with the localized fandom of 'Curly-Fu' (Benedict Cumberpatch as Sherlock) and 'Peanut' (Martin Freeman as Watson) (Yi 2012). The focus on slash – fannish and academic – replicates and reinscribes the male dominance and at the same time devalues the transgressiveness it can exhibit.

The feminist potentialities of fanfiction were recognized in the influential 'Pornography by Women, for Women, with Love' by Russ, and while there is a certain naivety to the essay it clearly links the way fanworks are a form of creative *and* feminist praxis for the creators and the readers (1985). It also very strongly links the sexual content of fanwork with psychological freedoms offered by the form when compared with other forms of writing. Several theorists (of which I am the most recent) have attempted this integration of a particular view of femininity, or femaleness, or creativity, into fanworks. The reinterpretations of slash as 'normal' desire by a fairly undifferentiated category of women – either as they appear within the community or analysed in the context of evolutionary biology situating the desire on a masculinity on part of the reader (Salmon 2015; Salmon and Symons 2004), Freudian influenced psychology as a rejection of heteronormativity (Foster 2015), or second-wave feminist theory as a liberatory act (Russ 1985) – do little to acknowledge the gender non-conforming works, or the way a female (or nominally expected-to-be-female) creator still continues the mainstream imbalance of the default white male hero into her own work. It also perpetuates the erasure of queer women within the work and as the creators. The presence of the queer woman in fandom cannot be ascertained merely by the work she creates, as several fan-led surveys have revealed the majority of fans identify in some way as non-straight while still writing male-male slash, clearly revealing sexual attraction to the protagonists is not the primarily or sole motivator for fannish work; my own data support these observations.

More recent theorists, like Busse and Hellekson, and Lackner and Reid, examine the ways the presence of the woman behind the works themselves moderates the male domination in the works they produce, and the media they work within (2014; 2006; 2009). Large-scale autoethnographic demographic surveys undertaken by fans and fan organizations tend to show the previous conception of fans as primarily straight, although with a much greater proportion of queer fans. This work, however, is based on assumptions about sexual identity and behaviour, which presume sexual desire is revealed in a linear fashion through media consumption, rather than the idea that 'what can inspire one reader to masturbate, can be read as an interesting study of desire by another' or that 'the interaction between the fandom can add an extra layer of excitement' to sharing the works (Kukka 2021, 59). These kinds of assumptions underlie significant amounts of fanwork, where the assumption of sexuality based on gender presentation, activity or behaviour outside sex, is as much a point of transgression as the act of writing fanwork. This transgression illustrates not just the politicized effects but a playful affect, where the works themselves and engagement with them are centred on deep play where a 'purely ludic affair can have serious undercurrents that reflect community realities and concerns' (Ancelet 2001, 144). The next chapter uses that focus on play to explore what it means for an adaptation to play with gender.

4

What does 'playing with gender' mean?

When fans adapt a media object to include regendered or gender-creative characters, my research found there was a sense of playfulness integrated with that experimentation. The experience of being female within mainstream culture provoked the 'gender play' within fanworks, and those works were concerned with the ways gender affects characterization. Negative responses to the adaptations – mostly the ones within mainstream professional contexts – were primarily based in a rejection of narratives that diverge from a male default and 'correct' characterization, with queerness playing a small part in both negative and positive approaches. The common thread of fans and their engagement with regendered work, or active disengagement with it, was centred around emotion and affect – a playfulness and desire.

A very obvious thread of optimism and positivity was present within the participants of my research; this informed the themes and tropes they spoke about explicitly but also ones I identified within their answers. Even where fans were negative about works – professional or fannish – and about other fans, there was a sense or an active expectation of improvement:

> Women are underrepresented in the mainstream works that generally become fandom mainstays. It's always been one of my biggest pet peeves, and I wish strongly to make an impact on that trend. I seek to identify with characters in fandom, and I personally connect better with female characters. They face the same, more commonly female, struggles–growing up know that your work is less valued, living in a victim-blaming and slut-shaming culture. I identify strongly as a feminist, so any form of literature that empowers women … (link to work redacted) … This illustrates the problems of gender stereotypes in Sherlock and in the wider world. Stereotypes fascinate and frustrate me. I am particularly interested in genderswap where the integral characteristics of the person do not change.
>
> (AS84)

This hopefulness, the drive to better themselves and the nebulously defined 'fandom' they are a part of, colours the way respondents engaged with questions about gender, identity and their own practices as fans. This hope may seem irrelevant but as I explain, the narrative nature of how fans engage with these works and their own identity gives that hope a less ephemeral quality as it becomes a promise to the reader that they too can survive the harsher parts of life.

Affect and regendering

Regendering as a form of adaptation often hewed away from ideas of fidelity instead it offered a way for creators and the audience to delineate what aspects of adaptation as a responsive process appealed to them. The survey of fans and creators included negative responses, and negative spaces where those responses were not volunteered (either in the survey or in the pauses during interviews); this illustrates the importance of affect and emotionality within the fannish counterpublic which holds itself separate from much of the critical nature of mainstream media response and analysis *but only for works within the counterpublic*. The performance of community within the counterpublic is a method of reinforcing the boundaries around it.

This delineation between the fans of regendering – operating outside the industry – and the professional adaptations such as *Ghostbusters: Answer the Call* is evident in the way critique is performed and received. The carefully anonymous critique of other fannish work is absent if discussing the commercial and professional examples. This is a manifestation of the affective economy of fandom, where the burden of 'proof' is higher for criticism aimed in-group. It is important to note that this is not a consistent practice, with work from Pande and Stanfill both pointing to negative aspects of fannish responses to fannish work where the critic is 'seen to disrupt operations of pleasure' and 'takes the hurt feelings of majoritarians as evidence of minoritarian violence' in relation to issues of race in particular (Proctor et al. 2018, 372–3).

The operations of pleasure are signified in my research as 'play' – this is used to signal where fans responses included the theme where play can be a serious interaction with the boundaries of self and the world, the 'special calibre of play … that leads to transcendence, creativity …' (Ackerman 2011, 26). As the data show in Chart 1 this 'play' theme is correlated with almost all

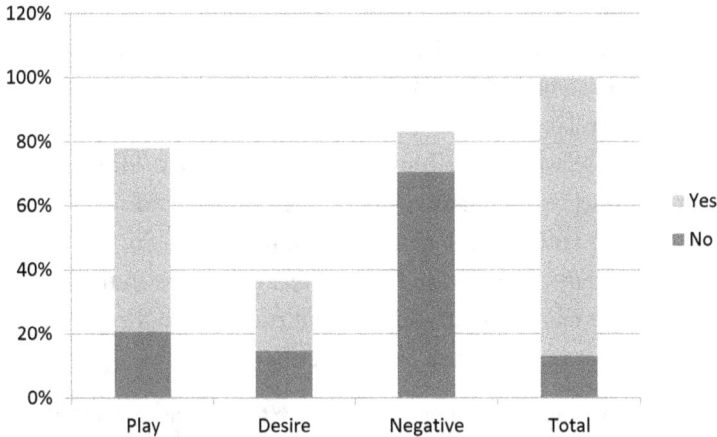

Chart 1 Creative practices and negative affect.

of the respondents who create regendered work, but a reasonable proportion of those respondents were also negative in their responses. Similarly, 'desire' encompasses not only sexual desire for erotic works, but a desire for a specific manifestation of character; not a simple wish for more women, or more sex, but a mindset where that desire is made manifest in work and that is reflected in my data.

The majority of answers from fans, in interviews and within the short comment fields of the survey, were eager to share both their experiences but also the ways in which positive outcomes were achieved within fanworks and by fandom. In interviews particularly, it was difficult for participants to answer question 10: 'What are some ways you have seen genderbent characters be less successful?'; my interviews were designed specifically to avoid personal 'rants' about works the respondents may have disliked, and to elicit as much constructive information as possible. This final question often provoked a kind of affective distress that can be attributed to my position as something of an interloper – as an academic, as someone reporting on fandom, fans were almost always aware of the ways in which fannish conflicts can become entertainment fodder (as in 'Survey!Fail') (Reid 2016). Or as Stanfill terms is 'a protective attitude in relation to outsiders' due to the high levels of emotional labour and the affective economy of fandom; niceness is prized as a communication method and even constructive criticism is a negotiated encounter (Stanfill 2013). This question was framed in order to specifically focus on characterization and wider tropes rather than on specific works.

Those that answered the question often referred to older works, ones prior to 'gender enlightenment', or referred to humorous errors, like gender change causing hair to become suddenly long.

When negative language was used (fear, bad, problematic, stupid) it was often around those works that transgressed those activist ideals, rather than about fans themselves. Similarly, when a trope was identified as negative, it was engaged with critically as a manifestation of identity. So, in particular, an interviewee – Catbus – objected to fanwork that engaged with trans characters, but their response was founded in ideas about education and exposure, and the need for more creators to be open to critique about gender:

> **Catbus:** Um so I think its not impossible to have the cismale to cisfemale swap as a successful genderbend but you need to be very careful and you need to talk to people, you can't just throw it out into the aether and expect that it's going to work.

Survey respondents who were negative about regendering often professed either an apathy towards the idea, or a lack of understanding 'I don't know why people would do that'. This was often expressed with the concern that regendering as an adaptive technique moved a character or story away from fanwork to 'original' in some fashion. Another area of concern for those respondents who were negative about regendering – even if they did engage in it or sought it out – was the idea that it is in some way homophobic, or transphobic. This has been expressed by fans in meta, specifically around the ways regendering is categorized and named (indeed, I explain in the Introduction why I use 'regendering' due to these concerns). Specifically, the term regendering was reacted to positively by several participants as avoiding the binary view of gender implied by 'swap', or the artificial conflation of sex and gender and gender performance as implied by 'genderbend' or 'genderswap' or even 'cisswap':

> I like regendered fanart; it's a fun way to play with the canon. [Off topic: I like the term regendering. Members of the trans community addressed the problems with using terms like genderswap quite a few times and I think this is a much nicer alternative.]
>
> (AS85)

However, even without concerns around the nomenclature fans were concerned about the ways in which fandom as a whole participates in sexist structures, knowingly and unknowingly.

Complicity in fandom's failures was also individualized – either as a previous lack of awareness or a fear of rejection. This was particularly stark when discussing issues of sex and desire. Some fans were open about their lack of desire for sexual material involving women (heterosexual, or lesbian scenes); others were repulsed by heterosexuality. More often though was a fear of that heterosexuality infecting their fannish works with heteronormativity and binarized gender roles.

Fans turning a mirror on themselves

An unexpected benefit to researching audiences and fans when it comes to regendering is that their creative practices are much more experimental and do not have to navigate the committees and production boards or marketing departments the professional adaptations do. To this end several respondents and interviewees explained that they had tried out regendering their own work as a kind of market test themselves. This shift also addressed that fear of heterocentric narratives unconsciously dominating their fanworks. One survey respondent specifically addressed this fear by 'experimenting' with two works, identical but for a gender change; the slash work was much more highly rated, read and shared, than the heterosexual:

> Experiment #1: I started a multi-chapter story that was male lead/OFC. In a slashy fandom, bound to be unpopular. So as an experiment I started a posting a swapped version of the story, identical to the first, except that the m/m OTP was crammed into it for no logical reason at all. Result: 3x the hits and kudos on the swapped story. People do love their OTPs, and to hell if it actually makes sense.

> Experiment #2 was this story, still ongoing, my take/critique on omegaverse …
> I had read a lot of omegaverse (in spn and occasional sherlock) with both fascination and horror. It seemed to be that that for the vast majority of the stories in the trope, the whole purpose and appeal of it was to turn male characters into females without the psychological ickiness of *calling* them females. …
> The idea was to critique this idea that biological determinism is somehow an acceptable excuse for blatant sexism throughout society. The story's had mixed to poor reception compared to some others I've done. It has some harsh tags and content, but I do believe the main reason is the genderswapping – people really don't like it, and when they see the 'she' attached the the two former male leads, I think people are backclicking as fast as possible.

(AS9)

An interviewee also noticed similar patterns in her work:.

> **Mariel:** My pronoun-flipped story has received a very tepid response. It's
> gotten hits but far fewer kudos than my other similarly lengthed stories,
> which tells me people are clicking on it out of curiosity and probably not
> liking it. I'm pretty convinced this is due to the genderbend aspect. If I
> posted the same story – the OTP running off together from a bad marriage
> in the face of societal discrimination – but simply made them back into
> 'he's,' I'm sure it would be far more popular. But I'm stubborn about my
> stories and I like the concept, even if very few others do too, so I keep
> working on it.

This functioned as dual evidence – the primacy of male-masculine narrativity and
characterization over the feminine, but also of fandom's internal discomfort with
its own senses of desire and need without focusing that through the masculine.
Scodari's work about science fiction fans rejecting many of the female characters
available, occasionally with emotive or contradictory reasons, is repeated within
fan counterpublics when faced with fannish regendered works (Scodari 2003).
However, due to the critique-adverse elements of those counterpublics, the
rejection is primarily through deficiencies within the affective economy rather
than explicit criticisms.

Big, bad canon

The respondents who identified particular works as problematic often chose
commercial works as examples, most frequently the example chosen was
Elementary. This is primarily due to it being the most prominent example
during the research period. Some respondents rejected it as erasure, but
often the objections were centred around character and characterization.
Even where there was support for regendering in theory, the practice of it
by *Elementary* was objectionable due to multiple factors; it was in some way
plagiarism or copying, it did damage to the canon, it was not as good as other
archontic variations, it demeaned women, it erased queer subtext in order
to heterosexualize the relationship, the casting was wrong, the genre (police
procedural) was wrong, the writing was bad or it was simply 'uninteresting'.
Many of these objections were combined, particularly those centred around
representation of women and queerness, and took the form of 'why not make

both of them women?' or fear that the series would be overtly gendered. Often these respondents had not watched the series but were simply responding to a wider fandom discussion of the series, and of how fandom approaches its own (Genovese 2019).

It would be remiss not to remark upon the racist undertones of some of these objections to Lucy Liu as Watson. They were primarily rooted in the dominant archetypes of Asian women as submissive, or as dragon ladies, with little in between (Feng 2002, 3). While Liu's acting ability was praised by numerous respondents her faults or inadequacies were remarked upon by multiple critics of *Elementary* as evidence the creative decisions were at fault, alongside the regendering itself (Coren 2012; Stagg 2012). In particular there was a small group who surmised that Liu should be playing Sherlock, rather than Watson, using racialized stereotypes of inscrutability/emotionlessness as their rationale (Genovese 2019, 153). None of this was intended to be overtly racist and most of these respondents echoed wider calls for more minority representation – or at least some kind of parity – but to them, this representation was wrong in some fashion (Genovese 2019). The implicit nature of critiques and criticisms of regendered work demands a closer reading of the texts themselves, as it is within the specific elements of the narratives – characterization, aesthetics, plot – that the resistance and othering of the mainstream take place.

Regendering and violence

This link between gender, relationship narratives and violence is also found in some of the interview and survey results, particularly those around gender representation for non-binary people. This included trans representation where errors in those stories were connected to the ways in which trans people, particularly trans women, are subject to social opposition. Here violence is correlated with the idea of 'surviving' the microaggressions, harm and mental health issues associated with gender non-conforming people. This was not only found in personal narratives about transition, or trans fans, but in answers and narratives from queer fans as well (albeit less frequently). In an attempt to capture this ethos, I focused on the issues these fans saw as battlegrounds – specifically sexuality, the gender binary and representation (of women, of trans women, of queer people). I then separated those responses via the three broad gender categories.

I found that queer representation was almost always connected with these narratives of representation and social change, regardless of the identity of the respondent, but was less connected with sexuality specifically than other ways of being queer. Dividing the overall concerns into three main themes, representation of women, representation of non-binary gender roles and sexuality illustrated the concerns more accurately. The majority of openly non-straight respondents (78 per cent, making up 11 per cent of total respondents) were supportive or demanding of seeing their sexuality within their media or their fanworks. Chart 2 details the responses according to the respondent gender.

The majority of respondents consumed regendered work with 67.27 per cent of gender non-conforming respondents actively created or consumed regendered works, 10.91 per cent rejecting them. This trend was slightly less than respondents who identified as female/woman/cisfemale, with 78.63 per cent consuming or creating those works, but also with 11.97 per cent actively rejecting those works. This is a more tentative correlation, but echoes much of the qualitative responses from participants, who identify their own experiences of gender and queerness as the reason behind their fannish works that explore those themes. Most striking was the way in which the gender non-conforming participants were the most concerned with all of these issues, even though they formed a minority of participants. This focus on the experience of gender from 'outside', from the position of the other, underlies the idea that the position of the 'other' is central to the practice of regendering.

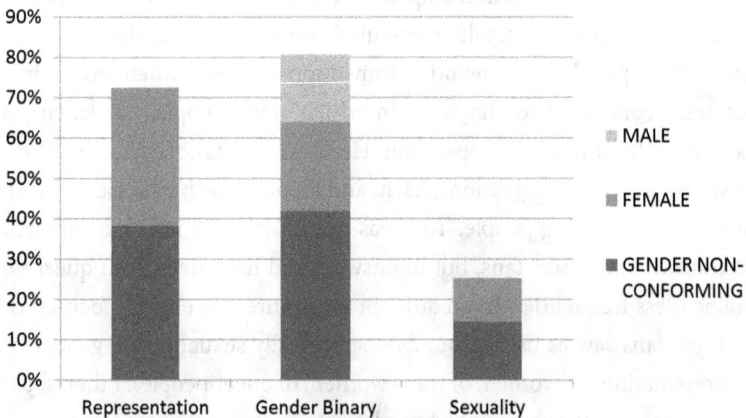

Chart 2 Concerns about sexuality, gender binary and representation of women.

Gender identities

The question of identity, of what part that plays in fandom and fanwork, is often delineated between the demographics of what fans identify as, and how this intersects with various theories of fanwork. Even more recent fan studies research often focuses on the demographics of the readers and creators, and why they would write what they write. What is more clearly evident in my research is the genesis of identity – an identity narrative created by and with fannishness that includes the media object and the counterpublic the fan engages with. This is very definitely stated by one respondent whose gender identity 'problems' were both soothed and made more evident by their engagement with fanworks, particularly regendered ones:

> Most het fic pushes me out by assuming a level of genderedness in the female characters that makes it impossible for me to identify with them. I need to see women being a lot of different kinds of women. I need not gender essentialism in my fic. … A woman written as having once been a man is automatically not being written within those strictures. … I am genderqueer, and for me, reading fic with genderswap is basically the only way I can express that aspect of my identity and sexuality. It's what kept me sane through figuring out my gender issues, realizing there is no way to transition to what I want to be even if I were willing to go through the social hell of a transition, we just don't have it. So fic with genderqueer themes is where that part of me lives. It's what makes it possible for me to go about the rest of my life as a woman and be happy, and love my very female appearing body and not want to change it, knowing that when I need to I can be a part of another life that I live in fiction.
>
> (AS42)

***

> Sometimes, they're fascinating as meta works, but a lot of times it's simply an opportunity to read something I want to (f/f sex, m/f sex) without feeling vulnerable. If they're genderswapped, then they have the parts that interest me, but I can still think of them as men and thus have a lot less concern that something terrible is going to happen to them or that any minor problem is a lead-in to the inevitable public humiliation, shaming, rape, or fridging. It's like a weird demilitarized zone for me: a place that is neither male nor female, where some stuff that is female-oriented can happen without the customary crushing punishment that is a part of being a fictional woman.
>
> (AS97)

This kind of identification with the fictional is common and drives a multitude of marketing decisions, remakes, letters to editors and purchases of merchandise. Gendered meaning in regendered work comes from relational aggression and comfort, messily enacted by the rest of the world. The body of the character forms a pattern for the policing of the world around it, but in each of the texts the person prevails. Their own sense of identity and inherent place in the world is made prominent, almost entirely through what they *do* within that world. In that context it is a remarkably neoliberal visage of gender freedoms, where the freedom of identity is mostly found in what work the person engages in, what they purchase, how they find employment. Even outside the usual structures of 'work' the characters find meaning in labour itself. These formations of identity through what one does, or loves, are not restricted to regendered fanworks however, but it is important to note how the idea of identity itself is constructed.

What separates many of these fans is not only the cross-gendered identification, but the way that cross-gendered identification is interpreted within their works about that character. The 'problem' of a lack of female characters is remedied by identifying with male characters who are regendered – as masculine women, as feminine women, as trans men, as trans women. In opposition to the theory that people, particularly young people, need to read within gender in order to find role models and inspiration, fandom explodes out gender to encompass the traditionally othered and unseen. In doing this however, the question of why those identities are othered and unseen remains paramount, unanswered but paramount.

Regendering as critique

One of the methods of answering and investigating this otherness was the regendering of the underlying assumptions of the narrative. The plight of the lone female character contrasted with worlds that are overwhelming female featuring a seemingly endless variation on the idea of what constitutes 'woman', focusing on and exposing women as the default character, rather than men. By regendering the focus these works warp the world they inhabit into one with a female default – default characters, default audience, default narrative focus. This is accompanied by an expectation of a primarily female audience – or at least one that understands and has lived a female or woman-identified experience. Where the assumptions of the narrative itself are regendered offer a significant repudiation to the 'default' masculinity Gatens and Spender detail in their work (1996; 1985). Even in works where there is a single female character of note talked about by respondents or written by them, they use that character as a lens through which to reveal the masculinity and maleness of the narrative they now inhabit. The trope of the 'lone good woman' is regendered itself into a kind of cadre of Cassandraic narratives where sexism and misogyny are reiterated into an unbelieving canon, with the presumed women of the audience a kind of Greek chorus who knows the truth and supports the dispossessed other in their prophecies.

More than one respondent gifted[1] to me a narrative of identity that relied upon not only the community of fandom, but on the experimentation of fans within their works, with gender and with sex. This was not unilaterally positive – where there is acceptance there is also a risk of rejection and vulnerability – but fans who participated in my survey and interviews were very clear about the ways their fannish habits were bodily ones, part of a digital life that was not confined to either a virtual space, or to a specific habit:

> I have personal experience with being confused by your gender/sexuality. For a very long time the only way I could think about what was going on in my head was through the characters and how they dealt with some of the same issues I have. Though I primarily identify as female I'm on the line of agender and am asexual. So reading about these people, or seeing pictures of these people, imaginary they may be helped greatly.
>
> (AS110)

***

> Gender is such a weird and complex concept – especially in the fandom, and in the tumblr community where everything you say can be considered offending to somebody's gender. Only after I spent my time in this community, following a few amazing people I started realising that all of this is not so easy, that we are such complex human beings and gender is a part of that complexity. I found out things about myself and about the others. I think that is the reason why I am searching for materials on changes in the gender of the characters and reading metas.
>
> (AS113)

---

[1] I specifically use the term 'gifted' as these answers were incredibly open, rich and broad, and beyond what was initially expected of the scope of this research. Their trust in me as a researcher was made clear by these answers and I cannot overstate the importance of recognizing this as a facet of both the autoethnographic grounded research I engaged in, but also the engagement of fans in their own autoethnographic habits.

This narrative timeline of identity and fannish habits expands the ways in which fanwork is linked to identity, as both creator and consumer of those works. These narratives encompassed both specific fandoms, and the ways in which fans identified themselves and their work, including changes in their approaches to work as their own personal identity shifted. These shifts were often messy, difficult ones, but in the narratives the fans developed, that messiness was growth, and was marked by growth in their fannish habits as much as their lives.

These themes, and self-identified tropes, within regendering show the way in which the seriousness of gender, of sex and sexuality and identity, is interrogated and experimented with through the play of fanworks. Regendering offers a specific manifestation of gender which not only affects character, and characterization, but the formation of the paracosms these characters inhabit. A narrative of transition – not simply gender transition but sense of self – permeates many answers. Romance and relationships function as Petri dishes for gender and character. Respondents clearly identified that relational intimate space as a way for them to explore gender, characterization and narrative, which was coded as 'play'. It also functioned as a psychological space for self-identification and examination, the way play functions in 'the real world' where 'distancing combined with the "just for fun" element of play facilitates a feeling of safety within which the individual can freely experiment with the identity in question' (Ibarra and Petriglieri 2010). Identities become inscribed and reinscribed through fannish praxis, both creative and consuming, and meaning is made through the personal identification with characters. Fans approach their work on multiple axes, with some prioritizing character and narrative, others the meaning made by those things.

Part Two

Case studies and analysis

This section brings together analysis of four works within a single archontic media field, along with analysis of two major mainstream adaptations that regender characters. Using fanworks to begin the analysis I draw on theories of gender, sexuality and violence within the canon affecting the representations in transformational fanwork. In particular I examine how regendering within Sherlock Holmes adaptations uses different forms – regendering both Holmes and Watson, regendering Watson, regendering Holmes and regendering Watson and Moriarty – to explore different focal points of gender and the genre of the canon along with archontic representations. The fear of heterosexualizing the homosocial male bond of Holmes and Watson is present in much of the critique of regendering within the archontic Holmsean mythos; however, the chosen adaptations (fanworks and the professional adaptation of *Elementary*) illustrate the breadth of possibilities. Using regendering to explore a historical aspect of queer, and lesbian, cultures, or how a heterosexual romance is affected by trauma, or gender dysphoria and the genderedness of the genre, are exhibited in the three fanworks. In *Elementary* the heterosexualizing element of a female Watson is averted not only by the platonic relationship between Holmes and Joan Watson, but also by the introduction of a female Moriarty who is intimately and sexually linked with Holmes and transfers that to Joan Watson.

However, these examples are predominantly positive, even within my overall conclusion that regendering reiterates the focus on the male narratives in mainstream media. When *Ghostbusters: Answer the Call* and *Doctor Who* regendered main characters the negative responses from fandom dominated analysis and reception. These two case studies explore the ways in which affection for the archontic and canonical media object can translate into not only negativity, but abuse and harassment, and appears to be taking an upward momentum in the acceptable actions of anti-fans. The initial responses to *Elementary* were a preview of the depths of anger and aggression faced when regendering is used as an adaptational technique, and how fandom – including academic fan studies and media studies – replicates not only the male default narratives but reifies and reinscribes them as normative.

A case study in fannish regendering

All the girls in the Gateways, and Johnnie had to fall for Sherlock Holmes.
(breathedout 2013a)

The difficulty inherent in media studies, particularly when including fanwork, is the sheer enormity of the field; for fanwork millions of texts, images and art pieces exist in thousands of archives and notebooks and private diaries. Selection of works to analyse is something of an attempt to find an example that represents the broader category for sociological research, but the influence of cinema and literary studies also focuses on unique or particularly good examples of the category. The work selected for close analysis as an example of fannish regendering is the *One Shape to Another* series by Having Been Breathed Out/breathed out (HBBO). It is a novel-length fanfic set in post-Second World War Britain, using lesbian regendered versions of the characters of Sherlock Holmes and John(nie) Watson, and does what many critics called for in previous chapters – both central characters are regendered. It was selected for a variety of reasons including its presence on recommendation lists as 'this is GOOD femmeslash', and that it is specifically cited in the fannish Wikipedia 'Fanlore' under the entry for BBC's *Sherlock* as an example of how fans have 'have dealt with the dearth of female characters' in the original works ('Sherlock (TV Series) – Fanlore' n.d.).

Several fanartists have created art based on the work, and the work itself has received a high number of kudos and comments on the fanfic archive AO3. HBBO's openness about her writing methods is also key to why this work was selected; she was previously a 'lit blogger' and this aspect of her creative process is clear in her authorial notes and online presence (breathedout 2017). These factors combine to allow her work to operate in the liminal space between the derided 'mawkish teenage-crush scenarios rife with misspelling and cliché' (Miller 2013) reputation of fanfic that underlies even essays praising the form – valuable only when commercialized – and the cultural capital of classically inspired pastiches or parallel narratives such as *Wide Sargasso Sea* by Jean Rhys, or *March* by Geraldine Brooks. This space allows for the work to exist as an exercise in intellectual creativity. Her Johnnie and her Sherlock operate within not just a fannish paradigm but deliberately engage with the gendered dichotomy between 'fanwork' and 'literary adaptation'.

As with many online fanworks, the novel includes author notes about her research, her inspirations and reading lists for those interested in her work; these notes include familiar asides to the readers, notes on her research, quotes from the sources she has used and apologies for liberties she has taken with history. These communications with her audience clearly assume that these are elements the readers will care about. The overarching narrative of HBBO's novel is focused not simply on the familiar role of the 'case' as a proxy for examining the world through the genre but also on the characters and how that case intersects with their beliefs and ideas as queer women who are survivors of the Second World War and who evince strongly radical views of gender, race and sexuality. Views that seem anachronistic in some fashion but are supported by the research HBBO undertook, and references in her author notes. This chapter will focus on how that regendering works within constructions of historical queerness, and shifting genre conventions, to reveal aspects of the canon, and the archontic works around it. Initially I will address the way in which HBBO constructs womanhood within the work as a regendered fiction, with the influences of the male originators within her text; I then analyse how that construction is mediated through sexuality – specifically the butch/femme binary. From there I explain how these constructions create a space not only for those regendered forms of characterization that expand the expectations placed on female characters, but also how that space is created through the sexual and romantic expectations of the genre and metatexts of fandom when read through that lens of regendering.

The series is rated 'explicit' due to the inclusion of explicit sex scenes; the co-option of media ratings by fandom gives itself boundaries, but it is also important to note that not all fans rate or add 'warnings' to their work in order to preserve the 'surprise' aspect of canonical works, but HBBO has. The work contains a number of sex scenes of varying levels of explicitness, and kinkiness (the kink scenes are those that are most likely to involve a warning, but also function as a tag for readers to find those works). This explicitness alongside the extended nature of her work[1] is not rare in fandom but belies the 'pornographic'

---

[1] It is not only novel-length, but similar in word count to *Return of the King* by J. R. R. Tolkien or *A Tale of Two Cities* by Charles Dickens (132 531; 134 462; 135 420 words, respectively).

tag often applied to that work, or the idea that acceptability or heterosexuality is the aim of regendering and precludes radical queerness. This dual focus on the characters as both regendered versions within a regendered narrative, and as sexual agents of their own, combines representations of regendering with queerness. My research into fans themselves revealed that this work in particular was a 'turning point' in some way for many who were suspicious of regendering as a practice. HBBO herself points to the desire to see one's own sexuality within literature as a creative drive, and while interviewees and survey participants rarely mentioned ratings, they highlight the sexual content of the work as an element that dictates their reading or writing. Cunnilingus, sex between women or desire for a specifically gendered body engaged in sexual contact is perceived as either a reason to engage with a work, or with regendering as a creative process.

One Shape to Another starts with an action scene where Sherlock encourages Johnnie to crash the motorcycle they are escaping on into an abandoned quarry. Sherlock's memory and intellect are paired with Johnnie's physicality, courage and devotion to the cause from the beginning of the text, but it is also non-linearly constructed. We know the pair survive the crash that is depicted in this opening scene, but we wait to find out how and why. Just as we follow along in Holmes's footsteps when he explains his deductions, realizing that this is of course the only explanation, we follow along HBBO's reasoning too, to realize her narrative deductions about the canon, about the characters and about gender and sexuality within and outside the text itself. The story takes place within an almost entirely female space; male characters come and go and of course there is the palimpsest of the birth of Johnnie and Sherlock from within the male dominance of the canonical narrative, but the story itself is about women, about women's spaces and lives. This does not mean feminine, or the assumed feminized space of emotion and intuition, as the characters retain a high level of their initial characterization; Sherlock is intellectual and dismissive, but devoted to Johnnie, and Johnnie herself is impulsive, reckless, while being more emotionally connected with the world around them. It also means that the story takes place within a space recognizably real, recognizable whole and with characters whose agency is not undermined, or elided by the prominence of feminine tropes, instead they are given a wider range of originally masculine tropes to subvert and transgress.

The initial characterization of male characters allows for and insists upon a certain level of gender-non-conformity that simultaneously becomes realistic due to the 'flow' from the familiar canonical character to the regendered version, and the increasing expectation of complex female characters with agency within media. As with Jamie in *Elementary,* masculinized behaviours need no explanation. The sexuality of both Johnnie and Sherlock is something of an explanation, but it exists in and out of the narrative as a provocation to action. Regendering both the characters and the milieu of the genre to the women-heavy Gateways – a lesbian club – provides a plethora of female characters which ensures no single action becomes a 'girl thing' as there are any number of reactions and characters to examine and represent forms of reality.

Crucial to this queer and gendered dichotomy is the landscape of the case within the work; it heavily features the lesbian subcultural practices of the era as researched by HBBO, with Butch and Femme as embodied identity categories different to contemporary B/butch, F/femme or even lesbian[2] communities. These categories – Butch and Femme – mimicked heterosexual relationships and heteronormative gender performances, and result in both Sherlock and Johnnie finding themselves as outsiders even within the subculture that superficially welcomes them, due to their inability to fulfil those roles. This insider/outsider aspect of their gender and sexuality performances – Johnnie as the visually obvious Butch woman who nonetheless desires to be penetrated, to be taken, and Sherlock for whom those identities are as transitory as her other performative disguises – is used not only to depict the historical elements of the work, but the contemporary ways in which gender remains unable to deal with liminal identities. The case itself, the murder of a woman who was active in the lesbian subculture but despised for her politics there and rejected for her Butch lesbian identity by mainstream London and Britain, requires both characters to leverage their ability to shift their identity performances, while maintaining the militaristic/detective skills of the canonical versions.

How the Mouth Changes Its Shape deals with those questions and perceptions of gender in two very specific ways; how the regendering intersects with the metatextual expectations of same-sex attraction/erotic content and compensating within the text for the necessary gendered shifts. HBBO shifts the characterization of Johnnie and Sherlock to compensate for gender, and the actions of the canonical Holmes and Watson. Of particular interest is the feedback

---

[2] I use this notation to include both the Butch identity, and butch as a description of gender performance – while often linked, they do not refer to the same concept. The use of masculine identified clothing by women as an aesthetic and personal choice which may be associated with sexuality but not necessarily is referred to a butch, while Butch is a specific lesbian identification with subcultural expectations around behaviour as much as attire. Similarly, femme is the standard feminized attire for women, while Femme is a specific lesbian/queer identification around performance alongside that aesthetic femininity.

of readers and the audience to this regendered work, which I use through this chapter to illustrate the ways in which regendering acts as a subculture within the fannish counterpublic yet recalls to its audience the mainstream cultures of queerness and masculinity inherent in the original work.

How the mouth changes its shape by breathedout

Rating: Explicit
Archive Warning: Underage
Category: F/F
Additional Tags: Genderswap, Alternate Universe – 1950s, Butch/Femme, Gender Issues, Gender Roles, Case Fic, bildungsroman, World War II
Stats: Published: 2013-03-02 Chapters: 20/20 Words: 132531
Summary: 1955. Under the placid veneer of suburban playparks and middle-class conformity churns a hidden London: femmes and butches dancing close in basement bars; clandestine love between women. To Sherlock Holmes, struggling private detective and mistress of disguise, it's a realm she renounced years before. To Johnnie Watson, daredevil ambulance driver turned auto mechanic, it's become a little too familiar. But when someone is murdered in the washroom of the city's most notorious lesbian club, the investigation will lead both women to reconsider their assumptions about themselves, each other, and the world in which they live.

Lesbian detectives

The closet the regendered Sherlock finds herself in is familiarly archontic – she is better than the rest of humanity, too intellectual for emotion, too distanced from the mess of emotions to fall into a relationship; all common aspects of the character variously highlighted by other adaptations, commercial and fannish alike. Her internalized sense of wrongness is also a closet locked by the social conventions of gender and sex in that era, the fears and disgust of masculinized women, of gender transgression and the role of women with society. Her earliest sexual experience is marred, irreparably, by those fears and that disgust – not hers, but the fears held by the girl she was involved with, Vicky Trevor. The internalized homophobia, exacerbated by and inflicted on Trevor, results in devastation for Sherlock. That too is familiar – the wound of an early relationship gone wrong only able to be healed by the new lover. But it is not only the romantic damage done which needs to be healed, but the social scars left by a society that marginalizes lesbians, and by lesbian subculture itself perpetuating a binary version of sexuality that still constrains the desires and bodies of those practising it (Johns et al. 2012; Rothblum, Balsam, and Wickham 2018). Even within the oft-presumed utopia of a lesbian society, those binaries are still enforced. When Sherlock attends The Gateways in her normal clothes, neither Femme nor Butch, she is subject to disapproval by one of the Femme women; 'And then Astrid – Sherlock thought it was Astrid, or maybe it was Sam – leaned over with a look like they'd all had, cat-eye liner and dark pink lips, and said into her ear "What are you?" sounding disgusted' (breathedout 2013a, 62).

Johnnie's introductory chapter is woven through with historical elements and the authorial notes include excerpts from texts about the Gateways, about lesbian life in the era, about the Metropolitan Women's Police Patrol, adding not only veracity to the text but embedding it within a narrative of queer history. HBBO explains narrative choices she has made based on this research, where she has diverted from it, and what the research has meant to her. The choices Johnnie makes within the text are grounded in the choices available to women in the era. Her experiences in the war are not created whole cloth, or in an imaginary version of history, but in the very real experiences of women, queer or not, as part of the Auxiliary Terrestrial Services as detailed in HBBO's authorial notes about her research. Johnnie's Butchness is not a legacy from the character she reworks but is a manifestation of character traits within a social matrix which assumes and shapes women's masculinity into sexuality and to a codified version of itself. The regendered Watson could be femme, or feminine, and in fact often is depending on which aspects of the canon character are being emphasized, but HBBO's narrative requires not simply masculinity, but the Butch identity in order to function both with veracity and intention.

The historicity of *One Shape to Another* means that the travails of war cannot be elided by the text. Johnnie's status as one of the few women to have 'manned' an anti-aircraft gun during the war (when the gunner passed out) centralizes her as a veteran, allowing her access to the canonical Watson's PTSD/shell shock, and simultaneous longing for the clearly delineated space of war. This longing for the battlefield transmuted to finding a sense of belonging in Sherlock's circle of influence is present in a number of archontic variations. Within *One Shape to Another* this longing is explicitly made sexual and presents the tension as akin to war. Johnnie calls their relationship 'the battlefield she'd forgotten she loved' (breathedout 2013a, 51), for Sherlock it is 'an ocean she refused to chart on the map' (breathedout 2013a, 53). Johnnie assumes her desire for Sherlock is unreturned and accepts this with the equanimity of queered otherness, the clearly delineated moments of homosocial and homosexual; of course, 'that she was drawn to Sherlock was no great surprise, and no great problem either. Johnnie Watson had loved, and lived with, enough women to respect a clear disavowal of interest' (breathedout 2013a, 57).

This does not stop her devotion to Sherlock, following the other woman into cases and violence and danger. The relevance of danger to love within the lesbian relationship is transferred to the explicit danger of the violent world around them, solving crimes and the closet providing the same risks; to fail at either is potentially deadly. The danger of heterosexual men is present only to expose the strengths of the two women; Sherlock's intellect and sleight of hand, Johnnie's physicality and willingness to do violence avert the most obvious attempt at a gendered violence against them. It is their own assumption of male identities within cases that provokes discomfort for Johnnie. Her identity as a lesbian is disrupted as she finds herself sexually attracted to 'Evan' even though she slips easily into the identity of 'Michael' when they investigate crimes that take place within those male spaces;

> For one thing, Johnnie had never (they joked about gold stars down at the Gates) had the remotest desire to go to bed with a man. But when she and Sherlock spent the week undercover as Evan and Michael, out-of-town executives at Mrs. Fitzpatrick's brother's advertising firm, she could hardly think for staring at the tailored navy wool suiting taut across Sherlock's backside.
>
> (breathedout 2013a, 57)

For both of them the relationship requires that they re-examine and reveal aspects of themselves that they had either obscured, elided or fearfully avoided.

The prospect of losing parts of oneself, of hard edges smoothed into oblivion by the act of becoming lover and loved haunts Sherlock and Johnnie both. The restrictiveness of gender, of gender performance and sexuality, is not only restricted to heterosexual relationships. This allows for a broader range of identification with readers, while illuminating the universality of human interaction codified and performed within cultures that may or may not be the reader's own. The re-othering that takes place situates the experience of maleness as that of the other; the men within the narrative are not-men. Some of these not-men are 'good' – they are Butches, or they are men who remain in the background, but others are aggressors whose masculinity is the vile, unnatural, subversion of women's masculinity, with their rapacious sexuality and abuse of women contrasted, unfavourably, with the 'suited and booted' women of The Gateways. Butches may be violent, may be aggressive, may be considered unnatural within 1950s Britain, or even within our own cultures, but within the narrative they are integral and necessary for women who are masculine, the women who love them and the communities they are part of. In this novel butch masculinity, not men, is the counterpoint to femininity and femaleness, and regendering does not make a feminine narrative, as much as it makes an inclusive one. Simultaneously, butch experiences within the work – particularly the way Johnnie's sexuality and sense of self are restricted by ideas of penetration and vulnerability that her partners have enforced – reveals the way that the unthinking rejection of femininity is itself as much of a restrictive process as the act of being unable to choose masculinity, and that these performances codified culturally and subculturally rely on self-policing gender and role as much as external pressures.

Within HBBO's works the apparitional invisibility of lesbianism in literature is rejected by the conscious eroticism inherent in this series. It cannot simply be read as just another aspect of fannish prurience or the abjectivity of female sexuality or the familiar risible judgement of fanfic as a specifically feminine pornography that Ogas and Gaddam, or Salmon and Symons claim as being explicable by something other than sexual desire (2012; 2004). The focus on the presence of eroticism in HBBO's work, and the appreciation of her fans for that presence, is not an unexpected or unwelcome diversion from the assumed 'normality' of other feminized works but an integration of regendering, queering and focusing the narrative onto women. As Reid calls it, 'a type of fascination with perceived perversity' (2009, 466) which underlies even the valorization of it as a reactionary subversion of male pornography (Russ 1985). This feminine fannish prurience, or the expectation thereof without any other indicators of it, is a facet of that assumption of what constitutes 'normal' work by women. However, within fandom itself, the sexual elements are expected, almost centralized despite the prevalence of non-sexual fanwork, but still conform in ways to this expectation of female ambivalence and absence. Specifically, for fandom, the representations of female sexuality are often still bound by a crucial imbalance of focus; women are paired off to create space for more representation of queer men, alternative sexualities are catered for in such a way as to retain a focus on men. Or their sexuality is dangerous in the most retrograde and classic of fashions; she is the trap into which a man falls, and it is only true love that can save him (the twist being the true lover is a man) (Schur 1984). These stories, and these absences entirely, are where blatant, erotic, sexually explicit depictions of queer women are radically relevant, and while not necessarily being a reaction to those narratives and erasures, they inhabit a space that is rejected by them. The familiar death of lesbians, or rejections, or heterosexual resolution, or the queer-inflected villains, is as much behind regendered and lesbian fanworks as the canon it works within and against.

At the same time, the eroticism is pornographic in its intent to arouse, to provoke a physical and physiological response in the reader. The integration of the sex into the characterization and the plot provides necessary elements to illustrate change and growth in ways that could not be provided outside the erotic context, given the intent to delineate the lesbian relationship from the homosocial woman. HBBO alerts her readers: 'warnings for specific sex acts in the endnotes section: it's a bit spoiler-y, but also a possible squick for some folks. So: choose your poison.:-)' (breathedout 2013a, 154).

This warning is not about the sexual contact itself, but about the forms it takes. Within the metanarrative expectations of fandom the erotic elements are almost incidental, and do not provide the narrative focus the way it does in what fandom considers to be pornography (with or without plot). These subcultural definitions are only occasionally defined, and are complex sites of differing opinions, and playful erasure and liminality where the boundaries between porn and plot are not as neatly inscribed as they are within other highly sexualized media. The then sexualized relationship between the author and the readers is queered by expectations of femaleness, but also by the non-standard relationships, imbalanced and multiplied between fandoms and fans, a site of contention, legality and eroticized play (Kukka 2021; Lackner, Lucas, and Reid 2006). However, the sensory aspect of the work cannot be elided as simply political, even when it does act as an element of the queer and lesbian representation against type and expectation, it is, by authorial fiat, intended to arouse and to explain. HBBO notes in the first section of the work:

> I added the underage warning because the first few chapters involve Sherlock's time at boarding school in 1943, but the one underage sex scene is, in my opinion, unlikely to be triggering or offensive to most folks. At various times the story engages with racism, homophobia, antisemitism and sexism, although I do my utmost to be thoughtful and sensitive about all of the above.
>
> (breathedout, 2013a, 1)

This is particularly the case given the intensity of the erotic scenes within *One Shape to Another*. When Johnnie unintentionally speaks her own desires, ones that she feels judged for as a Butch within their subculture, and attempts to cover her 'shame' with sexual activities – fisting and anal penetration – designed to overwhelm Sherlock as 'since Sherlock would already think Johnnie was broken she might as well be filthy on top of it' (breathedout 2013a). Within fandom, particularly fanfic, those acts don't count as particularly transgressive, simply a kink to be accepted (Busse 2013b, np). The erotic content is vital, as are all the other aspects of the work, but it is not just these elements that create meaning in the work, it is also the narrative methods HBBO uses.

The romantic elements of the text are crucial not just for the sexual/erotic components but as a form of revision. Making the (pseudo)platonic relationship explicitly sexual within fandom has been read by fan studies academics in a variety of ways; a sexual act, a feminist revisioning of masculinity and sex, creative anti-capitalist activity as per 'culture repairing the damage done in a system where contemporary myths are owned by corporations instead of owned by the folk' (Jenkins quoted by Harmon 1997). However, to change the detective genre to the romantic with no disavowal of either aspect acts at a metatextual level not only to reimagine the masculine as the feminine, in terms of genre, but to address the erasures of the genre itself. It reinserts the messy emotionality of life into the logician's dream of rational action; in a reversion of the 'masculinized woman' so feared in the contemporaneous universe of *One Shape to Another*, it feminizes the masculine genre while reworking what counts as feminine within the work itself. It redresses the imbalances of the original by regendering, and it also resituates the entire framework of gender performance within the female body. It also disrupts the assumptions of intellectual disinterest that surround fanfic, with myriad references not only to academic and non-fiction research, but also literary classics. 'It's, um, REALLY SHAMEFULLY OBVIOUS if you've read it, but a debt of gratitude is owed to Joyce's Molly Bloom for the style and all the yeses in the penultimate paragraph of the first scene' (breathedout 2013a, 89).

The borrowing of cultural capital with fandom has precedents, in the form of Shakespeare, and HBBO acknowledges those sources of inspiration alongside references to 1950s porn films, and the historical lesbian community's response to sex toys. Joyce's work is notoriously dense, difficult and subject to censorship for the sexual content; seemingly unlikely to inspire fanwork but HBBO's cultural capital, and openly shared preferences for literary works particularly post-modern authors, make the literary allusion unremarkable except for the necessary attributions. The author's adherence to genre restrictions allows for and encourages a kind of narrative reduction and by sourcing such disparate inspirations, by openly linking to and acknowledging them, HBBO uses fanfic to expand the metatextual genre of the canon, not just correct the gender, race, class and sexuality imbalances of it.

A place for women like me

Fanfiction allows the author to experiment; not simply stylistically or within canonical universes, but to tell a story entirely about women and women's experiences, one that rejects masculine attention, including male-masculine readers, and one that examines the minutiae and intricacies of lesbian life across historical eras. There is no expectation of a neatly quantified niche audience, for all the hope that there will be one within the counterpublic of fandom, no performance necessary to fulfil publisher metrics, instead HBBO is free to examine what she wishes to however she chooses to, without having to envision a market sector to appeal to. She describes her process needing that space:

> because what interests and excites me, both about writing fiction (currently) and designing garments (formerly), is challenging myself: finding a thing I'm not sure I can do, and pushing myself while I explore ways to do it. That kind of experimentation has a high failure rate, which means more time in revision/development; and it also tends to lead to end products that are more technically difficult and therefore don't sell well to anybody but a niche market.
>
> (breathedout 2017)

This freedom of fanwork allows for a Sherlock who loves, who approaches love and infatuation with the same rationality as they do anything else. A Sherlock whose initial forays into the art of illusion and disguise is an examination of the restrictions of gender and the performances of femininity. The freedom of fanwork does not require a defence of the choices made, not in the same fashion as within mainstream work; there are still metanarratives, and questions of popularity within fandom itself, that reveal how works are received. As noted by my survey participants, there is an attention economy within fandom that does prioritize and focus on male-masculine stories, one that the creators experiment with and consider in the creation and publication of their work. It is common for certain 'ships' or kinks to come with defences, or self-conscious acknowledgement of the perceived 'problematic' nature, but the works exist within a subcultural milieu that accepts, with some scepticism, those problems with the motto 'your kink is not my kink but your kink is okay' (Busse 2013b). For HBBO this manifests as Sherlock, the girl and the woman, who is allowed to be the unquestioned heroine but also conflicted and complex, unmanageable and flawed. There is no performance metric to be filled in order to thrive, outside the deeply personal and unique affective economic drivers that prompt a fan to create; some throw their work into the void with no care for its reception, while other feed from that economy and let it drive their work.

Yet, despite this lack of a quantified means to measure success, which often dictates continued commercial support within mainstream markets, fandom does have methods and means to measure an internalized idea of success. By those measures *One Shape to Another* is a success; the author has stated that the feedback from fans has been almost universally positive and even within a cultural matrix that rejects lesbianism, feedback about the sex scenes has been positive. The rate of 'kudos' and comments suggests popularity – 433 comments, 625 kudos, 415 bookmarks (after a technical issue necessitated re-uploading the fic), that while not comparable to the most popular slash stories (3189/39715/7261), or femmeslash stories (4793/21162/2984), is 'disproportionately' high for a lesbian-focused work. Specifically, the fairly flat ratio between comments, kudos and bookmarks is one that reveals readers are heavily engaged with the work, and with communicating that to each other. It is also important to note that of all the recommendations received through the survey, this work was the only work to receive more than one mention by name:

> my first genderbent fic was How the Mouth Changes Its Shape, by breathedout. I love her work, and read it because it was her. I wasn't seeking genderbent fic. And it was glorious! I now gobble it up. Reading complex female characters is very satisfying.
>
> (AS 214)

> Genderswapped Johnlock, historical AU in 1950's London, super detailed and fascinating world-building involving 1950s femme/butch lesbian culture. It does a lot more than just cisswap the characters – the setting itself necessarily involves an exploration of gender and gender roles.
>
> (AS23)

This focus on not only the quality of HBBO's work in general, but the complexity and depth of her characterization of Watson and Holmes in terms of that regendering illustrates the ways fans engage with her work in particular. Authors and readers have often remarked on the high level of approval they receive for slash over femmeslash, but *One Shape to Another* escapes this disproportionate response due to both the author's tendency to create only femmeslash, but also her cultural capital within fandom.

The case they solve relies heavily not only on the traditional elements of the archontic Holmsean methods and narratives, but on an understanding of lesbian subculture within the era. As a narrative it interweaves with the historical elements of queer representation for women, and the ways in which femininity was a necessary performance for social, financial and intellectual reasons regardless of one's natural butchness, contrasting heavily with the ways in which Butchness codified behaviours (social, emotional and sexual) within culture. The relative toughness of women is not measured by adherence to feminine performances, but by the ability to endure and remain whole. The characters who survive are the ones who see beyond the roles and performances enforced around them, recognizing them as performances. Sherlock's narrative arc is to overcome an initial kind of trauma around her lesbianism as an act, but also to see beyond, and find those who also see beyond the roles and performances inscribed on the bodies of women even within the relative acceptance of the queer community. Throughout the case they find themselves blurring those lines, and find others also blurring the lines, breaking and reforming those roles, not just within the community but metatextually as well; HBBO's characters are not simply re-enactments of the canonical, but queer the canon itself, confronting the audience with their own expectations of homosexuality, gender and the canon. The relative tenderness, fragility, of femininity is reworked within a culture of women as something both performative and real, as something that invites a performance of masculinity as strength but also, when envisioned wholly within a character of agency, contains its own strength. In the midst of a physical fight Johnnie and Sherlock argue the relative 'naturalness' of femme presentation, with Sherlock claiming it is '... not natural on bloody anyone' while Johnnie offers the coda that 'they weren't – all – femmes' as their fight moves from those larger ideals about presentation to the real problem of how performances of masculinity and femininity compromise their own relationship (breathedout 2013a, 102–3). The otherness, of both the Holmes and Watson characters, is not restricted to their gender or their sexuality, even as their expression of both is beyond mainstream and subcultural matrices.

Layers of difference, of otherness and outsiderness, are woven into the characters, linking them back to the canon and the archontic versions, but also to arguments and discourses around women and representation, women and lived experience. Sherlock is odd, even in the realm of the odd that is post-war lesbian culture; Johnnie is the only woman who shelled the Germans with heavy artillery. Both maintain their sense of self as other than; other than straight, other than even the relative expanses of queer, other than anything but meant for each other.

What kind of woman

What the canonical Holmsean characters would do in other time periods has been a feature of fanworks and adaptations since the early periods of the fandom. The historicity of HBBO's retelling is bolstered, along the way, by her authorial notes and asides such as 'let me tell you, my friends: it is extremely difficult researching the appearance and availability of dildos circa 1954 in Britain' (breathedout 2013a, 89), and her presence on social networking allowing readers to not only read along with her research but to have access to other aspects of the creative process. The performative aspect of fandom and fannishness adds verisimilitude to *One Shape to Another* for reader and writer (and researcher) through that open research process, and embeds HBBO not only as the writer, but as a community member. She shares her various sources for inspiration, often works with high levels of cultural capital due to her erudite posts on a variety of topics including the Bloomsbury Set, poetry, pornography and the art of writing. She also speaks about her focus on women and the experiences of lesbian and queer women particularly;

> I know everyone is probably tired of me beating this drum, but: *this*, in a nutshell, is why I started reading and writing fanfiction to begin with. Because I felt the persistent and conspicuous lack of complicated, embodied sex in the literary fiction whose prose excited me (a few exceptions notwithstanding); and when I tried to read mainstream romance it was so egregiously heteronormative and so narratively uninteresting (to me personally, no offense meant to romance aficionad@s) that I found it neither hot nor thought-provoking.
>
> (breathedout 2013b)

Rather than reinscribing what Moi calls a 'kind of intellectual schizophrenia' marked by 'a specific kind of defensive speech act' disavowing her femaleness, or queerness, HBBO situates those identities as a cornerstone of her writing and her work (2008, 264–5).

The initial reworking, where Holmes and Watson relocate to a different era, still clothed in their Victorian habitus, is skewed only slightly by HBBO's regendering. The situational aspects of the era – post-war scarcity (the Second World War rather than the canonical Second Anglo-Afghan War), the changing roles of gender (due to the socio-political upheavals of post-World War Europe, rather than the earlier stages of women's suffrage in the UK), the relative freedoms of war for B/butch women and resulting abjectivity of their presence – manifest differently for Johnnie and Sherlock than for Watson and Holmes. However, the reimagining and reinscribing of the characters maintain recognizable elements of their canonical selves such as Watson's military bearing, sexual prowess with women and support of Sherlock, and Sherlock's intelligence, deductive skills and reliance on Watson's support. Within HBBO's work, as in history, the masculine women are only valuable when it is necessary to use those masculine-signified bodies for labour; once women are 'freed' of the labour they are expected to perform femininity once more or be relegated to socio-political positions where that performance is allowed to be dropped. HBBO reimagines Sherlock and Watson as queer women and invokes the canonical Sherlock's attempts to reshape the world through detective work in the shared political drive of those post-war women. She depicts the cultural milieu of lesbian London post-war as one that reveals the freedoms offered in wartime for women and specifically for masculine women and lesbians. A freedom that is then subject to a concerted effort to reduce such subversions and transgressions once the social structures could be resurrected around the returning men. Rebecca Jennings's *Tomboys and Bachelor Girls: A Lesbian History of Post-war Britain*, Jill Gardiner's *From the Closet to the Screen: Women at the Gateways*, Davis Kynaston's *Family Britain* and oral history sites like *A.T.S. Remembered* appear repeatedly in HBBO's authorial notes discussing her recreation of this era, and how her choices intersect with the canonical versions. These notes appear at the end of each relevant chapter, with quotes from the texts referenced along with links to the works.

Within the female-female relationship narratives, as researchers suggest with slash and male-male relationships, there is a freedom from gender role restrictions. Within slash this is assumed to be a 'liberatory practice', as Russ, and Lamb, and Veith variously claim, as summarized by Hellekson and Busse (2006, 14). This liberation is then linked by this supposition to the theoretical positions of Salmon and Symons (and others), where slash is the result of inalienable differences between male and female 'mating psychology' (2006, 17, 21). The assumption is that without the expectations of heterosexuality, the creator is able to examine love and sex in a 'pure' state; however, the works themselves simultaneously defy gender roles and reify them by revoking the gender roles of the author and engaging them in the narratives. This rhetoric of spiritualized love is identical to the defences of homosexual relations in ancient Greece as reinterpreted by Wilde among others at the turn of the nineteenth century, the use of Plato in particular as 'covertly advancing the cause of homosexual emancipation' (Ross 2012, 8). In this case femmeslash, from that intimate act of regendering, also frees the author of regendered works from the familiarly gendered narrative space where male-masculine stories dominate. There is no masculine attention to court, no male characters to work around and with, no possibility for the threads of that imbalance to influence the narrative itself. HBBO does not evade masculinity, or even the spectre of it within Butch symbolism, as the heterosexual dominance of masculinity is repeated by the women of the Gateways, and by the standards of the queer subculture they inhabit. By regendering both Sherlock and Watson HBBO simply avoids having to shape the narrative around only one part of the duo.

HBBO's story weaves its way through the narrative spaces of Conan Doyle's texts – Sherlock's interest in chemistry, his apparent inability to relate to people on an emotional level, his dubious connections to the underworld and government, his approach to crime as war itself and his myriad wounds and memories, all find resonances in *One Shape to Another.* Alongside those characteristics, however, is the situational genderedness of them within the canon, and how those identifiers are forced to shift in the retelling. As a woman, HBBO's Sherlock would not have had access to the canonical Holmes's education. The narrative lampshades this deficit with the arrival of an educational theorist at the young Sherlock's school: 'Old Basil Smythe had made it *quite* plain, over the course of an agonising half-hour, that such chemistry and physics curricula only masculinised the girls' (breathedout 2013a, 9). This narrative refocuses, briefly, onto the restrictions upon women during this era and the effects this had not only on education, but on queer women specifically. This is supported by the authorial notes by HBBO where she quotes Jennings's work *Tomboys and Bachelor Girls,* and adds that 'the dilemma was often put to these women [lesbians] as a choice between stifling their same-sex desires and becoming fully emotionally mature, or continuing to pursue them and condemning themselves to a lifetime of emotional immaturity (not to mention loneliness and tragedy)' (breathedout 2013a, 30).

Rather than creating a rationale for the unique situation of a girl learning advanced chemistry during the era, HBBO clarifies the situational aspects of it, the rhetoric of 'masculinizing' women, the fear of the lesbian, of women's sexuality in general and the fetishizing of women's spaces. The lurid stories of masculine, voracious and rapacious lesbians using girls school, prisons, nursing stations and nunneries as hunting grounds are a fertile genre, and one revealing much more about the interlocutor than the subject (Castle 1993). The male Holmes deals with social opprobrium for being strange; female Holmes deals with entire avenues of activism and psychology devoted to destroying part of her in some fashion. It is implied, within the text and from the research I have conducted into fans, that this imposition of heterosexuality and gender conformity leads to a greater capacity for acting and subterfuge, and for Holmes, forms parts of her incessant 'watching' of humanity, unable to allow herself to join. Regendered fanwork and the cross-dressing subterfuge of Holmes are both a way for identities to be 'tried on'. One respondent from my survey specifically mentioned slash, and their theory that creative inhabitation of male figures is

> actually about women's engagement with their own imaginaries, their own desires, and their marked bodies. Reading and writing slash is in that reading already a way to engage in an imaginary genderqueer narrative, where we can (if we want to) identify and desire, be and want it all!
>
> (AS15)

From this fannish engagement with gendered identities, as with the gendered experimentations of Holmes and Johnnie within The Gateways and lesbian subculture, there is a sense of 'safety' within those cultures. The Gateways is where Johnnie can be 'suited and booted' in relative peace, and for at least one respondent fandom replicates some of that community;

> fandom is a place that can change, that i can change, the showcasing of erasure and discrimination i face in "real life", in a way i have a great deal of access (physically, technologically and emotionally, experientially) to. it makes me feel safe and accepted. and it's very enjoyable.
>
> (AS3)

One of the key features of HBBO's retelling is not simply this resituating of the characters within a new historical space and time, but within that specific queer subcultural milieu that now acts as confirmation, and rejection, of gender performance constructs:

> Butch/femme dynamics at the Gateways were very rigid. Several respondents interviewed in Jennings and Gardiner were (initially or permanently) turned off

of the club by the expectation of conformity to one side or the other of the butch/ femme divide. Others found it liberating, or simply an easy short-hand.

(breathedout 2013a, chap. 7)

The liminality of their sexuality spectrum between Butch and Femme is a space where they can remain queer and lesbian while challenging gender stereotypes; their experience of homophobia is not lessened by the regendering, or by their performances, and in fact is inherent to the story itself in terms of the necessity of solving the case – with its wider impact on post-war politics ignored due to the gender and sexuality of the victim.

What are you?

The performances of femininity and masculinity within the female body – Femme and Butch and butch and femme and everyone between – are associated with sexuality even without sexual behaviours. Fears of the masculinized woman were, and are, linked by researchers and 'concerned persons', with fears of the non-reproductive woman, the hyper-sexualized but non-fertile woman whose very presence would induce other women to follow in their lifestyle (Cahn 1993; Halberstam 1998; 2012)[3]. Simultaneously the actual sexual acts of those women were unspoken, erased and elided, even by the well-meaning, as though there is no difference between women who are friends and women who are lovers (Castle 1993; Halberstam 1998; Noble 2004). The unimaginative condemnation of lesbian sex, unexamined except as a performance for men that is separated from actual desire or pleasure for women except as object, is confronted within *One Shape to Another* by highly explicit sexual scenes. Like Castle, for HBBO's characters there can be no confusion between the homosocial and the homosexual when one is the latter; what one does in a homosocial relationship is different to a homosexual one, and what one feels and desires is different. This is made clear within the text as Johnnie's familiarity with women is one that occupies a sexual and non-sexual space; she is friends with women, and a lover, and there are delineations between the two acts. Through regendering Johnnie and Sherlock and sexualizing their relationship, HBBO is able to expand from

---

[3] Once again, it would be remiss not to mention that this homophobia aimed at Butch women particularly as transformed into a contemporary transphobia aimed at trans women as interlopers, or 'butch flight' (Mackay 2019; Rossiter 2016).

the seeming restrictions of feminine and female narratives to illuminate wider concerns about sexuality regardless of gender.

In contrast to the dominance of the name – Sherlock, and the Holmsean canon – they are not the centre, not with the presence of Watson, or Johnnie, as the counterbalance. Again, those essential elements of the character Watson are maintained in *One Shape to Another* – the military history and bearing, the reckless courage, the devotion and admiration towards Sherlock, the devastating charm and attractiveness to women – just filtered through gender. The military history is one of ambulance driving, signals and communications, relentless misogyny erasing both the danger and the sacrifice Johnnie made. Rather than being a surgeon, she is a mechanic, shown to be as adept with engines as any archontic Watson is with human bodies, and it is talent which repeatedly saves both characters (although she does also have some familiarity with nursing). Rather than having courted women across three continents, she is the woman who 'once talked the legendary Diana Dors out of her £200 cocktail dress in the washroom of the Gateways for a barroom bet' (breathedout 2013a, 42) and whose attentions and charm allow her access to expertise and spaces. Her reaction when confronted with another lesbian at the Gateways who is known to have 'met and idolised Adolf Hitler' is to be disgusted that she would be allowed to interact with the community, as 'I put my *life* on the line, and so did half the women in here, and so did Smithy, and now she just stands there,' Johnny gestured, breathing hard, 'serving Allen drinks' (breathedout 2013a, 67; italics in original).

Using the structure and metatexts of fanfic, HBBO directly addresses the centuries of habitus that erase and elide lesbians; even the relative freedom afforded by no actual laws against lesbian sexual activity within the era of the work is highlighted and tempered by the social policing and economic necessities of passing and feminine performance required of women regardless of sexual identity. Even for the presumed 'butch' careers, HBBO shares with her reader that 'uniforms were feminized, extracurricular activities were monitored and women officers who were seen as presenting as too "butch" were told to femme up or pack their bags. This, in traditionally masculine, athletic professions' (breathedout 2013a, 119). The authorial notes layer meaning into the text, acting as a way of reading and communicating the text politically and socially. The discourse between the reader and the author is very much about the live author, who, to quote Tansy Rayner Roberts's speech at 2015's Continuum convention, 'is right there! Just ask her!'. HBBO pre-empts the critiques often aimed at lesbian narratives, that there is some inherent unreality to a woman-dominated social life or that there is some genderless utopia within lesbianism and refuses to remain 'dead' to the reader. The notes serve not just as educational asides, but also as socially aware dialogues on fandom, queerness, sex and women.

Sherlock's drive to find company in her otherness, her singular oddness, mimics the sociocultural space of the fan and fandom. The popular narrative is that here in fandom, the fan finds othered women just like herself; no longer alone she has peers as odd and displaced as she is. In fandom a 'young urban dyke shares erotic space with a straight married mom in the American heartland' as part of the complex, queered relationships between fans in their spaces (Lothian, Busse, and Reid 2007). In this environment HBBO, and other transformative fans, use the rationale of regendering to refigure that affective imbalance. However, it reinforces that imbalance by focusing that labour on the male and the masculine narratives and on regendering them. This paradox makes close reading vital in understanding gender within regendered narratives; in *One Shape to Another* the narrative focus is closely held on not just the characters, but how their gender and sexuality as lesbian women manifest within the boundaries of the established canonical and fannish character narratives and expectations, and within the historical setting HBBO has chosen.

In *One Shape to Another* HBBO has used not only the common tropes and signifiers of fanfic like the historical AU, shipping, authorial asides, notes and acknowledgements updated with links to fanart, alongside the canon of commercial Sherlockian work, queer literature, post-modernism, lesbian media and erotica/pornography, to create a narrative that uses and investigates those things through the experiences of women who do not perform gender 'correctly'. This variability of gender role performance can be read as a responsiveness to the canon and to the fandom itself; by remaking the universe of the text almost entirely female there is no way women's experiences can be erased and no need for women's narratives and lives to be condensed into a singular kind of character and story. The queer components of the narrative not only situate *One Shape to Another* within a broader genre of lesbian romance but also allow HBBO to illuminate the intricacies of gender role performance. The 'freedom' of slash and femmeslash from heterosexual binaries is revealed within *One Shape to Another* as a manifestation of desire not as a reflection of either queer experience or queer literature.

One specific aspect of her presentation worth highlighting is the presence of violence. The position of the queered regendered character, who in the canonical versions is a vector and a victim of violence, inherently contends with the social role of violence against women, against lesbians and within our communities. While HBBO situates her regendered characters within a milieu that narratively excludes much of male violence, outside a few key scenes, the aftermath and ongoing effects of previous experiences are included as a way in which women bond and strengthen their communities. However, the presence of war, in this case a war that was won, that is over, provides a foundation for the characters and for much of the case that they investigate. In the following chapter I will analyse more modern interpretations, where the experience of war – as a woman – is one that does not provide a community of survivors; instead, the experience of war marks the characters as much as gender, in a multitude of ways. Additionally, I analyse a work that regenders Sherlock in a way – rather than changing his gender it explores how the character would evolve as a trans man, and how the violence against queer and trans people creates trauma. These explicit experiences of war and transphobia, with PTSD and the knowledge that the conflict is never-ending, are inextricably linked with the experiences of women and trans people in 'peacetime'. Through their experiences of violence, harm and surviving those terrors as integral to their experience of gender (even when that gender is a coercively assigned one, to be negotiated around and moved through) the characterization of the original works is explored and expanded, played with and critiqued.

6

Gender is a battlefield

The breadth of fandom's regendering, in contrast to professional adaptation, is the capacity to focus deeply on a singular character while exploring how gender is manifest in the original work. This regendering is not simply male-to-female or cisgender. The two fanfic texts I have chosen for analysis in this chapter have several commonalities – they are Archontic Holsmean narratives, regender one or more characters and feature gender as a means to explore the default assumptions of the original canon and its genre. *Compatible Damage* (CD) by branwyn is a modern retelling based heavily on the BBC Sherlock adaptation, regendering Watson but maintaining many of the canonical signifiers from that archontic iteration where the role and meaning of being a veteran are linked to the work of the genre. The other work, *Seems So Easy for Everybody Else* (SSEfEE) by etothepii, also bases itself heavily on BBC *Sherlock*; however, it reworks the narrative to centre Sherlock's transition as a trans man, complicating the default narratives of the genre but also the ways in which the original and archontic versions are gendered. In particular 'stories featuring characters with non-cisgender identities are the least common occurring queer narratives on AO3' (Dym, Brubaker, and Fiesler 2018). Works that regender rather than 'genderfuck' works which use 'science fiction and fantasy tropes to alter and reimagine characters' sexed and gendered bodies' while also addressing kinds of transitions are rare but also significant in the metanarratives and counterpublic genre conventions (Busse and Lothian 2009). These two works address and complicate ideas of binary or static genders, using the archontic Holmes along with other narratives familiar to the audiences.

CD also features a kind of courtship, lengthy and drawn out and orthogonal to the assumed implications of a heterosexual relationship springing from a regendered character pair. For Joanna Watson, her experience of war makes this connection to Sherlock more than simply a romantic or sexual preoccupation, it is instead a lifeline, repeatedly linked with avoiding suicide but also her vision of herself as a weapon. While this militaristic preoccupation can be seen as a natural extension of Watson's position as a veteran, and Sherlock's conception of London being at war within itself, readings of the texts within the metanarratives of fandom reveal the metaphorical nature of the battlefield of love as being somewhat less than metaphorical.

The implied and expected reader of these narratives exists not only as a close, and trained, reader but also in a state of flow. Aspects of characterization do not need to be explained, the author can expect the reader will understand that Sherlock is Sherlock Holmes, with all the Archontic iterations stretching out fore and aft and bolstering the representations and the critiques she is weaving into the work. In that state of flow, where the reader is enmeshed within the narrative due to their familiarity with the canon, and the Archontic variations, she is able to integrate the unfamiliar elements of the narrative – not simply the change in gender, but the way that regendering affects the narrator and the themes of the text itself. This makes the politico-social elements of the text integral to the reading of the work and not simply as a kind of creative feminist praxis, but as a narrative tool aimed at the reader and the fandom itself, critiquing the metanarratives of fandom.

Modern fandom, historically within fan studies at least, owes its inception to a kind of capitalist version of storytelling and subversion; however, there is also a longer history outside the concept of media fandom as it was conceptualized, born from the loins of television and zines. Castle refers to the groups of women who entered into lively conversation with authors during the 1800s, writing to them to plead for changes in the narratives, and rewriting those texts for their friends and circulating their corrections (Castle 2013; Chamberlain 2020). In this way, authors like branwyn and etothepii join with a long literary history of subaltern readers reacting to and criticizing texts through rewriting the focus of the work, by revisioning and reworking the narratives to their own ends; either by changing the narrative to satisfy their own desires for justice, for romance, or to illustrate the blithe ignorance and imbalances of the original. Fans become part of this history with their work, and even though those narratives are often long gone, hidden in archives or lost entirely, the spirit of that interaction lives on in modern fandom.

Activism around gender identity domestic violence, reproductive justice, rape culture, intersectional elements of racial and ethnic violence reveals the personal landscape as one fraught with incredible risk and danger for women and those who are gender non-normative. Even before modern ideas and waves of feminism, the deadly potential of sex and love was well understood by those for whom birth and pregnancy presented much higher risks than in many modern cultures; similarly social risks were much higher also. This is the backdrop against which these stories paper themselves; not simply the canon, or the Archontic version, or fandom, but centuries of history, and specifically not history of the subaltern. The stories link all of these elements together with their own reinterpretation of the Archontic Holmesean narrative.

Burn London down

In the interconnected stories of the CD series, branwyn focuses heavily on Watson as the veteran, weaving that narrative into modern day versions of Conan Doyle's cases. Joanna Watson's characterization is tied intimately with being a veteran much like many archontic iterations, and the experience of being a woman veteran in an overlay. Her gender changes very little in terms of the nouns, the names; veteran, Afghanistan, shoulder wound, shot, surgeon, PTSD, therapy, follower, Captain; however, the experience of those as a woman changes each and every aspect.

Compatible Damage by branwyn

Description: Being deceivers, yet we are true; unknown, yet well known; dying, yet behold we live; punished, yet not killed; sorrowful, yet always rejoicing; poor, yet making many rich; having nothing, yet possessing everything. 2 Corinthians 6:8–10, tr. Laurie R. King.

Stats: Words: 85,011 Works: 3 Complete: No Bookmarks: 573

Part 1: The Skeleton Winter

Rating: Mature

Archive Warning: Creator Chose Not to Use Archive Warnings

Category: F/M

Additional Tags: PTSD, Suicide, Angst, casefic: The Dancing Men, Genderswap, Attempted Rape

Stats: Words: 29577 Chapters: 11/11 Comments: 149 Kudos: 1664 Bookmarks: 414 Hits: 48275

Part 2: Let Sense Be Dumb

Rating: Mature

Archive Warnings: Creator Chose Not to Use Archive Warnings; Rape/ Non-Con

Additional Tags: casefic, Genderswapgirl!john, PTSD, Kidnapping, Class
Issues, Self-Destructive Behavior, A Case of Identity, incest themes,
Childhood Sexual Abuse
Stats: Words: 39212 Chapters: 14/14 Comments: 357 Kodos: 1647
Bookmarks: 208 Hits: 51236

Part 3: The Silences
Rating: Mature
Archive Warning: Creator Chose Not To Use Archive Warnings
Additional Tags: Genderswapgirl!john, casefic, The Gloria Scott, The
Abbey Grange, Domestic Violence, Blackmail
Stats: Words: 16222 Chapters: 6/6 Comments: 230 Kudos: 1201
Bookmarks: 155 Hits: 34944

In CD Joanna is traumatized, repeatedly, from childhood onwards. Her
experiences enmesh perfectly with the construction of a female character who
would become an army surgeon, who would take a flat with a man she doesn't
know, who would seek out danger and find peace in risk. The character herself
faces this, recognizing that she

> plunges headlong into danger, exposes herself to risk on purpose because there's
> nothing as sweet, as rewarding, as the moment when Sherlock comes charging
> in to save her. … she only felt at ease in the world when she was in danger.
> There's a wound in her so deep and old she'd forgotten it, failed to recognize that
> in every brush with destruction she was putting a plaster on a bullet hole. It's the
> source of the static. She'd mistaken the symptom for the disease.
>
> (branwyn 2012)

Branwyn follows the tracks and trails left by trauma, specifically gendered kinds
of trauma and the way the aftermaths of those traumatic incidences (rape, abuse,
homelessness, assault, war injuries, PTSD) are gendered by communities and
cultures. She also examines the ways in which that trauma, the scars left behind,
maps out strengths and a kind of resilience common to the experience of women
as a class in the way 'she'd learned to take all her fear and helplessness and rage and
convert it into courage, determination, and forward momentum' (branwyn 2012).
The ability to endure, to continue, to swallow anger and hurt and act, is how the
canonical aspects of the Archontic Watson's courage under fire become Joanna's.
     She is less traumatized by experience than by the aftermath and the otherness
she feels where 'Everything Joanna Watson used to be bled out of her under the
glaring eye of a foreign sun' and she is left 'wondering how she is meant to live in

a world that so obviously no longer has any place for her, when she no longer has the strength of will to make a place for herself' (branwyn 2011). The importance of honour, and dedication, occupies significant amounts of character space for the CD – Joanna phrases her dedication to the honourable cause of Sherlock Holmes as 'enlisting in his private army'. The complex question of how to serve returning women veterans focuses, in real life, on their experiences of violence and often on sexual trauma. Joanna belies that rationale as a career soldier, that familiar masculine character who is unable to adjust to civilian life. When that trope becomes regendered, it exposes the ways in which the originals are highly gendered in their representations even if the perceptions of the character are more neutral. Joanna's history of sexual trauma and treatment that meets the definition of assault or harassment, are represented as the background radiation of misogyny the author expects that the reader will understand.

The spectre of the heterosexualizing of the partnership between the male Sherlock and the female Watson is cracked through by the way she is distanced from her body as a woman, only feeling 'in her body' in situations that revolve around violence that recall she was a 'woman of action even before she became so spectacularly broken'. Her attraction is cemented in being seen as who she is: 'Not just a short, wasted woman with awkward chin-length hair and dubiously feminine scar tissue, but the lost soldier in search of a new mission' (branwyn 2011). Joanna's body reflects her discomforts, as it is one that 'could be mistaken for someone's mum' but has 'taken a bullet, and more beatings than she can count' and has lost the muscularity that is 'more than is strictly feminine' and simultaneously mourned for making her more attractive but 'frail' (branwyn 2012). Her bodily musing is something much like the 'mirror scene – a narrative convention in trans representations of all kinds' where Joanna's nonconforming body is reflected as an archive of a body whose intelligibility requires a vulnerable visibility (Rose 2020, 31–2). It is also fragmented by Joanna's self-perception as 'not a woman, but a ghost haunting a woman's body' (branwyn 2011). Her capacity for violence is rewritten into the masculine 'brother-in-arms' who allows her the rationale for lawful killing.

The relationship is repeatedly marred and problematized by Sherlock's emotional distance, as someone who 'never quite grasped that emotional wounds don't heal on the same schedule as flesh wounds' yet also 'goes mental when she's in danger' (branwyn 2012). His feelings are unacknowledged by both Sherlock and Watson beyond the defensive recognition Watson signifies as occurring 'because in a world where appealing to a man's sexuality can lead to marriage or to murder, every woman over the age of thirteen is a master of observation and deduction' until the end of the first entry in the series (branwyn 2011). When they come close to the romantic, in a trope where during an argument they stand toe-to-toe, Joanna notes internally that

> people don't do this sort of thing unless they're either going to fight, or fuck and not only can't she tell which Sherlock has in mind, but her own thoughts are caught between making a tactical assessment of his weaknesses, and wondering whether, if she touched him now, he would melt, or else ignite like one of his experiments gone awry

only to go on and diffuse the situation with tactical tickling (branwyn 2011). The result of which leaves her feeling 'like a girl in a fairy tale, she's broken the spell, and Sherlock is once again a mad, brilliant, sputtering child' (branwyn 2011). The diffusion and the undignified reactions interrupt the familiar violence of romantic tropes (particularly within action or crime narratives). But it is branwyn's Sherlock who states, 'And what is a marriage, after all, but a loyal unit of two people, sworn to defend each other against all enemies?' But it is one, also, as noted by his brother after a kidnapping and attempted rape where 'caring for a woman is rather like caring for a soldier. On some level, one will worry for her. Constantly' (branwyn 2012). When they do finally move into a romantic and sexual space it's immediately after Sherlock discovers Joanna with her gun and realizes that her suicidal ideation is linked to boredom, to inaction. Their bond is one where 'you let me be who I am, and I need that like I need air' (branwyn 2011).

The Sherlock of CD is a familiar one to many archontic iterations, he is brusque, aware of the interpersonal and emotional but places himself at a distance. When Joanna notes his obtuseness about his attraction to her, it is a variation of that. This emotional blindness, when placed squarely within the realm of a heterosexual partnership, or even a heterosocial one, highlights the ways in which the kinds of canonical and archontic behaviours of Sherlock are commonly masculinized in a multitude of narratives. Watson's emotional intelligence has been referred to as womanish, feminine, since the early days of the fandom (Stout 1941) but branwyn's explicit regendering of Watson removes that inability to connect from the male realm of the detective novel to the familiarly romantic narrative woven through her story. This accomplishes a critique of the ways in which intellect and intelligence are masculinized within narratives and wider media, but also makes it clear how limited that makes the narrative and the character.

The valorization of rationality, of logic, is skewered by the regendering of such a familiar narrative. As in HBBO's retelling, where Sherlock removed herself from the messy realities of love because her early experiences as a lesbian were shrouded by period-typical homophobia (internalized and external), retelling the Holmsean narrative with a female Watson highlights the expected reader affinities and affordances. In CD the knowing voice of the narrator punctures the pontificating and patronizing logic that allows and enforces maladjusted behaviour from male characters, and punishes the women around them. Consciously and performatively within the narrative it creates an implied reader who knows exactly what the female characters have endured – not necessarily by direct experience but by being alongside. The narrative assumes women exist as a class, shifting in and around intersectional aspects like race, class, ability, ethnicity and sexuality, but that women as a class have a shared experience of the world. It is this class that is the implied, intended, reader also. Men and male experience are deliberately constructed as the other within both CD and how the mouth changes its shape, using the narrative, characterization and metanarratives around the work, media and fandom.

This knowing and judgemental narrator within CD is coded female, and angry – not necessarily a woman, or the right kind of woman, for all the references to chromosomes and growing up female. Instead there is no space made by the narrator for the elisions and revisions of masculine inattention, of rationality's rudeness, and those things are instead laid bare for the reader as inexcusable errors of intellect and attention. There is no excuse, within the Holmesean genius, for not understanding women, yet the canon and the Archontic versions often feature this as an element of his intellect. Branwyn draws attention to the ways in which this actually lessens his abilities, lessens his intellect, echoing, metatextually, the ways in which the erasure and ignorance of women and femininity across numerous disciplines and fields lead to weaknesses within those areas.

This explicit othering, and the naming and rejection of the male gaze, is woven into the experiences of being women and the expected performances of femininity within the text. Authorities loom large, with expectations of gender policing manifest in both actions and inactions; women aren't meant to be on the frontline (like men) thus women do not need arms training (like men) thus women who train like men, who are injured like men, are suspect for their transgression of the roles they have been given. Joanna struggles with this, and her own internalized need for that risk and danger. It is filtered through trauma; for her the risk focuses the damage and the danger onto its correct vector, her body, while also providing emotional resonances in the way those around her react and care for her. It is also a commentary on gendered violence and the way women who are like her are underestimated: 'A man who ceases to see a woman as a human being is equally unlikely to see her as a threat' (branwyn 2012). In the first story it is that mistake, along with knowing that while 'she's not a trained hostage negotiator … but she's trained for this sort of thing all the same, simply by living 35 years in the world with two X chromosomes. Wasn't that the first lesson society taught a girl, how to please a man?' (branwyn 2012). The regendering allows for a Watson who is as emotionally sensitive and acute as the original but who chooses to 'weaponize those lessons' of womanhood.

The well-worn objections to the 'bossy woman' alongside admiration for the 'leader' who is presumed male – and drilling down through those objections to layers and layers of intersecting axes of oppression – are critiqued within these regendered narratives by taking those admirable masculine-male characters and laying them at the foundation of the female character. The way these interactions within the narrative work echoes the way in which real women's lives and experiences are policed, but also how in media, fandom and other discourses female characterization is policed for those transgressions. A policing and enforcement that is not confined only to women – Pande's work illustrates the way nonwhite fans are subject to the same kinds of behaviour, and as the next section illustrates, so too are gender non-normative people. Joanna is female, but consistently outside and 'unusual for a woman' who aligns 'Soldiers, doctors, women' as a category, who says 'Who'd be a proper girl?' (branwyn 2012).

What does it matter?

The representations of women and non-normative genders are included within the schematic of 'regendering'. While Sherlock who is a trans man has not changed his gender, and indeed there is no confirmation that canonical Sherlock is a cis man at all (or heterosexual, which has much greater traction as a 'what if' to be explored than gender identity), the transitional experience in *Seems So Easy for Everybody Else* (SSEfEE) by etothepii reaffirms and reworks the expectations of gender within the narrative itself.

Seems So Easy for Everybody Else by etothepii

Rating: Teen And Up Audiences
Archive Warning: Creator Chose Not To Use Archive Warnings

Additional Tags: Trans Sherlock, Trans Male Character
Stats: Words: 14882 Chapters: 1/1 Comments: 161 Kudos: 3371
Bookmarks: 898 Hits: 25204

Rose describes how 'in addition to providing a form of trans entertainment, i.e. an in-group entertainment for those familiar with trans, transfic also, albeit not always successfully, as will be shown below, functions as (cis) education. And finally, through its inherently collective approach to storytelling, trans narratives in fanfiction call into question the very opposition between cis and trans' (2020, 25). Like other transgender fanwork it 'pushes back against the heteronormative, hypermasculine tension' of the original media object (Dym, Brubaker, and Fiesler 2018). This retelling of the Sherlock 'origin story' examines the experiences of gender from the liminal spaces, the margins of the binary model and the edges of sexuality as well. Much like the videogame narratives of transgender characters, SSEfEE rewrites 'canonically cisgender characters as transgender without making significant changes to a (game's) narrative' (Dym, Brubaker, and Fiesler 2018) – Sherlock remains estranged from his family, has a difficult relationship with his brother, a long-standing drug habit and is drawn to the predictability and control of detective work. In SSEfEE etothepii follows a young Sherlock, designated female at birth and named Sophie Charlotte. Textually the story uses the pronouns of Holmes's external identity – she until transition, he afterwards. While this, in terms of a biographic representation, is contrary to accepted and preferred practice (use the gender pronouns of the post-transitional person's preference) it centres the narrative neatly on the character themselves, and the transitional experience that does not conform to the popular transitional story of 'I always knew' but instead focuses on the uncertainty and tensions of the process itself.

> She tells herself it'll change. She tells herself that she'll change, that one day she will see herself in the mirror or reflected in the eyes of someone else, and think, yes, this is me. This is who I am.
>
> She can't see it happening, no matter how hard she tries.
>
> –
>
> He gives up arguing with himself about it, eventually.
>
> (etothepii 2011)

The young Holmes knows they are different – they are smart, they are curious and they act well outside the accepted roles for young girls. At which point does this transgression and misbehaviour become symptomatic of being designated the wrong gender, rather than of the essential inequality of the role itself? And within a character like Sherlock Holmes, already well outside the expected norm, what is it that shapes the difference into a kind of conformity?

> There are things that she wants, things she's always wanted, that she'd thought were impossible. You can't change something that's already happened. And, maybe she's wrong, maybe she just doesn't believe women are truly equal to men, and that's the problem. Maybe she just has low self-esteem caused by having no friends during her prime socialization years, and thinks that being a boy would have fixed it.
>
> It doesn't make any sense. Sex is just the body. The body is just transport for the mind. She's above the demands of her body, so why does she want to change it?
>
> And even if she does want to be male, what does it matter? She can't actually change her chromosomes, just force her body into a facsimile of masculinity.
>
> It's costly and inconvenient and not really that big of a deal, because even as a woman, she's sure she can get her way and do what she wants with minimal interference from others. It wouldn't even be much of a difference, because it's not as if trying to change it would do that much.
>
> (etothepii 2011)

The way etothepii's text follows the concrete experiences of transition from designated female to his male identity allows the author to illustrate the way in which behaviours are perceived differently between men and women. What Sophie does, what she can achieve, what she experiences, change as her presentation masculinizes. This work of exploring his identity shift shows that 'despite trans narratives' engagement with and predication on social norms relating to gender, they can be seen as employing an additional mode of engagement, namely one that trans-es gender discourses' (Rose 2020, 26). When Sophie fully transitions to Sherlock, his experiences, while still as an outsider and as a gender minority, still retain and use power and privilege that had been inaccessible prior to that transition. The length of the process – first presentation changes, then there is a social transition, and finally a medical one – slowly increases reader awareness of the ways in which the canonical elements of Sherlock's character are only really accessible to the male version and for the female, even the imaginary projected version of Sophie-who-did-not-transition, there is a lack of the real, of social recognizance. For all of the canonical and Archontic Sherlock's inability to become part of the seething sea of humanity, as a man he is allowed this space as an extension of his masculinity. For a woman, that rationality and distance are unthinkable, only explicable in the shadow of trauma, but instead of the expected kinds of feminine trauma to explain those 'flaws', etothepii uses transition and transgender traumas. Rose aligns this with Walker's narrative extraction in that 'the impact of trans experiences on how we read and make sense of the narratives surrounding us, allowing us to tease out and foreground aspects of our favourite characters that remain invisible from cis perspectives' (Walker 2019; 2020, 27). Those tendencies of Sherlock's remain a manifestation of the masculine, and the trauma is that of gender dysphoria, misgendering, the internal conflict of one's body at odds with one's self.

Depicting and representing liminal gender spaces as ways of interrogating out own assumptions of cisgender defaults is made possible through the medium of fanfiction or adaptive works. The audience is presented with a version of the familiar, but whose gender creates a tension with the canonical, with the reader's expectations and with wider discourses about gender. Rose illustrates that the works and their focus explore the cis-normative 'resulting in disorientation, which is both a threat and a chance – a threat to the binary order and a chance to open spaces within and beyond this order, without neglecting but rather by foregrounding trans embodiment' (2020, 26). Readers are forced to understand their own complicity in the gender binary, their own acts enforcing and reinforcing the constructs within and outside the text by the layers of meaning woven around the supporting characters – in SSEfEE the well-meaning but ultimately non-understanding concern of Mycroft whose eventual acceptance is marked by significant aggressions against Sherlock along the way.

Yet SSEfEE retains a kind of essentialism of gender performance, even if transition is nominally gender diversity in action. Sherlock's transition is away from the kind of misfired, error-ridden experience of female he has endured, to something that better fits his vision of himself. However, those visions of self are boundaried and contained within a binary and within gender roles. Our understanding, as readers, of Sherlock as a specific kind of masculinity – logical, rational, detached and removed – is integral to our understanding of Sophie's transition to Sherlock. Rose says this kind of 'The social scrutiny of bodies and the resulting pressure to conform to expectations link the fanfiction's trans focus to other experiences that bring about feelings of shame and personal deficiency' (2020, 30). It is not simply about what is masculine and male, but about the internal sense of self being manifest in the body, the need to be a certain kind of person that links the trans narrative to the more widespread experiences of the readers. We know who exists at the end of the transition process, so the points during the transition process that illuminate Sophie's discomfort with her gender – not simply the treatment she is subject to, but breasts and menstruation and male attention and the expectations around those things – are exhibits of gender dysphoria. But those points are not enough to rationalize transition, are not simply unique to gender dysphoria, and it is the external framework of fanfic, the metadata and metanarratives, that prompts the reader to experience and interpret those ideas as aspects of transgender narratives rather than as a discourse about the restrictive roles and behaviours expected of women and young girls (Willis 2012).

Regendering is disruptive to the Archontic elements of the narrative, not just because of the gender change but because what remains of the gendered aspects of the canonical and Archontic representations is then subverted and undermined. The conflict and tension between binarized gender and non-standard representations and perceptions of those representations add complexity to the Archontic Holmes and readings of the canon. The presentation of gender, made complex by transition and transgression, is metatextually familiar; fandom is a nominally queer, feminine, space but also includes relatively high levels of gender diverse people and the concepts of transmen and genderqueer women are not new. However, the twisting of the familiar narratives of transition – I always knew I was a boy – into etothepii's loving and nuanced representation of confusion, of uncertainty, about that maleness, shifts those common representations of gender diversity into something not only appropriate to the Archontic Holmes but also broadening those representations.

Not a woman

Both of these works rely strongly on essentialism, in character, to excuse and to sequester their characters from that wider pool of women. Like Irene Adler in the canon, Joanna and Sophie are not women, are not like other women (indeed, Sophie is not even a woman, Joanna is a ghost in a woman's body); their uniqueness demands that they are removed from that class and quarantined safely away. They are a veteran, whose experiences from not just the war but from childhood abuse, knowing intimately 'the helplessness that comes with looking at a living victim and knowing that even giving her answers isn't going to fix the mess that's been made of her life' (branwyn 2012). They aren't even a woman, they are a man who 'dares to grow his hair long. It's not too long, just barely enough to curl, and even when he shaves his jaw smooth, no one looks at him askance, squinting as if they can determine his sex by staring long enough' (etothepii 2011).

The gender liminality of regendering is made clear in the fannish representations; however, in commercial and professional adaptations there is a much more normative representation of gender. The next chapter deals with *Elementary* and the regendering of Moriarty. This character, as a regendered adaptation, explores the violence and othering embodied by a female villain. She faces many of the same judgements and constraints the fannish examples do, but exhibits them differently due to both the commercial/professional aspect but also her motherhood and femininity as a villain.

7

Elementary and regendering the classics

In *Elementary* Jeremy Lee Miller and Lucy Liu play Sherlock and Watson, respectively. It also stars, in a recurring role, Natalie Dormer; she initially appears as Irene Adler but is then revealed to be Jamie Moriarty; both characters appear in limited ways in the canonical texts but who are repeatedly focused on by adaptations. As Irene Adler she is The Woman, as Moriarty she is the Napoleon of Crime. As both, she is a disruption to the expectations of the genre, of Holmsean adaptations, and the gendered presentation of violence in television. To understand the expectations of the genre, and Holmsean adaptations, this chapter will examine the ways in which *Elementary* interacts with other retellings of the canonical stories, and the ways in which Dormer's character changes from the initial introduction to her performance in the later seasons, including central tropes of feminine gender performance – motherhood and love. So while 'the female heroism of the warrior woman is both masculine and feminine which subverts cultural tendencies to represent gender categories in rigid, binary terms,' she is identified as 'recognizably female, even maternal ... furthermore, her feminine qualities do not inhibit her fighting prowess in any way, while her masculine traits do not diminish her humanity' (Bennion-Nixon 2010, para. 5). The necessity of the violent female figure to have a reason for that violence, to exhibit a cause deemed just, to be maternal if not a mother, to be feminine, means that for the regendered character a balance must be struck between the original violence and the feminized version. The importance of the regendering within *Elementary* intersects with the depiction and representation of cinematic violence in a multitude of ways, and the manifestation of narrative sympathy for those characters within the texts themselves.

The tension between the playful facets of fanwork and the more serious notion of adaptation was evident when *Elementary* was first launched. Originally it was conceived as a US 'version' of the BBC's *Sherlock,* but the showrunners plans were rejected. Given the out-of-copyright status of the original Conan Doyle works (as much as this was a point of contention for the later stories and for his estate) the CBS network elected to create their own modernized version. This both allowed, and demanded, a greater distance from the BBC version. Beyond location changes (*Elementary* locates itself within New York and occasionally the wider United States or internationally, *Sherlock* is in London and the UK primarily), *Elementary* made one large, and contentious, change – Dr John Watson became Dr Joan Watson. This regendering, and changes in her biographical identifiers, caused enormous amounts of disagreement for fans of both the original and of *Sherlock*. Multiple essays were written defending both of those works from the perceived insult of feminizing the ladies man veteran, or Americanizing the narrative (Bennett 2012; Coren 2012; Stagg 2012). Once the show was released many of these complaints became muffled, particularly those regarding the 'heterosexualizing' of a narrative many see as in some way queer[1], and the 'damaging' of the canon or the characters. Some of this is due to the ways the show very deliberately sidestepped those concerns, and the way genre plays into the perception of the show. The series continued to play with the canon, and with audience expectations, including the regendering (in a way) of Professor Moriarty, and the regendering (in a way) of Ms Hudson (who is textually a trans woman, played by a trans woman). These more-complex-than-expected ways of intersecting with gender, genre and format, have stymied much of the criticism targeted at the regendering itself.

One of the enduring criticisms of the show is familiar to many of the more negative approaches to regendering evident in my previous chapter about fan responses; it isn't *really* an adaptation; it merely uses the name with no real connection to the original. This critique privileges the interlocutor's version of the 'original' and what they consider to be the foundations of identity, so it is unsurprising that a change in gender is perceived as to be so foundationally shattering as to render any work 'original' but also suspect, due to its co-optation of those canonical signifiers, in a kind of trademark infringement or misrepresentation. Even though the body is fictional, 'is a site where flesh and speech or knowledge fold within and through each other as an expression of self' as an element of discursive materiality (MacCormack 2008, 12).

Important to the understanding of the characterization of any Holmsean narrative is the fandom, and all of the other adaptations, and the fanaticism that

---

[1] The question of queerness and Holmes/Watson is still subject to ongoing analysis, so I hesitate to make any claim for or against it within the canon.

springs up around those adaptations (Pearson 2007, 98). From the beginning of the works the fans have been a part of the mythos (Eyles 1986); the black armbands after Sir Conan Doyle finally threw his hero from the Reichenbach Falls, and the rumours of said hero's resurrection being due to royal bargaining, are not unfamiliar emotional responses to the modern audience. There has been a long-standing drive to adapt these characters to the fan-producer's contemporary desires, adding materials to the archontic Holmes (Stein, Busse, and Hills 2014). *Elementary* references these other adaptations, firmly situating itself within the wider archontic field of fanwork, from playful references to less serious adaptations (such as the opening cinematic directly remaking a key scene from *The Great Mouse Detective*) to the original works themselves (episode names such as *The Five Orange Pipz* directly reference Conan Doyle's story *The Five Orange Pips* but diverge from it significantly) (Taylor 2013). While definitively a commercial project, it approaches the process of adaptation in a way familiar to fanworks – through a complex intersection of play, politics and pastiche.

Regendering the villain

By regendering Moriarty, the overarching villain whose relationships with Watson and Holmes are complex, sexualized and integral to the series, *Elementary* disrupted many expectations from the modern expectations of a classic. As both (Jamie) Moriarty and Irene Adler, the 'evil mastermind' of the canonical character and the contemporary iterations of Adler are subverted and defined by gender, and it also reveals how that intersects with expectations of gendered violence. The spectre of women and violence is central to the detective and police procedural genres that *Elementary* crosses, and an analysis of the ways in which the regendering affects that violence from the point of view of the instigator as much as a victim. As the nemesis, Moriarty is almost unrepentantly violent, orchestrating murders and tortures and leading an international crime syndicate. Despite this, her violence is rarely visually represented – only *her* performance around it. She is responsible, at a remove. This essay examines the manifestations of her self-described 'innate' violent tendencies with her position as both soul mate and nemesis of Sherlock, and her status as a mother. The televisual aspects of her violence are depicted most clearly in her relationship with Holmes or Watson, and in her relationship with her daughter; intimate and closely cropped to the domain of women. Similarly, her violence also works in and around the cinematic history of queer signifiers for antagonists, such as her gender transgressions, obsessiveness and violent tendencies, and her flamboyance once she reasserts herself as a criminal mastermind. Of note is the differentiation between her performance of the damaged woman and her subsequent position as the bad man with her transition from lover and victim to the caged criminal genius and subsequent maternity.

The affect associated with adaptive work is comfort; Van Steenhuyse suggests it is an immersive context, a familiarity that is then traded on for increased identification and a more sophisticated reading of the text as the audience can be relied upon to know the broad details of the canonical work (Van Steenhuyse 2011). This then allows the adaptation to expand upon, or change, or twist, those elements so that 'they are transported to a universe that confirms a wide range of expectations, but also offers them something new' (2011, 6). In regendered work this is not simply just about character, or genre, but also about the ways gender is characterized within the work, within media and within genre. Jamie Moriarty takes upon herself the mantle of the *male* criminal genius through that regendering, while retaining the femaleness of Adler, and the myriad ways that manifest in the original and in the many other adaptations of the work;

> My first instinct was to kill you. Quietly, discreetly. But then, the more I learned about you, the more … curious I became. Here, at last, seemed to be a mind that rivalled my own, something too complicated and too beautiful to destroy. At least, without further analysis. – Jamie Moriarty to Sherlock Holmes.
>
> ('M.' 2013)

The division, artificial as it may be, between the personal violence of the criminal and the institutional and systematic violence of the mastermind is one that *Elementary* introduces in numerous episodes and personifies in several of its recurring antagonists. Most obviously, the figure of Moriarty inhabits a space both personally malevolent and institutionally violent – they are a manipulator of nations, head of an international crime syndicate, while also murdering people 'on the page' and off. The spectrum of violence occupied by Moriarty is broad and one that, while intimately focused on Sherlock, is not simply defined by the relationship between the two characters. There is the third member of the group – Watson – but also the world itself. The perceptions surrounding Moriarty, who is simultaneously powerful at a systematic international level but unknown, faceless and unknowable to the public, are layered in with gender in *Elementary*'s version of the character. The intricacies of the relationships between Holmes, Watson and Moriarty underpin almost all adaptations, and those versions become part of the wider mythos themselves; *Elementary* adds to those Archontic narratives and to wider discourses around the experiences of women in media and in television. The character of Jamie is one who builds on not only the canonical Irene, the canonical Moriarty, but also the myriad adaptations and the perceptions and receptions of women as love interests, women as criminals and women as figures of violence.

The canon, the adaptations and the spaces between

The Derridean Archive of meaning drawn from not only our experience of a text but all that accompanies it intertextually is particularly acute within Holmsean adaptations. Within this framework Jamie Moriarty is not simply a singular character within the confines of the stories or *Elementary* but exists within the wider audience perception of the archontic Holmsean narrative, expanding upon, relating with and to the other archontic versions. By combining the two characters *Elementary* deals with the inherent misogyny of the original's The Woman – who defines '… Holmes's dismissive view of the whole sex', and the implied sexism of the archontic Adlers as '… stunted re-visionings of female subjectivity' (Primorac 2013, 94; 107). It also addresses some of the issues for actresses, and roles for women in wider media; Dormer herself has been quoted in interviews talking about the role of Moriarty as one she relishes: 'we don't have enough young, female antiheroes. We don't accept women as antiheroes the way we do the men …' (Higgins 2014). By examining these aspects of *Elementary* as an adaptation, and how they interact with other adaptations and the wider media, the scope of Moriarty's violence can be ascertained.

Regendering, as evident in the characters of Joan, Jamie and to a certain extent Ms Hudson who is a trans woman in *Elementary*, offers a deconstruction of gender via the simultaneous examination of the engendering of the original character through the changes in the derivative work, and the manifestation of gender performance in the regendered cipher. It also begins to occupy the absence of non-male, non-white characters being identified by researchers and fans as endemic to mainstream media, and experientially rejects it as harmful. The show runners, including Doherty the Executive Producer, have mentioned the imbalances of the original and why they sought to make those changes to the gender and race of characters because their adaptation modernizes the mythos and situates it in New York; a cast dominated by white men would have some authenticity with respect to the original work, but would also be entirely inauthentic for the new setting and historical period (Bennett 2012).

Even with the more egalitarian notions about the archontic Holmes and the elimination of a hierarchy in the context of the adaptations and fanworks, the canon still takes precedence for many and the relevance of that canonical origin of the characters is necessary to examine the ways the adaptations work with and around them. Canonical Holmes professes no love for Adler, but he is consumed by The Woman. His idolization of Adler can be likened to tropes of courtly love, emphasized by his patriotic engraving of 'V.R.' (Victoria Regina) in bullet holes on the wall of his lodgings, and the strict standards of propriety and romantic notions of that 'gracious woman', but also reveals the limitations of the source, bound as it was to ideals and understandings of the day (Doyle [1892] 1986). To have Holmes 'beaten' by a woman could only happen if the woman were exceptional, unique and able to be placed upon a pedestal and removed from the wider class of women. The canonical Irene Adler appears briefly but demands outsized attentions for the effort. She is one of the few people who bested Holmes in his area of interest, identifying him and his work, disguising herself to escape his notice, thoroughly disconcerting his emotional equilibrium by maintaining a sense of honour where Holmes' client has little (Primorac 2013, 99). The textual and historical elements of her characterization in the canon as an adventuress, as a mistress, as to the nature of the incriminating evidence, provide a rich ground for archontic adaptations. Only Adler has beaten Holmes, and only Holmes has beaten Moriarty.

In *Elementary*, however, Holmes and eventually Watson have 'solved' the mystery that is Jamie. It is one of the few retellings which both regenders Moriarty *and* sexualizes this relationship via Moriarty's alter ego of Irene Adler. Her gender presentation is explicitly and knowingly performative, in that she acknowledges the treatment of her persona as Adler is different to the false masculine front of Moriarty. In a reverse of a common adaptational and cinematic trope of Adler/The Woman being the tool being wielded by Moriarty/the crime lord (both BBC's *Sherlock* and Guy Ritchie's *A Game of Shadows* do this) Moriarty is in truth a tool, a persona, just as Adler is, to the ur-character Jamie.

There are several modern adaptations that feature Irene and Moriarty as linked on some level; in *Sherlock* she is reimagined as a blackmailer, who uses her professional skills as a dominatrix as fodder for her work; she is also a lesbian who falls in love with Sherlock. In the Guy Ritchie *Sherlock Holmes* film series, she is an agent provocateur, who is used by Moriarty as a tool against Sherlock, ultimately dying (or appearing to) by Moriarty's hand. In *Elementary* she is Jamie Moriarty an art restorer/thief and ultimately the canonical crime lord – Adler is the cipher, a persona adopted by Moriarty, and Holmes's ex-lover and soulmate. Adler's relationship with Holmes is sexualized and romanticized from the beginning, but Jamie's is not. These contemporary Archontic representations provide as much fodder for *Elementary* as the original as the show plays with representations and hints at the other adaptations through a variety of means: the names of characters like 'Del Gruner' whose namesake in the original has the more unwieldy 'Adelbert Gruner'; episodes such as 'A Giant Gun Filled With Drugs' where the phrase 'I believe in Sherlock Holmes' is repeatedly mentioned – a phrase originally linked with the finale of Season 2 of BBC's *Sherlock* and the fannish reaction to Holmes's apparent death; the title credits that reference the animated adaptation, and the writing containing references to shows with links to the Holmsean mythos, ranging from *Get Smart* and the shoe phone, to using the actual phrenology prop from *House* (a version of Holmes who is a Doctor). This gives their decisions about the presentation of Irene and Moriarty a greater weight and conscious understanding of the Archontic elements of the work (Stein, Busse, and Hills 2014). *Elementary* destabilizes these expectations, and the canon, knowingly, by regendering more than one character, and offering these 'Easter Eggs' to fans. It also subverts the expectations of the fans – loosely defined as those who know the mythos – as much as it subverts media expectations and canon.

Jamie's sexuality is not as pronounced as it is for many of the Archontic Adlers, but it remains a part of the character. Primorac identifies Adler's characterization as honourable in the canonical texts (even as she is a 'dishonourable woman' as per the contextual adventuress codifying sexual promiscuity) and that it is Holmes's cynicism which causes his underestimation of her in the original (2013). The sexual nature of Adler is an undertone in the canon to the modern reader unfamiliar with the signifiers of the era, although she remains an eroticized figure with 'compromising images' she diegetically rejects the identity in favour of respectability (Doyle [1892] 1986). This is replaced in modern adaptations by blatant sexuality combining with emotional reticence (or 'self-diagnosed sociopathy' as per *Sherlock)* causing the underestimation in the modern adaptations; a hearkening to that neo-Victorian trope of female sexuality, even as it modernizes the container it is in as a thoroughly capable fighter or dominatrix (Primorac 2013, 89–90). Her eroticized nature as a lesson on the immorality of the aristocracy from the canon becomes overtly sexual and sexualized in the adaptations and from there makes it into the archontic Adler. Creators of adaptive works receive this sexuality as a feature of the Archontic Adler and something that must be considered in their versions of the work; the writing, the casting, the costuming (such as the nudity of BBC's Adler and her wardrobe of sexual costumes including the leather and crop of a dominatrix). Thus, in many recent adaptations, and indeed most of them, the Archontic Adler becomes something of a femme fatale – sexual, tied intimately with Holmes, deceitful and ultimately in need of his intellect. Primorac has criticized this, and has remarked that this is a reduction in Adler's characterization from the canonical where 'the blatant and much overlooked loss of Victorian female characters' agency that takes place in the process of "updating" Victorian texts in contemporary screen adaptations through the – now almost routine – "sexing up" of the proverbially prudish Victorians' (2013, 90).

The aggressive sexualization of the character is very much a facet of modern film, and this disproportionately feminine lens is applied almost without thought given to canonical Adler's use of masculine clothing as a disguise or her ultimate goal being anonymity (Primorac 2013). In *Elementary* this is almost reversed, with Adler returning from the dead, and her power increasing as she is revealed to be Moriarty and in spite of the highly feminizing revelation of motherhood, her relationship with Sherlock, and being incarcerated, she remains powerful. Yet her relationship with Joan is as important as the relationship with Sherlock. Her characterization remains a comforting memory of the canon but instead of another representation of women as tools of powerful men, it delivers a representation based in the archontic Moriarty's power – a mostly masculine-male image – and contains it within a woman. The problems, the powers, the personality, so familiar from the canonical texts (and other adaptations) are regendered, allowing for the audience to experience the expected Moriarty in the guise of Jamie, expanding the space and representation of Adler (and Moriarty) to encompass the regendered version. This transition, from Adler to Moriarty, from Irene to Jamie, is something more than simply a surprising reveal of a recurring antagonist; it is the reworking of an iconic character through the versions and habitus of femininity the canon, the genre and the archontic adaptations are steeping in.

Irene to Jamie

Tell me, is that how you learned to be one of them? By learning to care how your actions seemed in the eyes of another? – Moriarty, to Sherlock Holmes.

('The Diabolical Kind' 2014)

Jamie's performance as Adler, and as Moriarty, offers very concrete examples of the performatively feminine. Her gender is not simply a result of her genes, her physical body, but is a complex relationship of semiotic presentations, conversations, physical embodiments and acts, and adjusts around other characters, including the sexual relationship with Sherlock. Unlike most other adaptations, *Elementary's* Sherlock is introduced as a sexual being (removing handcuffs from a ladder implying their use with a visiting sex worker, and a series of sexual relationships with women throughout the series) yet he and Jamie are not depicted engaging in sex; her character is de-eroticized as she moves from the archontic Adler – who he does have a sexual relationship with – to the archontic Moriarty.

Irene is initially 'the dead woman'; her death prompts his investigations into Moriarty, into M, prompts his drug addiction. It is revenge for her murder that pushes him into torture and his own intimate acts of violence. When she is reintroduced as having been held hostage, rather than murdered, Dormer portrays a woman who is terrified. She is the victim of terrors, unspoken and un-examined, crying and screaming in fear. The familiar visual representations of female victimhood are played out with great detail and aplomb – the oversized shirt, the fearful gaze and shaking hands, and the reactions of those around her who seek to protect her and heal her trauma. Watson and Holmes particularly are drawn to her, protecting her, and embark on their investigations to ensure she remains safe. Holmes also exhibits a kind of barely restrained violence, exhibitions of his love disrupted and thwarted by another man's violence, in his investigations into her kidnapping – until she is revealed to be Moriarty.

The transition from Irene to Moriarty occurs within the intimate space of the bedroom, the intimacy of an ex-lover's gaze that strips away the identity Jamie had adopted. Sherlock's familiarity not simply with Irene but with her body is what proves to be the clue that reveals the connection between the two characters. The scene takes place within a bedroom, as Irene dresses. The intimacy of the scene is highlighted by the positioning of the characters, by their movements around the set and the way Sherlock's restrained anger flares briefly as he grabs Irene; in response she leaves, still retaining a familiar kind of feminine victimhood in her partial nudity and flinching away from Holmes, until she kills the assassin attempting to kill Sherlock. With that act she takes on the mantle of the predator, not the victim.

From here she very deliberately begins to act outside the confines of expected gender roles. She says after shooting a would-be assassin; 'as if men had a monopoly on murder' to explain the deficiencies of men unused to violent or competent women ('Heroine' 2013). This explanation works metatextually as well, to alert the audience of their own comfortable, but false, assumptions and expectations. She is dressed in a military-styled jacket, and walks around Sherlock's space with a sense of ownership, ignoring his gunshot wound in order to lecture him on her prowess, and to taunt him:

> I'm saying I'm better. And, that's why I let you live, back in London – you were not the threat I'd made you out to be. So I … concluded my experiment, and resumed my business. You then proceeded to prove you were inferior, by disappearing into a syringe. – Moriarty, to Sherlock.
>
> ('Heroine' 2013)

Jamie's connection with Sherlock is at the heart of their interactions in the series but after she reveals herself, that connection is shifted somewhat to Watson. In the scene where Sherlock fakes an overdose to lure Moriarty out of hiding, the originator of the plan is not Sherlock himself but Watson. In the scene he says, 'You said there was only one person in the world who could surprise you … turns out, there's two' referring to Watson and her capacity to supplant both of them in investigation ('Heroine' 2013).

Moriarty's (and Dormer's) performance and appearance in this scene are heralded by the very phallic symbol of her gun barrel entering the room before she herself does, and the weapon itself being used almost as an extension of her hand as she gestures and postures throughout the scene. She is also dressed in a military-esque jacket, which draws obvious parallels with the canonical Watson and other adaptations; in BBC's *Sherlock* Watson is introduced and murders, with military precision and bearing, a man who is a danger to Sherlock in the very first episode. The gendered expectations of competition, of a love triangle between the two women, are subverted by the way Moriarty uses violence against and for Sherlock and Watson.

Moriarty's own underestimation of Watson is deeply rooted in her assumption of gendered standards of behaviour even though she simultaneously rejects them for herself. In *Elementary* we see an Irene, a Moriarty, who puts herself on the pedestal, and because of this, underestimates the women around her. When she does come to terms with Watson's skill, a kind of transference of attention occurs. It is a portrait of Watson's face that dominates the room that is Moriarty's cell, which is placed between Sherlock and Jamie as they discuss the relationship they have. Sherlock continues a dialogue with Jamie via letters, but it is Watson whose face, whose decisions, deductions, dominate the psychological spaces around Moriarty. Ultimately it is Joan Watson, with a kind of feminine intuition that realizes the latest complex plot from Moriarty is aimed at neither Sherlock nor Watson – it is actually to save the hitherto unknown daughter, Kayden.

Mama and mastermind

It is not only the triad between Sherlock and Joan that dominates the emotional landscape of Moriarty's self-professed lack of connection; in the second series Jamie is revealed to have a child. Contrary to dramatic expectation it is not Sherlock's (although he does have a connection with the father). The reveal of her maternal nature is not medical in nature, or even coldly logical deduction about Moriarty's body or her history; it is Joan's emotional intelligence that deduces the connection between Jamie and Kayden, the kidnapped child. The transition comes full circle with this revelation; the canonical Irene takes the mantle of respectability by a marriage of love to a common man to fulfil the gendered expectations of her class – she moves on from her life as an 'adventuress' for the love of a 'better man' than the King, presumably it, one completed by reproductive duties (Doyle [1892] 1986). In *Elementary* the ghostly Irene present in Jamie legitimizes her violence with the role of mother. By illustrating both the lengths she will go to in order to protect her child, including self-sacrifice and murder, *Elementary* ties together all of Moriarty's previous and future actions with this desire through the continued existence of her criminal enterprise as a means of fostering out that protection.

This is one of the greatest transitions *Elementary* makes with their Moriarty; not only a woman, but she is a mother. Her maternal 'instincts' are depicted entirely within the realm of violence – when her daughter is kidnapped, she engineers an incredibly complex plan, involving not only deception and assault, but at one point injuring herself to escape and rescue the child, who is then returned to her adoptive parents. The expectation of maternal affect is made visible only through personal violence. The kidnapping is prompted by Moriarty's institutional and systematic violence against other criminals and even entire countries; she responds not just with the familiar motherly protectiveness but with internationally syndicated crime. Yet she does not take upon herself the mantle of active motherhood, returning the child to her adoptive parents. Dormer commented on the presence of sociopathy and violence as only excusable by the mother in response to the dangers her family faces – 'we accept women being complete cunts if they're doing it for a child' – and that Moriarty is not bound by those restrictions (Higgins 2014). She does not find in herself a capacity for love, romantic or maternal, and returns to prison leaving both Sherlock and her daughter under the care of her criminal empire, and their replacements for her.

The veneer of motherhood often haunts any representation of women; a kind of Schrödinger effect whereby a female character is also always possibly a mother figure, either textually or subtextually, as motivation in some fashion. If the spectral qualities of motherhood are not obvious, the audience, the critic, responds to their absence – why isn't she a mother, why doesn't she want children, why is she not fulfilling the expected role? Motherhood must be the happy ending, the closure on the question of feminine performance even within the realm of violence, or without it the character becomes monstrous. The canon of Conan Doyle offers maternal figures to reflect upon, and the mantle of responsibility and respectability for women relies on the correct performance of motherhood. In *Elementary* Moriarty assumes, or rather *reveals*, her motherhood but does not perform it outside a kind of protective violence aimed at allowing her daughter to assume her place within the human world that Moriarty disavows, without Jamie becoming *more* monstrous than she already is, in terms of gender transgression and violence.

The underlying motivational factor behind the maternal character is depicted as love for her child, a need to protect that child. Motherlove maintains a small cross section of behaviours and aberrations from it are notable for their transgressions – the brutal, the protective, the absent mother, are not positive examples of motherhood on screen (Karlyn 2011). Moriarty subverts this – it is her existing institutionally violent tendencies that lead to her daughter being kidnapped, and it is her deeply personal violent tendencies that rescue her. Self-sacrifice is evident, Moriarty's own body being violated at her own hand, the symbolic blood of birth being reframed as a semi-suicidal gesture that escorts her daughter from the realm of the dead back to the safe life once more.

Elementary only reveals Jamie's motherhood as a reason behind her sudden interactions with the police and with Sherlock. But it is Joan who notices Jamie's emotional reactions when the phone call with the kidnapped child is played, even though Moriarty's words are hardly indicative of it 'quite lovely isn't she? You can only imagine how frightened she must be' ('The Diabolical Kind' 2014). Sherlock overlooks this, limited as he is to the concept of Jamie the criminal mastermind and ex-partner: 'the woman is a riddle wrapped in a mystery inside an enigma I've had sex with'). It is Joan who realizes that Jamie is a mother, it is Joan who tells Jamie that 'You think you're in love with him. Only you can't be sure, because as much as you claim to know about the world, love is something you don't quite get' ('The Diabolical Kind' 2014).

The familiar trope of the love triangle is strong enough to be an expectation, part of the habitus and familiarity that the audience brings to the text, but it is subverted within *Elementary*. Joan and Sherlock maintain an emotionally intimate platonic relationship, one that Moriarty struggles to understand because even though she has previously been in a relationship with him, hers was a ploy to disrupt his investigations into her criminal actions. The effect of this is to refocus on Sherlock but he is no longer the fixed point around which the women orbit until one reaches ascendance (via romantic love, or sex) but is instead the medium through which those women exercise their subtextually sexualized frustrations with each other.

Love and other things difficult to understand

The potential of romance has been present in the Holmsean narrative since its inception, after all; 'it was worth a wound – it was worth many wounds – to know the depth of loyalty and love which lay behind that cold mask' (Doyle [1892] 1986). Several modern adaptations, and contemporary critiques, have chosen to allude to queer readings of that subtext within the canonical work, such as the dance scene in Ritchie's *A Game of Shadows*, or earlier in *The Private Life of Sherlock Holmes* where Sherlock tells Watson that 'yes … you're being presumptuous. Good night' when queried about his sexuality (Wilder 1970). Elementary came under particularly harsh criticism for the assumption that by regendering Watson they would heterosexualize the relationship, 'reducing' it to a romance (Coren 2012; Stagg 2012). However, *Elementary* avoided a sexual or romantic relationship between Watson and Holmes, instead textualizing and sexualizing the connection between Holmes and Adler, and loading the relationship between Moriarty and Watson with queer subtext in a regendered form of Kofosky Sedgwick's homosocial triangle (Sedgwick 1985, 18).

> Would you be surprised to learn you've been on my mind, Joan Watson? – Moriarty to Joan Watson.
>
> ('The Diabolical Kind' 2014)

The homosocial triangle is regendered and reworked within Elementary to focus on the two women with a man at the heart of their relationship with each other. This connection is made explicit in Moriarty's transference of attention – '… I'm drawn to things I don't understand. Same as Sherlock. Once I've figured you out, I'll move on. Same as Sherlock' ('The Diabolical Kind' 2014). This is bolstered by the enormous portrait dominating her space, the way Joan identifies what Jamie feels for Sherlock being 'love' yet not making the connection to Jamie's own fascination with her. Similar to the earlier episodes, where Jamie saves Sherlock, in later episodes she saves Joan also – this time using her connections to protect Joan from assassins sent by yet another female criminal mastermind (one far less capable than Jamie as she falls victim to Jamie's assassins). The violence is at a remove, not yet the deeply personalized interactions Jamie has with Sherlock but is still coded within the feminine realm of 'emotional entanglement' and still the 'same as Sherlock' in its intent.

With Jamie's (re)gender the queer subtext of the Sherlock-Moriarty rivalry becomes explicitly heterosexual. Yet, simultaneously, the feminine qualities of Watson that become female in Joan and contribute to a surface reading of sexual tension and competition that then become queerly coded in the new Watson-Moriarty rivalry. The competence of Joan, deployed against Jamie, interacts and intersects with one of the great fannish conundrums about how seriously should Watson be played – is the character competent to Sherlock's hyper-competent, or a bumbler to account for an even more dramatic difference? Jamie maintains her own competence, undermined not by her femininity but by underestimating Watson's investigatory techniques due to their femininity, her own missteps resembling those of the audience and critics.

The scope of female violence on-screen often manifests alongside lesbian signifiers and gender transgressive acts; this is particularly relevant to *Elementary*'s representation of Moriarty given the queer subtext between her and Watson. The queering of villains has a long and infamous history, particularly in cinema. Within the archontic Holmes the BBC's *Sherlock* includes an openly lesbian Adler (who eventually falls in love with Sherlock) and a queerly coded Moriarty. Jim, as Moriarty is known, signifies his queer tendencies as an act, and '... refuses to present himself to be read' from that performance (Fathallah 2014, 7). Fathallah concludes that the queerness – of Moriarty, of Sherlock, of the text itself – haunts the narrative, waiting for the closure of a heterosexual exorcism of the spectre. Similarly the queerness of Jamie Moriarty is a ghostly apparition, like Castle's examinations of the ways in which lesbianism occurs through literary history (1993, 91), but one that has not been foreclosed upon because the openness of both the format, and the way the text of Elementary includes the possibilities and probabilities of queerness in the text itself. Even though Jamie is linked with Sherlock, she is also linked with Watson, at a level beyond that of friendship or even romance; Joan, who displays heterosexual behaviours, is also complicit in this homosocial triangle, haunted by the unspoken palimpsest between 'I solved you' and 'I love you':

> I would never kill you. Not in a million years. You may not be as unique as you thought, darling, but you're still a work of art. I appreciate art. What I can do, what I will do, is hurt you. Worse than I did before. I have reserves of creativity I haven't even begun to tap. So, please, for your own good, let me win. – Moriarty, to Sherlock Holmes.
>
> ('Heroine' 2013)

Ultimately Jamie's violence, like her sexuality, is a borrowed suit. Most of Jamie's on-screen violence – the murders she perpetrates, the explicit assassinations she has ordered – was confined to that realm of the personal. Even though textually she is acknowledged as ordering multiple assassinations, committing international fraud, destabilizing entire national economies, those often happen off-screen or are referred to at a remove. The violence for which the character in their original form is known for is adjusted for gender and gendered expectations within Elementary. Even though the series destabilizes the gendered characterizations of the archontic narratives it still adheres to these expected performances of gender and violence. Moriarty is a mother: her violence is motherly protection of her daughter. Moriarty is a woman in love: her violence protects those she loves (even if that love is subverted by the homosocial triangle). Moriarty is a criminal, internationally wanted active and feared mastermind: but her violence at a systematic and institutional level is off-screen, implied, inferred, discovered, not depicted in all its gory aftermaths – unlike the male original, or many of the male adaptations.

Similarly, Jamie's sociopathy is adjusted; she maintains a maternal nature, a desire to understand, balanced by Sherlock's own attempts to 'become one of them'. The two characters exhibit similarities and connections that mean if one is to be condemned so must the other, thus binding the two characters further together and forcing the audience to examine the ways in which psychopathy and violence are gendered. The space she is written into belongs to the familiar habitus of the masculine, and without the masculine the character struggles to exhibit all the familiar traits as they are read and perceived by the audience through that spectre of femininity and warped through that reflective, reflexive, gendering. The regendered aspects of her characterization – not simply the change to 'woman' the writers and showrunners made, but the ways underlying aspects of the narrative, the structure and the interrogations the text makes, are also changed. These all force the audience to revalue their relationships with the canon and with other adaptations. But this revaluation still works within a greater social complex around gender, and the very specific ways that manifests in mainstream media, in genre television, in police procedurals, to shift the representations and depictions of women, but not to entirely rework them. The reaction to her as a regendered character was even less overt or negative than that of Joan, which may suggest some level of acceptance of regendering; as the next two chapters show, this has not been the case.

8

Ghostbusters: Sex and science

In 2016 an all-female reboot of the 1984 *Ghostbusters* was released, *Ghostbusters: Answer the Call* (from here *Ghostbusters* refers to the 1984 release, *Answer the Call* to the 2016 film). The original film had been a critical and commercial success, considered one of the highest grossing films of all time when adjusted for inflation, with multiple re-releases and becoming one of the iconic 1980s films. Starring Bill Murray (Dr Paul Venkman), Dan Akroyd (Dr Raymond Stantz), Harold Ramis (Dr Egon Spengler) and Ernie Hudson (Winston Zeddemore) as ghostbusters in a New York beset by destructive ghosts, it was an unexpected success for Columbia Pictures. The marketing and release strategies created iconic visuals and sonic landscapes, with the tagline 'Who you gonna call?' and the terms 'ghostbusters' becoming parts of everyday language in the United States and elsewhere[1]. The franchise spawned from the original film encompassed sequels, videogames, toys, costumes, a popular drink and other assorted ephemera that was consistently available from 1984 onwards. There were also crossovers with other popular franchises, and re-releases for home entertainment, cementing its status as a rare 'cult blockbuster'. While not as popular, the sequel *Ghostbusters II* (1989) and the videogame adaptation *Ghostbusters: The Video Game* (2009) performed well, and the animated series ran for several years – the parts of the franchise that involved the original actors, scripting and other production by original crew. The 2016 reboot did not fare as well.

The decision to reboot the franchise was influenced by the perceived 'flop' of the sequel *Ghostbusters II* in spite of its commercial success, as it did not reach the same cultural peak as the original. The studio dismissal of the film, and the feelings of cast and crew, stymied attempts to make a third. In particular Bill Murray was reluctant to appear, and Reitman (director) also felt the project was

---

[1] Indeed, to the point that searching for academic work requires significant winnowing due to the popularity of the term across many disciplines from paediatric medicine to finance.

a failure. After the death of Harold Ramis, Reitman decided to sell the rights in order to reinvigorate the franchise (while still maintaining an interest via the production company Ghost Corps). This signalled a transition from the aptly eponymous 'hauntology' where a 'text renders a state of time out of joint' that 'sees only the past … and limits the possibility of future invention' (Kennedy-Karpat 2020, 290) to the much broader possibilities of adaptation. This led to Paul Feig directing *Ghostbusters: Answer the Call* as a reboot, a film that 'incorporates broad strokes of the property while also incorporating its own narrative' (Bryan and Clark 2019, 149). It starred Melissa McCarthy (Dr Abigail Yates), Kristin Wiig (Dr Erin Gilbert), Kate Mackinnon (Jillian Holtzmann) and Leslie Jones (Patty Tolan) as the four eponymous ghostbusters.

The reboot functions as a shift in narrative canonicity; it positions itself and the original as 'a story' or 'a version', which can add increased depth and relevance to a franchise (Nolan's *Batman* is often considered the most successful example of this model that launched the contemporary cycle of reboots) but in the case of *Answer the Call* resulted in a complex negotiation of childhood, nostalgia, gender, Hollywood and star culture. Even though the myriad sequels, animated versions and games performed similar corrections and alterations to the original canon, they were specifically secondary to that original narrative. The reboot, however, renders the original inauthentic in a way, unreliable, and 'in contrast to the affective nature of nostalgia, adaptation and other media multiplicities function textually, circumscribing nostalgia within certain recognizable forms' (Kennedy-Karpat 2020, 284). The adaptation or reboot positions itself as equal to that canon narrative and in the case of *Ghostbusters* also becomes a signifier of gender conflict on a wider societal level as it regendered the characters. *Answer the Call* was subject to high levels of negative press from very early in production, and ultimately led to active harassment of several cast members; most notable Leslie Jones was subject to revenge porn, racist abuse, hacking and death threats.

As a case of regendering in the professional field, *Answer the Call* requires a two-fold approach (at least): looking at the film itself as a remake of *Ghostbusters* where the film is regendered, rather than a character; and the way in which the reboot was received and perceived by fans. In analysing the regendered work of *Answer the Call* it is imperative to compare it with the original; what has been changed, how is it changed, what thematically is different and how are commonalities expressed? In particular the presence of sexual comedy, which had been a focus of Reitman in his previous work *Caddyshack* and *Stripes*, part of a trend in 1980s Hollywood of vulgar and crude slapstick being merged with other genres (sport films and war films respectively, teen movies as a general rule) (Chaney 2021). While not limited to only the 1980s, there is a repeated resurgence of the style as can be seen in *American Pie* in the late 1990s, the Apatow oeuvre and others in the 2010s (Jeffers McDonald 2012). In contemporary film Feig's works – *Bridesmaids* in particular – can be seen as modern inheritors, shifting the focus from the objectification and pursuit of women to centralizing female sexual and romantic (mis)adventures while not shying away from gross-out humour and raunchy elements; a focus on the 'homosocial elements' (Bowler 2013; Kies 2017, 266; Warner 2013). However, the reimagination of *Ghostbusters* as a family film, something assisted by the nostalgic fans who recall dressing up as children in the 1980s, and watching the animated show, leads to tension between not only the way women are represented in the original film, but how to translate the 1980s sex comedy elements of a horror-comedy to a 2010s audience. This comparison then leads us to what the regendering has offered comedically and narratively within *Answer the Call*, what happens to the thematic concerns of the original if the ghostbusters are women. There are 'important repercussions for queer audiences and queer readings of the film' (Kies 2017, 265) and because while Feig and Mackinnon avoided the overt acknowledgement of queerness it was an explicit palimpsest via the actress (Yamato 2017).

The extremity of the fannish response to the film is integral to examining how regendering is received and interpreted by the audience. Not simply because it is one of the biggest and most obvious examples of regendering in professional film, but because the fannish response formed part of a much larger movement. The negative responses have been linked to Gamergate, toxic geek masculinity, and the alt-right, and critiqued as such in much of the research around the film (Bryan and Clark 2019, 150). However, the fannish response is part of a broader movement in fandom, one of nostalgia which 'represents a dialectical confluence of temporal identities' between the child and the adult (Proctor 2017, 1115). The impulse to separate out audience from fans, where the audience is aggressive and the fans are supportive, where the individuals making threats, hacking websites, narrating multiple videos decrying the existence of the reboot are the 'audience' and somehow separate to fandom as a subculture to be researched is one that implies a genderedness to fandom and to behaviour. Even 'suspensionist' research labels the narratives around the fannish response as 'orchestrated' by media into 'a cultural firestorm, primarily hinged on a minority cluster of misogynist comments, often given oxygen by Feig's discursive interventions on social media' (Proctor 2017, 1112). It is important to acknowledge that the fans of *Ghostbusters* who attacked *Answer the Call* and its cast and crew, are fans, not simply aggressors or trolls, even when their responses are misogynistic. The behaviour of the *Ghostbuster* fans is neither unique, nor restricted to specific fandoms or forms of fandom; Proctor – who published the aforementioned suspensionist research – also claimed in a separate discussion piece that 'we fiercely protect our treasured objects from outside incursion, even as we are intimately aware that these are symbolic, psychic attacks' (Proctor and Brooker 2019) as an integral part of being a fan of an object. This nostalgic defensiveness is woven into fannish work, creative or otherwise and while it may occur as a form of misogyny, not all examples of nostalgia are easily or entirely dependent of misogynist critique.

The nostalgic project of fandom is one that reiterates and reinscribes media properties as ways of configuring identity and reacts to critique (or remake) of those properties as an attack on identity. As Kennedy-Karpat describes 'nostalgic response readily adheres to texts first experienced during one's youth. A fan claiming that any given adaptation, remake, or franchise extension "ruins their childhood" (to cite the mildest version of this refrain) is essentially nostalgic in their complaint. But what is being betrayed, and at whose expense?' (2020, 285). This in and of itself is a function of hegemony as it is primarily linked with white supremacy and the creation of an ahistorical imagined past, and from there with misogyny and a longing for 'the good ole days' that never truly existed. The deification of media and consumerism as identity is not just limited to the misogynist and alt-right factions; however, regendering may challenge the more overt misogynist aspects but can replicate the hierarchical power structures and embody them without critique or elaboration on the underlying inequalities of that structure.

Original vs remake

The form of humour from the original is highly predicated on the comedic forms of the four actors; Murray's improv background, abrasiveness and studied disdain, Akroyd's eccentric and earnest goofiness (very much an aspect of his neurodivergence), Ramis's deadpan wit and Hudson as the unflappable everyman character. In the 2016 reboot this is replaced by McCarthy's improvisational physicality, Wiig's expressive high-strung reactivity, Mackinnon's madcap disconnected weirdness and Jones's edgy and insightful bombast. While similarities in their roles can be observed, the underlying ensemble work on the original's humour is less obvious in the reboot, with all four actresses (and the director) constrained by the directive for 'family friendly' (Douglas 2017; Ferber 2017; Yamato 2017). This necessarily reduced the sexual humour of the original as well as any confirmation or overt moments of queerness; it particularly reduced the often confrontational and explicit comedy of McCarthy and Jones.

Ghostbusters (1984) opens with what we recognize as a classic case of sexual harassment by academic faculty, one that undermines the actual research. When the Dean dismisses the team and cancels their grant, he names Dr Venkman's approach to science as being a hustle, a grift. His neoliberal academic approach naming the problem being Venkman's scientific unreliability belies the casual misogyny of the academy, and the film itself. Indeed, after the initial scene where Venkman pretends a young college student is psychic (while unfairly electrocuting her male companion), he asks the librarian who had been haunted if she was menstruating and when questioned insists 'I'm a scientist'. The casual misogyny of the era, particularly evident in comedy film, is well on display from the opening moments of *Ghostbusters* (1984). The issue of regendering the casual and unmoored sexual bigotry of the original presents a problem not simply in the general lack of audience enjoyment of the form, but the way misandry is perceived as more monstrous, a true abruption of expectations versus the humorous puncture of them. The audience affordances have shifted, and the regendered ghostbusting team must navigate those changes alongside the echoes and nostalgic reverie of the original. When Dana throws Venkman out of her apartment as he aggressively hits on her, there's no clear way for the reboot to mimic either the purported humour of the scene (in the contemporaneous audience) or even the broader 'sense' of the scene.

The shifting sexual mores and ethics lead to some of the less successful elements of 2016's reboot, including the replacement of Janine the extremely efficient, intellectual, racquetball playing secretary with Chris Hemsworth playing Kevin, the painfully non-intellectual actor who is sexually harassed by Dr Erin Gilbert (the Venkman-esque academic who is initially unconvinced in spite of having done paranormal research previously). Kevin's obliviousness is played for laughs against Gilbert's aggressively inappropriate innuendo and commentary. The ghostly sex scene is absent entirely, as is Dana (or equivalent) and thus the contemporarily normal romantic entanglement with Venkman. Kies refers to this as replacing the 'testament to heterosexual reproduction' from the original with 'a celebration of the power of women's friendship as much as it is rife with queer possibilities' (2017, 266). Yet the film is constrained, unlike fanworks or even *Elementary*, by a directive for family-friendly that insists on the heterocentric idea of queerness as sexualized and unsafe.

Alongside this is replacing the villains of the original – the maligned EPA whose bureaucracy and book-bound regulations have resulted in wide-scale paranormal infestation – with a resentful incel-type character seeking to end the world. The class elements become turned around, in many ways, with the besuited and over-enunciating EPA agent threatening the hard-working physical labourer ghostbusters for their (admittedly dangerous) ghost containment strategies becoming a bellboy menial labourer who loathes the ghostbusters for their gender, their success and seeks to burn the world out of spite. He resembles in some ways Louis Tully from the original, in both the failed masculinity and the invocation of apocalypse. The shift from the neoliberal business first 1980s aesthetic and ethos to the girlboss neoliberal feminism of the 2010s not only refocuses the question of gender but adds into the moments where original is projected awkwardly against the reboot. The female ghostbusters face discrimination and succeed in spite of it but that in and of itself is 'contrasted with the inferiority complex of a loner working-class white man' (Kies 2017, 266). While 'the appeal of the Ghostbusters lies in these aspects: the everyday man can see himself in these heroes, and imagine their own success' the replacement of these 'everymen' with 'women of colour (Leslie Jones), of a different sexual orientation (Kate McKinnon), or to those who do not fit into traditional standards of beauty (Melissa McCarthy, Kristen Wiig)' gave rise not only to the disgruntled fan, but the awkward positioning of credentialled academic women with a small business teaming up to overcome the working-class bellboy (Bryan and Clark 2019, 148, 152).

The replication of the *Ghostbusters* as a tale of small business and the working class overcoming not just the supernatural but the 'dickless' EPA is one that positions the female ghostbusters as a neoliberal success story:

> The film's logic suggests that the corporation is just as vital to American interests – economic, security-wise, and in other ways – as it always has been, thus the neoliberal system should keep running as-is; but if you want to throw stones and break glass ceilings – via gender, sexuality, race, etc. – go right ahead since it will not alter the fundamental structure corporate capitalism or challenge neoliberalism itself.
>
> (Clare 2017, 8)

This lack of challenge to the structure of neoliberalism alongside the 'thrown stones' of regendering simultaneously empowers the structural elements of patriarchal normativity while appealing to the aesthetic possibilities of representation. Clare goes on to call the feminism of the film 'weak' noting the way 'It is only the individual man who is the perpetrator of sexism, not the larger structural forces that create and sustain gender and sexual inequality' (2017, 8). While Kies points out that the women of ghostbusters overcome the perpetual disdain of academia, the government, even the military, the focus on the individual man as a misogynist antagonist is one that does sidestep the structural inequalities. While the 'clapback'-style conflict with the antagonist is entertaining, the antagonist himself is resentful of his position within society; the difficulties of underemployed, mistreated and constantly struggling customer service workers are hardly unfamiliar to contemporary audiences. The insistence that the ghostbusters of *Answer the Call* are everywomen, just like the originals were 'not simply ciphers through which the audience was introduced to the world but also the trope of the "everyman" character, which the (often male) fans could relate to' (Bryan and Clark 2019, 148) falls flat due in part to the class signifiers in place that exacerbate the 'fears of no longer being the target audience of properties that had previously been important to certain, often male, fans' (Bryan and Clark 2019, 148).

This is also obvious in the way the films end; the original shows a crowd roaring in approval of the ghostbusters, with the triumphant kiss between Dana and Venkman, and the presentation of the heroes as down to earth New Yorkers (albeit ones blessed by a row of priests and hailed by media). Their final battle is punctuated by absurdity, the iconic Stay Puft marshmallow man exploding to cover the actors in white fluff as they earnestly mourn the loss of Dana and celebrate her actual survival. In the reboot the neoliberal feminist element turns the finale into an action film, admittedly one with a similarly iconic scene – this time Mackinnon licking her guns – but the women are not subject to either the same challenges or the absurdity. Kevin, inhabited by the antagonist, forces the military and police to dance as he raises the iconographic dead (including what seems like a Vodoun figure, and historical figures but mostly blandly horror zombie ghosts), and attempts to drag the women to the afterlife allowing for friendship to save the day. The triumphant support of New York is not a cheering crowd, but the ghostbusters somehow having a (very expensive) clear view of the city where support is written in lights, quite literally. But without the potential for death, the stoically endured humiliation of the marshmallow fluff, or the working-class aesthetic, the humour is made hollow and, in many ways, mean-spirited for audiences who had identified heavily with the working-class triumph of the original.

Science and gender

Part of the effect of regendering *Ghostbusters* was to regender the scientists depicted in the film. The representation of female scientists has suffered from both the default male stereotype of the career but also how Hollywood tends to depict women as a rule. By regendering the specific male scientists (and lone everyman character) *Answer the Call* tackles the difficulty in representing the female scientists outside the acceptable tropes and stereotypes that are Hollywood's stock in trade. The scientists who become ghostbusters are egotistical, obsessive, abrasive, regardless of gender, but representing female characters in this manner is somewhat more difficult due to the audience expectation of femininity.

The result of femininity as an expectation in the representation of women, even within industries that are male-dominated, leads to either a very specific kind of hyperfemininity (see Megan Fox as a female mechanic working in a bikini, or Alice Eve's appearance in her underwear in *Star Trek Into Darkness*). The presumed masculinity of the field needs to be remedied by reminding the audience of gender conformity, often via style choices, but also the presence/ marked absence of maternity, nude scenes, romance and often the prioritization of male narratives in the film or marketing (Flicker 2003). To avoid those elements is to invite the potentiality of queer and gender non-conforming representation. In the case of *Answer the Call* this was done deliberately by Mackinnon and Feig for the character Jillian Holtzmann, who evidences disinterest in the 'hot secretary', dresses more masculinely than the others and casually flirts with other women (Lang 2016). She is also aggressively non-normative, a 'glorious weirdo' and very much a regendered version of Akroyd's Raymond.

The regendering of *Answer the Call* opens up characterization for the female characters. Even Patty Tolan, the non-scientist character akin to Hudson's Widdemore, has post-graduate qualifications in history – which, much like the original's quotidian skills, act as a common sense or 'grounded' alternative to the theorizing of the others. The 'glorious weirdo' element of Holtzmann and her mentor Dr Rebecca Gorin who is revealed later in the film are similarly regendered versions whose on-screen behaviours and characterization are expanded by being an adaptation of the original. Dr Gorin being played by Sigourney Weaver continues the appearance of the original actors within the text, differentiated from their original characters and in this case, shifting Dana from the object of Venkman's pursuit and target of possession to an authority figure whose scientific endeavours mark her as still the other. The correlation between Venkman and Dr Gilbert replaces the predatory male academic and his dubious ethics and research with a woman who is struggling against the masculine normativity of her field. The scientific woman is not only subject to the same issues as her male counterparts, but also those specifically about femininity and womanhood. When Dr Gilbert asks if her outfit is 'too sexy for academia' the witch trial aspect of femininity is re-established, as there is no definitive way to avoid the process of being judged.

The spectral fandom

The idea of women as unfunny, or less funny, than men is one that is sustained regardless of evidence. When attempts are made to quantitatively measure humour, women 'surprisingly' performed better, 'a finding that is "surprising" in light of the ubiquity of messages prohibiting women's performance of humour' (Caldwell and Wojtach 2020, 348). In regendering a comedy film that is widely understood as not only a classic, but one of the highest grossing films of all time, with long-standing cultural and critical relevance, the conflict between the gendered reception of humour and the necessarily confrontational effect of the reboot is explosive. While this may seem like an overstatement, the harassment and abuse of the cast and crew were extreme and seemingly outsized. The position of women as 'other', as not the norm, creates the mirror image of men as default and to regender is to destabilize the expectations of normative society. This destabilization, alongside the consumer criticisms of reboot/remake culture, Hollywood's creative bankruptcy and *Ghostbusters* as a very influential cultural touchstone, resulted in much of the conflict the film and its crew experienced.

Humour, as a concept that requires an audience, is subject to gendered perceptions. When degendering humorous captions, researchers found that women were at least as funny, if not funnier, than men if their confidence was high. The researchers then went on to suggest that

> complaints about the women's lack of funniness, including the vitriol hurled against women who use humour professionally (e.g., the all-female cast of *Ghostbusters*), is backlash-based discrimination against women for stepping outside their traditional gender role. When journalists, documentarians, and internet trolls claim that women are not as funny as men, then they may be telling more about themselves than about women's actual capacity for humour.
> (Caldwell and Wojtach 2020, 350)

Tellingly, these researchers repeatedly used the example of *Answer the Call* as a situation with extreme elements of gendered perceptions of humour that were affected by the position of the film as an adaptation that 'treads on hallowed male comics' ground' (Caldwell and Wojtach 2020, 348). They also drew attention to the way the perception of women as unfunny has concrete effects on how women are treated in daily life.

Film and other media are often used as signifiers for identity, from very early childhood onwards, and nostalgia for them 'shapes sometimes profoundly – our relationships with people, places, objects, and texts' (Kennedy-Karpat 2020, 284). Research into children's play and literacy suggests that 'these film memories or stories are clearly also expressions of identity' (Parry 2013, 115) even media that is 'post-object fandom' and before the child's time can become integral to play, and from there how a child relates (Parry 2013, 88). The post-object fandom itself shifts the media object from a continual iterative process to one that has been reified, and is less a social experience of fandom and more an internal one (Williams 2015). *Ghostbusters*, through its truly widespread iconographic, sonic and linguistic effect on not just the immediate audience but a continual process of fan-building, cemented those aspects as not just fannish ones, but signifiers within identities. The film is a 'totemic object … that opens up a mnemonic conduit to an idealized history' specifically in terms of personal identity (Proctor 2017, 1112). This signifier of selfhood is primarily affirmational, in the way it seeks to replicate the original rather than transform it, to use Hills' categorizations (Hills 2015a). These elements influence how the nostalgia and adaptation intersect for the audience, where 'audiences can reject new intertexts whose changes upend their nostalgic relationship to existing text(s)' (Kennedy-Karpat 2020, 286).

Nostalgia itself has become something of a fannish identity, shifting from the antiquary and kitsch collectors to media audiences – 'totemic nostalgia' as defined by Proctor, who claims it as a non-toxic manifestation of fandom and self (Proctor 2017, 1113). This was most obviously at play in *Stranger Things*, another 1980s accented horror product that very much leaned into the nostalgic elements of recognition and identity signifiers, from playing Dungeons and Dragons, the set design, to the Halloween outfits from the first season being, unsurprisingly for the group of four boys, the ghostbusters. This 'embrace and reconstruction' of the past is an element of a nostalgic obsession, but Bartlett points out that it can function not just as a way to make meaning of the present, but also to escape contemporary society for a rose-coloured view of the past as 'not so much a foreign country as a panic room. It's understandable that we should want to retreat there when the present looks frightening' (2017, 18). The tendency for Hollywood to mine the successes of the past and other mediums in order to fulfil the production and monetary drive of the industry has been commented on for decades, and has resulted in a glut of reboots, remakes, sequels, prequels and adaptations dominating the Top Ten lists, and to a certain extent release schedules (Allen 2012; Loving 2012). This element of Hollywood nostalgia – not just creatively but commercially – has led to something of a backlash from fans even though as 'where nostalgia attaches to texts, "history matters" because nostalgia matters to many fans' decision to open their wallets' (Kennedy-Karpat 2020, 287). Proctor suggests that the totemic 'might extend into malicious toxic fan practice' which may or may not be a part of broader toxic cultures online (2017, 1116).

The adaptational dominance of Hollywood media is not always one that fares well – after all the question of 'sequels better than the original' remains something limited in acceptable answers – but as generations shift within the industry, the drive to remake and adapt the media of our own childhoods becomes real as fans become professionals. This is most often made obvious in long-running serials and series, or adaptations of other media, but those fans who become producers and professionals are also marketing and making their work for other fans and for 'newbies'. The issue with the reboot of *Ghostbusters* was likely exacerbated by the way the original had not only become part of wider vernacular, but also the steady schedule of re-releases, non-film adaptations and the nostalgic drive of the audience. Even 'the early response was negative, arguing that the casting of women fundamentally destroys the basic nature of the Ghostbusters as "everymen"' and 'the very idea of casting women as Ghostbusters is taken as sacrilegious, with the 1984 film being held up as an unimpeachable classic' (Bryan and Clark 2019, 154, 155). The nostalgia for the original was situated heavily in the idealized vision of the 1980s, heavily influenced by the portions of the community who decried helicopter parenting, political correctness and other societal shifts away from the neoliberal politics of that decade. It became 'a culture war between the genders, with Ghostbusters a valiant last stand, at least until the next last stand occurs' (Bryan and Clark 2019, 156).

Unsurprisingly, there has been a new addition to the franchise, *Ghostbusters: Afterlife* (2021); one that not only brings in nostalgic production elements (the director is Jason Reitman, son of Ivan) and as much of the original cast as possible, but vividly evokes childhood, and nostalgic elements. The trailer is replete with iconic signifiers from *Ghostbusters* against the backdrop of a golden lit Oklahoma, and a diegetic link to the original events via a family connection. Along with the release statements from Reitman appearing 'to echo the same complaints of the toxic respondents: that the 2016 Ghostbusters was not produced for the "true" fans, but to appease the larger corporate overlords, or some alleged conglomerate of Internet feminists' (Bryan and Clark 2019, 157) the division between audience, fan and the gendered representation of both becomes clear. The ghostbusters themselves are no longer central and instead Reitman developed a 'teenaged-girl ghostbuster' concept and praised the actress he cast for her fannish devotion to the franchise. As a sequel, rather than a reboot, *Afterlife* evokes not a nostalgia for the film as much as for the fans who grew up watching, rewatching and defending their identity-signifying media property from potential harm. Kennedy-Karpat states that 'the studio's response indicates the lengths the industry will go to mine (some) fans' nostalgia, underscoring both the fiscal stakes of adaptive nostalgia and the willingness to cater to misogynist bigots if executives believe that they will generate the surest profits' (2020, 287). Once more this delineates some essential difference between kinds of fans and implies some level of catering those who are too nostalgic, who attack cast and crew and who are misogynist bigots. This is not an unfair assessment; however, it is not limited to nostalgic fan bases, nor the obviously misogynist bigot fan, and is in fact endemic to all fandom along multiple intersections. It does not rely on nostalgia – although that may feature heavily – but on the way the media object becomes identity. The 'fans' recruitment of nostalgic narratives as a mode of meaning preservation and to offset self-discontinuity and ontological anxieties anchored to the totemic object' (Proctor 2017, 1120) is one that raises the stakes for responses and perception of a media object, but also aligns the media object with the wider sociological concerns the fan may have about gender, or race or class.

Transnational gender and identity

Answer the Call faced international censure, in this case the issues that led to it not being released in China. While the original was also not released theatrically in China, the market has shifted to significantly rely on that international release in order to bolster profits. The claim was made that the films were banned based on the technical rule of 'promoting superstitions or cults' but the supposed lack of interest due to the non-release of the original and its sequel were officially cited (Lang 2016). The international market was also connected with the decision to not openly identify Holtzmann as queer; in many ways 'family friendly' has come to not just include the sections of the audience who identify any level of queerness as inappropriate for children (or often anyone) but also the state homophobia found in many of Hollywood's overseas markets, including China (Lang 2016).

The thematic conflict of the film is one that predicted the fannish response, in particular the anti-fans where 'the fantasy of these (business) women triumphing over white male resentment was already prefigured in the startling hostility of a white male audience who fetishized the original film and objected to the new Ghostbusters sex-changes and gender-bending before the film had even been released' (Clare 2017, 15). Regendering not only made sense to Feig as a means of separating the reboot from the original film, but also brought the male-dominated film into contemporary cinema culture through the vast increase in roles for women within the franchise. His desire for more roles for women was at odds with the way the original was, however unconsciously, a gendered identity and reception moment for fans. The fannish response to the adaptation was primed for negativity by the 'totemic nostalgia' that does configure *Answer the Call* as an attack on the totemic object, but also on fans.

By connecting the concerns an individual may have around gender, race, class or other identity components with a media object, and then leveraging it into a defence of that object, the totemic nostalgia becomes something more than simply affect. The use of media criticism around popular fandoms or controversial media objects 'as part of a political persuasion tactic' has been linked to international geo-politics and Russian trolls or bots. Bay's study of similarly vitriolic fans of Star Wars revealed that while 'it is not fair to generalize and paint all of the *The Last Jedi* detractors as alt-right activists, racists or misogynists … the findings above show that a majority of the negatively-poised users included in the study do express such sentiments' (Bay 2018) and it is likely *Answer the Call* would have similar results. This is due to the similar ways in which non-white actors on both projects were treated by the audience, specifically the intense online harassment and racism. Bay also points out that while a minority of fans were negative, half of those negative tweets came from politically motivated fans or bots (Bay 2018). Fandom and the media have always been politically charged spaces; however, using the nostalgic impulse to further socio-political activism has become increasingly obvious particularly online.

Totemic nostalgia and fannish academics

This reification of the nostalgic impulse depicts 'the male and female, who decried the reboot as "ruining their childhood" or criticized the manoeuvre as a way to defend the fan-totem from external assault' as 'benign and innocuous rather than explicitly toxic' (Proctor 2017, 1129). The more quantitative research by Bryan and Clark analyses the way much of the critique focused on fat-shaming Melissa McCarthy or linking the film to feminism as a kind of sociological attack on men and masculinity, which undermines the purely psychological defensiveness rising from totemic nostalgia (2019). Bay's work revealing the almost even split between the actually negative fan and the opportunistic use of the totemic object by political agitators also undermines that idealized notion of the benign and innocuous fan whose identity has been marred by the regendered work (2018). While also being academic work about fans, Proctor's paper '"Bitches Ain't Gonna Hunt No Ghosts": Totemic Nostalgia, Toxic Fandom and the Ghostbusters Platonic' reveals an element of the autoethnographic impulse by aca-fans: it is a fannish object itself (2017). While focus on a singular academic paper about *Answer the Call* and the fannish response may seem somewhat indulgent, it is an attempt to illustrate the capacity for researchers – particularly those within media or fandom – to be subject to totemic nostalgia and for it to affect our work. To uncritically present the fannish argument of affective distress to *Answer the Call* is one that erases the actual harm done to Leslie Jones in particular and can be seen as an extension of fannish totemic nostalgia into the realm of research. Proctor's view on fannishness as including some form of 'protective' impulse that necessarily involves affective distress at any 'attack' on it is echoed by his stance that 'sub-sections of fanboys have also been discursively constructed as "bad" fans, aggressive, inappropriate and negatively masculinized' and that such constructions need to be 'addressed more rigorously by fan studies scholars'

(2017, 1135). The propensity to delineate that behaviour by gendered binaries is one that does erase the toxicity enacted by women towards other fans, creators and celebrities which is often correlated along the unexplored intersections identified by Pande (2018). The reality that fans across the gender spectrum engage in toxic practices, online or off, is evident in both the research and lived experiences of many scholars.

Proctor's analysis uses the phrase 'bitches ain't gonna hunt no ghosts' in it's title – a line from the film that reveals not only the misogyny aimed at the very concept of female ghostbusters evokes but also the toxicity of YouTube comments who agreed with the sentiment – alongside uncritical reproduction of claims by anti-fans. In particular the idea that critiques that were created before the release of the film, based either entirely on the concept of an all-female reboot, or a reboot at all, are free from misogyny or toxic fan practices, in this case specifically focusing on a video by James Rolfe. As Caldwell and Wojtach illustrated, the perception of humour is affected by knowing the gender of the caption creator, and that many respondents in their study did assume men to be funnier than women; it is naïve to suggest that the presence of women in a reboot would not affect the response of the audience (2020, 349). Proctor omits both the YouTube channel name (Angry Video Game Nerd) and niche focus on retro videogames, which could reveal the kind of politicized critique identified by Bay as 'cognitive dissonance' (2018). This kind of politicized critique is often linked not with nostalgia, or the importance of the object to identity but the strongly held political belief and 'the expectation of it to be respected, represented or even amplified in pop culture fandom' (Bay 2018). The prevalence and presence of 'fans' whose fannish behaviours are linked to 'divisive political discourse' rather than pop culture, or a media object has 'primed these fans with a particular type of political messaging that is in direct conflict with the values presented' (Bay 2018). While Bay's work focuses on *The Last Jedi*, the relevance for any 'controversial' fandom is clear: fans are not uniquely outside the political sphere, or uniquely progressive, and as academics this is necessary to account for.

The nostalgic project of fandom is not restricted to the totemic object, but totemic nostalgia includes a broad array of narratives beyond the object. Proctor claims that the totemic nostalgia explored by Hills suggests a 'move towards a nuanced understanding of fan complaints that a new text, such as *Ghostbusters* 2016, is perceived as a colonizing threat to trajectories of the self' because those claims are common within fandom, even if the fan is 'well aware that their childhood is safe and secure in real terms' (2017, 1117–18). Beyond the use of the term 'colonizing' to characterize an unwanted or disappointing adaptation, this claim does not concern itself with intersections of gender, race or class. To highlight the 'opprobrium and mocking' and 'outer fandom othering' performed on fans who 'communicate their vexation' through claims of 'soiled and ruined' childhoods due to the release of *Answer the Call* (regardless of if the fan has seen the film, if it had been released) emphasizes the affective distress but does not engage with what structural hegemonies are at play in the media object centred identity (Proctor 2017). This distress is suggested to be symptomatic of 'a wider cultural perspective that fundamentally misinterprets and misunderstands the affective mechanics that fuel the engine of fandom'; however, the view of adaptations as uniquely or specifically subject to the totemic nostalgia of fannish responses experienced by *Answer the Call* is one that ignores the political machine of nostalgia elsewhere. Proctor suggests this means that it is obvious that fans who criticized *Answer the Call* were acting in line with both this affective distress and a creative critique of reboot culture, while separating that response out from the 'reactionary actants' at fault for the 'toxic fan practices' (2017, 1122).

The secondary focus of Proctor's analysis also repeats the claim that the 'cultural firestorm' was 'orchestrated by Sony Pictures, including Paul Feig, as a marketing strategy to deal with the fallout from the debut of the trailer' (2017, 1131) without contextualizing or challenging the claims. Indeed he goes on to reiterate them in his plea for academics to look closer into the kinds of 'hoopla' created by media 'cherry-picking data and effectively manufacturing an online controversy for marketing ends' (hoopla here referring to racist commentary about actor John Boyega) (2017, 1132–3). He then uses the video from Red Letter Media about *Answer the Call* which suggests the claims of misogyny have been overblown in regard to the response to the trailer. Red Letter Media also released two videos about *Answer the Call*, one regarding the lack of humour of the trailer and the other 'theorizing that the studio engineered the social controversy around the film to promote it' (De Herder 2021, 434). In broader terms, Red Letter Media's use of 'computer software to excavate the discursive assemblage' (Proctor 2017, 1133) is a part of their 'discursive practices' that 'use articulations of working-class and shlock movie culture to construct a channel identity that appears to resist corporate Hollywood while maintaining a series of contradictory double articulations that may perpetuate oppressive hegemonic social practices' (De Herder 2021, 435). Bay's work also contextualizes that while the negative responses are a minority, 'one in three negative fans express misogynist, anti-progressive, anti-social justice or conservative views' and that there are 'deliberate influence measures' used to persuade fans with misinformation (Bay 2018). The minority element of the negative fans also does not preclude the damaging attacks on Leslie Jones and other marginalized professionals.

Regendering was mostly unexplored within the *Answer the Call* as a form for humorous interactions with either the diegetic or the archontic franchise aspects, but even if the film had leaned into the humour of Jones, Mackinnon and McCarthy in particular, and pushed against the imposition of family friendly, the audience reaction and fannish nostalgia were determined to be negative. It is seated not only in the aggressive totemic nostalgia for the original – blurred through decades of fannishness – but also that 'the laughter stops when masculinity is threatened … because of women taking on male legacy roles' (Hermes and Kopitz 2021, 82–3). As a film, *Answer the Call* may have been a flop, or at least disappointing and losing an unknown amount of money for Sony, but it has provoked significant amounts of conversation about reboot culture, regendering, gender in film and toxic fandom online. A year after the film's release the newest Doctor Who regeneration was announced to be a woman and while Whittaker avoided much of the excessive harassment and abuse faced by the actors in *Answer the Call* the response was aggressively negative in many spaces.

9

Doctor-Ess who?

Doctor Who, like *Star Trek*, occupies a breadth of television that encompasses the very early days of small-screen narratives to the prestige polish in contemporary streaming. As such, the series has had to contend with shifting social, technological and political ideals. *Doctor Who*'s 'hiatus' as such was interrupted by a resurgence of fannishness with the modern era Doctor, initially played by Christopher Eccleston. As Hills notes, 'the "brand" of *Doctor Who* has, quite simply, never become absent for the programme's cult fans' (2013b, 14). Importantly, the lengthy history of the franchise resulted in the 'New Who' including the 'new producer and creative force Russell T Davies being an avowed fan, as are others working on the programme – and this includes the tenth Doctor, David Tennant, who is a self-confessed fanboy' and later on Peter Capaldi, the twelfth Doctor being linked to a fan letter he wrote in his childhood. This fannishness was held as a kind of authenticity that would strengthen the link between the new and the old (Hills 2018). In spite of my own lack of fannishness I have strong memories of being terrified as a toddler of the theme music (excellent work on the part of Ron Grainer and Delia Derbyshire) as my mother was a fan (Nguyen 2017).

The central conceit of the series is the way the Doctor is changeable, he regenerates; initially a response to the illness and difficulties working with the actor, the shift has come to signify kinds of Doctors, who are different in their approaches to life as much as their appearances are changeable. The fandom for the Doctor as a character is highly grounded in affective response to a specific Doctor, as noted by their numerical designation. 'Across fifty years of its production we are faced with not only a wide range of stories that program makers borrowed from, but also widely ranging strategies they followed to make their adaptations' (Harmes 2014, xviii) has come to include regendering with the Thirteenth Doctor in series 11 and 12 of the modern iteration. Until then, in 2018, the Doctors have all been male (aside from the Charity Special).

The recasting of the Doctor as a woman was pre-empted by the similar regendering of the Master, his nemesis (Yodovich 2020). This changeability is linked to the success of the series as a cult television classic, which also affects the gendered representations of fandom and the companion figure (Jowett 2014). The cult aspect of the show finds significant meaning in the production aspect of the series and in particular the fannishness of the professionals in the modern iteration. This, however, also includes negative reactions particularly to the regendered work. As with many other critiques of regendered work that insists the issue is not regendering as much as the failures of the creators at 'doing it right'.

Masculinity is integral to much of the representation of the Doctor; however, it is a specific kind of alien and othered masculinity. Nonetheless the presentation of the Doctor is woven through with specifically national forms of masculinity, until the modern iterations. Even then the masculinity is simply filtered through class representation, or the ageing masculine body, until the Thirteenth Doctor. The difficulty of representing and presenting the decades of habitus and masculinity through the regendered body is made clear not only by diegetic moments remarking on gender, but the way the fans have responded.

Bigger on the inside

The habitus of the Doctor is one of constant change, configured around the eponymous Doctor and his Tardis – 'bigger on the inside' – and varieties of adventures. Originally considered an educational program, the series expanded from that mandate (if not the 'quarry somewhere in Cardiff') to feature more monster/mystery of the week, problem-solving and the ongoing problem of an alien relating to humans and other aliens. The adventures over the decades of the series included many historical moments on Earth, but also the rest of the universe, complicated time travel, potential galaxy-level apocalypses and the mysterious roots of the Doctor. The perpetual changes of the show supported significant shifts in characterization and narrative of the Doctor and the universe itself. However, even this persistent form of change – timelines, narratives, characters, ideas, backstories – does not create an audience or fandom as set on the consistent regeneration at the heart of the series. The franchise itself is cult in form, as defined by Hills, and 'typically focuses its endlessly deferred narrative around a singular question or related set of questions' about '(non-) identity of its (anti)hero' (2013a, 101, 102), and the audience concerns itself with those questions. Hills also highlights the fannish reification of *Doctor Who*'s 'flexibility' (2013a, 39) but that same format elasticity finds its limits in personifications of the Doctor that are too much the other.

The consistent approach of *Doctor Who* as a form of adaptation itself where although 'fidelity (meaning faithfulness in adapting a work) and being original when writing or creating a dramatic work have traditionally been cherished and valorized, but in the case of *Doctor Who*, either quality can sometimes be hard to locate' (Harmes 2014, xiv). The way the television series is part of a wider transmedia franchise, with well-established audio drama productions, literary texts and an ill-fated film is strictly adaptation, but more than that the franchise is a 'cross-media creation, in dialogue with a wide range of sources, ideas, and creative impulses' (Harmes 2014, xiv). This expansive creative impulse of the franchise includes contemporary modes of creation, and that dialogue can be strained with tensions around what the 'real' is of *Doctor Who* and that clash between fidelity and originality. As with the extensive fandom of Sherlock Holmes, the length of time the franchise has run alongside the way the media object has become a specific cultural touchstone, facilitates the responses of the audience and fans to adaptational techniques that interrupt their sense of flow.

The affective nostalgia for the series is grounded in not only the kind of 'totemic nostalgia' Proctor reifies as a kind of necessary fannish trait, but also the sheer amount of canon – fifty-six years and counting (Proctor and Brooker 2019). The weight of that history and the way it is woven into fandom and lived experience even of non-fans create an affective impulse that can be translated into a toxic misogynist response where 'Doctor Karen' is alienating fans due to her gender, 'terrible writing', and 'disrespect' to the canon, the history of the show and the childhood of the fans themselves, and also contributing to the downfall of the BBC themselves, due to the regendering (Nerdrotic 2021). This is in contrast to the viewing numbers that reveal similar numbers for Season 11 and Season 10, and Season 12 averaging similar numbers as well, albeit smaller. The backlash against the concept of a female Doctor began prior to the series being screened, much like other examples of regendering, and were considered regendering a 'weapon' of intersectional feminism's presumed attacks on men as a gender, and the creative bankruptcy of modern media. The totemic nostalgia is not simply for a media product, it is a nostalgia for a presumed past where the individual's preferences, tastes and ideals are dominant.

Production and cult fascination

The *Doctor Who* series has a surprisingly small amount of ephemera compared to many other fandoms, and a strong DIY movement (most notoriously knitting The Scarf) (Hills 2014). The signifiers of fandom are centred on singular elements like the sonic screwdriver or the Tardis, so it is no surprise that the more obvious the style choice the more likely it is to become iconic, as in the leather jacket of Eccleston vs the bowtie or converse shoes or scarf. Even these elements are more difficult to create within the regendered version, whose gender does not preclude individualistic style choices and whose iconic visuals must differentiate themselves from the expected 'fashion' of the female character onscreen. The rumour of Funko Pop dropping the licence to the show was repeated on several negative pieces about the Thirteenth Doctor and was attributed to the audience dislike of female Doctor portraying the ephemera of the franchise as integral to the success of a franchise, and the issue being about the gender, or the portrayal being undermined by the 'stunt' casting.

These production-side elements are also at play in critiques of the Thirteenth Doctor. Chibnall as the showrunner was sidelined in much of his previous work on the franchise's sibling show *Torchwood* (Hills 2013b) and is often seen as the 'problem' with the regendered series. The seeming conflict and tension between Davies and Chibnall as showrunners, writers and creators is positioned in both that series, and the fannish analysis of Series 11 and 12, as due to a fault of Chibnall as a creator who aims to be an auteur but is ultimately 'a "tenant" written out of Torchwood's author function' but whose contributions to *Doctor Who* are deeply suspect if not outright damaging (Hills 2013b, 217). In addition 'over its long production history, *Doctor Who* has had very few women directors, and even fewer female writers with none since 2010' (Jowett 2014, 86) which obviously affects how the series creates the long-held canon that is the origin of the totemic nostalgia that then provokes fandom to defend their memory objects. Indeed, 'according to Steven Moffat, female fans do not want a female Doctor' but he was contradicted by not only other writers, but fans themselves. Yodovich's study of feminist fans of *Doctor Who* after the announcement of Whittaker's casting revealed that 'they eagerly supported the casting shift in heated discussions with their opponents, who were usually male fans' (2020, 1248).

Many critiques position Moffat, or Davies, in conflict with Chibnall, as a way of delineating eras based on creators in order to elide gendered objections. Lewis, Marwick and Partin's research into online harassment examines response and critique videos as forms of online harassment that not only provide a rationale for harassment, and argument for the 'irrational and immoral' nature of the target, but also provide 'attack vectors' based on marginalization (Lewis, Marwick, and Partin 2021, 735; Marwick 2021, 6). The totemic nostalgia of the assumed-default male fan, who is threatened by both the destabilizing of gender enacted by regendering, and the interloper assumed-female fans positions the divide not only as gendered and centred on authenticity, but also a binary; you either are a 'real fan' who defends the immoral/irrational 'attack' on your fandom/self (as per Proctor) or you are inauthentic, reframing regendering or expressed desire for regendering as a politically motivated cultural vandal who is motivated by imagined misandry. In this way, 'attacking an out-group responds to a perceived symbolic threat and reflects a desire to protect one's group status and thus self-image' where the symbolic threat is against the symbolic self within the totemic object as well as the group status of 'fan' being subject to boundary defences and violations (Marwick 2021, 4).

The series as a 'cult' favourite also signifies elements of gender; cult tv featuring women often focuses on extreme elements like sexuality (Elvira) or sexuality (*Rocky Horror Picture Show*) or sexuality (Morticia Addams) or violent deviance (Wednesday Addams). The cult favourites of cinema and television are reliant on non-normativity, which relies on a default ideal of normative – which is often white, and male, thus 'sexual content has often taken a conventional form, intensifying rather than questioning the norms of cinematic depictions of gender' (Austin-Smith 2019, 143). Simply being non-white, and non-male is enough to be other, but to move into cult favourite requires something more than just otherness within the media object. The affective promise of the 'cult' media object is one that prioritizes a kind of otherness, a distance from the normative, even if the programme itself is reasonably normative. The object is defended not only as a beloved object, but as a moral choice, and as such the defence of it is not simply about the media object but about the self. In this defence the fan is defending 'a fan's attachment against external criticism' rather than some form of objective critique centred on the object. It is centred on the fan themselves, and is rooted in the way that fans, as a group, 'cannot agree on what *Doctor Who* is or should be' (Haslett 1994:10 in Hills 2013a, 38).

Gender representations

The modern revival answered many questions about the Doctor and his past, but also explored the connections between the Doctor and his companion – who is usually one of the only consistent female characters within the narrative. The representation of the companion has been the subject of many essays, along with academic work, that focus on gender, belonging and the role of women in *Doctor Who* and other geek narratives. 'Commentators and scholars have noted that female companions in particular have a "decorative" function in the series' from the 1973 decision to introduce Sarah Jane Smith as a more contemporary and independent Companion, to the current tensions around the introduction of sexual tension between the Doctor and his companion (Jowett 2014, 78–81). In addition to this the diegetic conflict where 'the Doctor is a lonely traveller in need of friendship, and at times uses the female companions' illustrates not only the companion as a necessarily subservient to the protagonist, but an unsettling repeated process whereby a woman is abducted by a man – which is later lampshaded and called out by companions (Jowett 2014, 82). The function of the Doctor means that 'companions, especially female companions, tend to be emotional, passive or dependent so the Doctor can function as their champion and rescuer' and that attempts to introduce similarly powerful female characters have failed as they do not 'fit the existing dynamic' (Jowett 2014, 83–4). Even River Song replicates the pattern where the female companion sacrifices everything, including her life, to wait for the Doctor in one way or another.

The companions have also allowed for more explicit representation of queerness – the Doctor himself is often non-romantic, non-sexual, even with the romantic implications of the modern Doctors. 'Christopher Eccleston, David Tennant and Matt Smith playing the Doctor all offer different versions of masculinity and heroism just as the various female companions offer a range of femininities' (Jowett 2014, 80) and in 2004 finally including non-white femininity in the form of Martha. The ninth Doctor acquires the 'companionship of Captain Jack Harkness (John Barrowman), a man from the fifty-first century who considers himself "omnisexual" but who is primarily represented as bisexual, if not homosexual' (Barron 2010, 138). This can be attributed to the length of the hiatus and that 'there has been a focus on representing female and queer companions in a positive light in order to reflect growing social and cultural movements' (Gilbert 2017, 106). In her promotional shot the Thirteenth Doctor embodies some of that range, 'her costume, which included high-waist trousers attached with suspenders and rainbow-colored stripes printed on a dark t-shirt, hinting to gay pride' (Yodovich 2020, 1251). Cornell suggests that there has always been a queer presence in the fandom itself, even if the show itself largely avoided the topic until the modern iteration (Cornell 1997). The default patterns of normative media – the white male protagonist – allow a space for the companion to embody the other, in her femaleness, or queerness, or non-whiteness, and to be non-normative as a woman. The introduction of a regendered Master, or Doctor, unsettles the expected balance between normative defaults and otherness within the narratives.

Attraction to The Doctor, in his forms of Tennant and Matt Smith particularly, is well established within fandom. In spite of the oft-used statistics that illustrate queerness on the part of fandom, this does not preclude attraction to men on the part of queer women. Similarly while the 'fandom is predominantly male, and its official fan-producers are also predominantly male' this too does not preclude same-sex attraction (Hills 2013a, 149). This is often evident in the particular affective connection to an iteration of the Doctor, along with the presumption that a female Doctor would fail due to the sexual interest in the male Doctors. This is interesting in contrast to the apparent quantitative queerness of fans, alongside the presumption that the maleness of the Doctor will appeal to women regardless of taste but a woman Doctor will not, and similarly that the male Doctor will appeal to the male audience regardless of sexuality. The maleness is perceived as central to the Doctor not just as a character element, but as a representation of canonical and childhood history, and also as part of a heteronormative function of media. In spite of this, when the younger Matt Smith was replaced by significantly older Peter Capaldi, vocalizing desire for the Doctor resulted in 'male fans of the series promptly attacked and discursively disciplined these allegedly "inauthentic" female fans' (Hills 2018, 205). The gendered fannishness also includes political alignment assumed to be congruent with gender, as 'when a female fan also identifies as a feminist, she is perceived as a double threat in science fiction fan communities' (Yodovich 2020, 1245). This threat to the canon, the original and therefore the identity of the 'real fan', is due to the inauthenticity through spoken desires, and the assumed cultural politics around gender, and face the same 'defence' outlined by Proctor as an integral part of fannishness (Proctor and Brooker 2019).

What a man/alien

The historical element of cross-gender identification with the Doctor belies complex feelings about gender primarily on the part of male fans identifying with the female Doctor (Hills 2013a, 167–8). The industrial and social aspect of the audience affect the adaptation, even without regendering, where 'the first Doctor lacks the epic heroism of his later self, and is portrayed as extremely patriarchal and attached to outmoded gender roles' in contrast to the Twelfth Doctor (Hills 2018, 211). The shifting narrative of the cult television form allows for character modifications that allow the franchise to remain relevant to the audience, but 'whether defined primarily as a genre, or as a set of ritualized practices that coalesce around a group of privileged texts, the term "cult film" is one used most often in relation to the cinephilia of young straight, white men' (Austin-Smith 2019, 144)

The masculinity of the Doctor has been examined as a feature of class, where he is an 'eccentric gentleman' whose regeneration as the distinctly Northern and 'working-class' was an appeal that worked to secure an audience far less interested or represented by the middle to upper class 'English gentleman' (Haslop 2016, 209–10). The question of gendered class is absent, with the Doctor remaining stubbornly male. Eccleston as the Ninth Doctor and Capaldi as the Twelfth both decontextualize the masculinity of the Doctor away from class but retain a specific genderedness. In the case of Capaldi, age was also subject to tension 'as an older actor taking on the twenty-first-century role, he was subjected to considerable paratextual anxiety that he was too old to play the part' (Hills 2018, 204). Hills also suggests that 'a "both/and" image of masculinity persisted across Capaldi's tenure, as his version of the Doctor both displayed paternalistic masculinity and disrupted masculine power/authority in a number of ways' and 'is periodically feminized narratively' (2018, 205). The gender non-normativity is linked with his age, but his final moments on screen are his acceptance of his regeneration, and welcome to the new, meaning 'masculine authority is restored' by his 'rational detachment' (2018, 212).

The Doctor is a character who embodies a kind of quirky anti-heroic default; it may seem counter-intuitive but the default masculinity and whiteness of the anti-hero hold space for that man to be non-normative (quirky) in a specific way, and 'this disruption of standard action heroism can be seen as attractive to a female audience' (Jowett 2014, 80). Who the Doctor is, or what, is a continual focus of the 'deferred narrative' and subject to revision. Even though 'over

26 years a fairly comprehensive sense of the Doctor's identity was eventually arrived at, only to be destabilized in the final few seasons (1988–89) where it was hinted that previous programme knowledge was only partial' the fans create a canonical version of what the Doctor should be (Hills 2013a, 101). These qualities, in flux due to the regeneration narrative, are used to explain how the female Doctor is wrong due to her embodiment/continuation of the destabilized identity. The regendered quirky anti-hero, however, hews much closer to the manic pixie dream girl trope than to the power fantasy of the nerdy hero as per the Doctor. She is still rarely the protagonist (*Amelie* is likely the most obvious cinematic example of the manic pixie dream girl protagonist, outside the swathe of children's books featuring heroes like Ramona Quimby). By regendering the Doctor, the series has to contend with the way the quirkiness of the Doctor becomes ineffectual when represented in the form of a woman. Similarly, the power fantasy of the Doctor, who is invulnerable/immortal, extremely powerful, intelligent and often non-normatively masculine; Tom Baker's scarf, the converses and bowties, the joyous positivity and the tears, all combine to create a protagonist who embodies a kind of masculine power fantasy unlike that of action heroes in Hollywood. Regendering this power fantasy seems like it should be reasonably straightforward, but it still relies on the male character as default. Regendering the power fantasy reveals the schisms and difficulties around binary gender roles in society.

Doing this as a woman

The Thirteenth Doctor helmed seasons 11 and 12 of the 'New Who', which by the latter season had dropped to some of the lowest ratings of the modern era. It is impossible to delineate how much of this is due to actual poor performance, given the breadth and range of adaptation inherent to the series, and how much is centred on the experience of the audience. Regendering, while offering unique and insightful ways to engage with and adapt original works, does provoke significant backlash by audiences.

Diegetic responses to the gender shift are possible within *Doctor Who* without breaking the fourth wall or otherwise affecting the narrative. When she remarks on her new gender it is with wonder at first, saying 'Oh, brilliant!' but quickly forgetting until reminded 'sorry, half an hour ago I was a white-haired Scotsman' (The Woman Who Fell to Earth, 2018). During later episodes it becomes much more pointed, with the cultural restrictions about gender influencing the Doctor's actions on earth. In the episode where she is facing the witch trials she exclaims 'these are hard times for women! If we're not being drowned, we're being patronised to death!' aligning herself with the women in the audience as much as historical and fictional ones (The Witchfinders, 2018). This genderedness is unremarked, and unmarked, when performed by the default white male Doctors but with womanhood comes marked gender, and gender performance.

The historical imbalance and unfairness of the witch trial remain relevant to regendering, and gender. When the Doctor is regendered, many moments and aspects of the show are highlighted in critiques in spite of their presence in other seasons and iterations. The impossibility of passing the witch trial becomes the impossibility of delivering an adaptation good enough, correct enough, or respectful enough if it contains a regendered character. The backlash against regendering is becoming more acute, more prone to the politicized agitation identified by Bay (2018) in their research into *Star Wars* fans. The level of vitriol and judgement is not only linked to the totemic nostalgia and psychological identification at play for fans, but to broader political and social movements around gender and race.

The dual aspects of *Doctor Who* as a cult TV phenomenon and as a contemporary adaptation of not only the original series but of other genres, stories and narratives, create a specific narrative for the audience. The show has accompanied fans from early childhood to old age, with fans becoming showrunners and stars, and has cemented itself as part of embodied and lived experiences:

> As people's location in family/educational/employment structures becomes increasingly varied and thus offers fewer anchors for constructing and maintaining personal identities, fandom returns us those resources in terms of both ('real') fan communities and ('fictional') fan/object relationships.

> (Harrington, Bielby, and Bardo 2011, 581)

This long-lived fandom, the continual change of the genre conventions and the main character, seems to suggest an adaptational technique like regendering would be less of an issue for fans, given previous regendering including a series antagonist in the contemporary series, or the charity special written by Moffat who became the New Who showrunner. But both of these moments of regendering cement the cult media tendency to intensify gender normativity.

The regendered Master becoming Missy while also becoming an ineffective antagonist and eventually being murdered by her own self for allying with the Doctor, or Joanna Lumley Doctor allying herself with the Master and being excited by her vibrating sonic screwdriver with 'three settings'. The beloved fourth Doctor, Tom Baker, quipped at his retirement 'It's time for me to let another man – or woman for that matter – have a go' (Caines 2018, 23), sparking concern and furore and taking over two decades to actually come to fruition.

When the Doctor is regendered, without the distance and non-canonical havoc of a charity special, the focus shifts to gender in a way that illustrates the default expectations of the audience of not only the character, but the media they consume. The playfulness of regendering in adaptation forces the audience to confront their own gendered ideals. Alongside this, reactions to the regendered work outside counterpublics like fandom-creator spaces demonstrate the unexpected confrontation with the gendered space of the original disrupts the narrative flow. The response to the regendered Doctor has elements in common not just with the fandom of *Doctor Who*, but also the increasing community of online commentators who aggressively defend iconic 'geek' objects as not just totemic nostalgia, but as masculinity itself. Like many other examples of regendering, the negative reactions occur before the media itself has been released and are centred on the expectations and the assumptions of the adaptation, and the affective distress of the fan who has integrated the media object into their identity.

Conclusion

The process of my research involved significant unearthing and acts of vulnerability, from me and those who responded to my call for participants and shared their stories with me, and those whose works make up the genre of regendering. This responsiveness demanded that I both hold a space for those stories to be told and to evolve through that retelling, but also that I mirror their openness. The internal conflicts of fan studies between the more sociological and data-driven work that seeks to quantify and understand the audience, and the critical analysis forms within media and literary studies, develop lines of tensions between those approaches. The theoretical framework offers a way of understanding gender-creative work but does not erase the way that it is subversive and transgressive, in both the fannish form and the commercial one. Negative responses to both illustrate why it is an act with feminist readings, and that destabilizes gender as a category and performance.

My own tendency and drive to approach fanworks as an artefact for research akin to any other literary or media product are at odds with some methods for approaching fan studies but the increasing popularity of fandom as a training ground for creatives is only increasing. The prevalence of well-written, insightful and deeply thought-out work is matched by the hastily scribbled auto-erotic fantasies that encompass much of the mainstream view of fandom, but both extremes are worthy of research. They form the exceptions, and the outer edges, of an enormous body of work that illustrates the intense interest audiences have in reworking media to fulfil their own desires, thus neatly demonstrating both those desires, and the missing moments of the works from which they spring.

Regendering as a creative praxis offers layered meaning to the creator-audiences of fannish counterpublics, and to professional creators. This layered meaning is particularly concerned with what their own identity does for that work; the fan using regendered fanfic to explore and explain gender to themselves and their peers, or the fan using regendered professional works to expand criticism from the media to their perception of feminism. The two approaches are opposed politically; however, regendering is the commonality that shows the adaptation process is not simply concerned with fidelity or originality. Regendering as adaptation is a political moment that provokes a broad range of responses depending on the counterpublic it is received by, but also by shifting modes of criticism and politics.

For fandom, as classically determined to be transformative, primarily female, and engaged, creative praxis engages not only the literary and media basis of fanwork, but also its socio-political frameworks. Regendering transgresses and subverts expectations of behaviour, as an affirmation of the fannish counterpublic and the metatexts of fannishness. Feminist theory regarding performativity and otherness, particularly as it pertains to media and gender, integrates with the transgressive actions of fanwork and resolves as a method for the counterpublic to create an 'other' of the wider non-fannish public. This 're-othering' is a foundation for the formation of the counterpublic and integrates even that gender-creative transgressive and subversive works but maintaining that 'other' even within seemingly contradictory or conflicting works.

Other forms of gender-creative fanwork are also an important site for this re-othering. In particular the Omegaverse or A/B/O fanworks, with their were-creature-associated erotica counterparts, are a specifically unique facet of gender-creative work, and one that very much has foundations in taboo eroticism, the intriguing abject nature of 'monstrous' bodies and how gender and reproduction function at societal levels. In a similar way the Alternate Universes where people are born with BDSM 'identities' interrogate structures while avoiding gender. In terms of otherness these works are sources of intense conflict around the erasure of women alongside the queerly signified bodies of the characters depicted. The queer female fan is often elided in favour of examining her homoerotic and homosexual male works for relevancy to heteronormative structures.

Fans, specifically transformative fans who engage with and create fanworks, were the primary respondents for my research. This necessarily reduced my data pool to those within the counterpublic of fandom, albeit including professionals and also the experiences of those fans outside their own contact zone. Their experiences provided significant data for who appreciates and creates regendered work but also what it meant to them to see it in fanwork and professional adaptations. The fanwork I included allowed me to illustrate the expansive nature of regendering in media that is not constrained by marketing or other departments, but also as a response to this data. The regendered work most meaningful to those fans at an individual level was done by other fans not the commercial industry. While regendered commercial work was seen as a good shift in industry norms, it was unable to negotiate the complex tensions of gender identity.

Fanworks are exhibitions and explanations of what makes one Other but also what makes one part of fandom, self-conscious and performed vulnerabilities and markers of difference. The experience of fandom, however, varies from this in many ways and for many reasons. A common site of community fracture is the affective economy – what fans say they want appears to be mismatched when compared to the attention and emotional labour they devote to the works. The outcry for female characters expressed in critiques and 'fancasting' is only matched in fandom by the sheer negativity female characters are exposed to when they are either deemed failures or unacceptable in some fashion; too loud, too brash, too aggressive, too sexual, not sexual enough, boring, too girly, too ineffectual, too much entirely. Where, even with the mechanism of resistance via fandom, '… such fans give lip service to an egalitarian vision in a general sense while campaigning against it in a specific case' because the focus remains again, on male characters and their relationships (Scodari 2003). Or, even more damning, by silence, by the absence of the female characters from the works created.

Professional regendering is often a response to older narratives lacking the gender equity modern audiences expect while still intending to retell that story. *Elementary, Ghostbusters: Answer the Call*, the Thirteenth Doctor and the audience reactions to those show the ways in which adaptation and gender influence both reception and production for professionals but rely on a canonical masculinity in order to have that effect. This effect illustrates the dominance of that masculine default but also highlights regendering as an increasingly popular option for adaptation in a media environment dominated by remakes, reboots and sequels. The presumption of flow, and familiarity, conflicts with the necessity of uniqueness or originality as either a creative practice or an artefact of copyright. Professional adaptations are also subject to a much broader audience reaction, and this includes the negative aspects.

Copyright and other market influences can have varied effects. The necessity for CBS to differentiate *Elementary* more from *Sherlock* meant they regendered John into Joan, and not only did that result in seven series of police procedural, but it also explored parts of the Holmsean mythos often ignored – his drug addiction, his family – and the highly subtextual queerness of Moriarty and Watson. The drive for a family friendly *Ghostbusters* reduced much of the comedic appeal of its stars, and actively erased queerness from the intended text. The creative possibilities of regendering are linked with queerness in many ways, and while this is often noted as a way in which the commercial possibilities are limited, in and of itself this is a reiteration of the masculine default. It is also unsupported as 'the response to *Ghostbusters* appears to have had a rather limited impact: the 2017 casting of Jodie Whittaker as the Thirteenth Doctor and the success of the female-lead *Ocean's 8* in 2018 reveals limits to the hypermasculine readings of canon and tradition, regardless of how deeply entrenched the 1984 Ghostbusters film appears to be in the cultural consciousness' (Bryan and Clark 2019, 157).

The tendency to divide fans into binary camps is rapidly becoming irrelevant to the study of what fans do. While the productive fandom, those who create fanworks and who form communities around those works, have been gendered female it is not strictly delineated according to those binaries. Male productive fans exist, and indeed – what is fantasy football but a large fannish rpg when (primarily) men engage in a communal restructuring at a creative level? Similarly, what are critical videos and essays? Audio-visual versions of the metafiction previously found in mostly textual format. The idea of the 'good' fan is also one that necessitates a 'bad' fan, but more troublingly it creates a valid target for either protection or retribution. The categorization of fandom is useful to the quantitative examinations and data-driven work of sociology, or marketing, but as numerous studies have shown that does not measure the effect of those fans. It also provides a more troubling tendency where fannish points of tension are shifted into the academic space, where the autoethnographic and qualitative aspects of fan studies can allow for an uncritical replication of the tension, rather than an actual research project.

Negativity, from anti-fans, from political or social agitators, from those drawn in by the contagious trolling or misinformation, from those genuinely curious or concerned, has become a signifier of fannish intent. To be a fan is no longer signified by engagement, or even production, but by activity on behalf of the fannish object. Similarly, the importance of the object is now tied to identity – queer subtext becomes representation, representation becomes a rationale for defence of the media object. Criticism, rather than critique, manifests with socio-political engagement over the creative praxis. Regendering is a particular lightning rod for negativity stemming from social and political models of media, and defence of the psychologically formative media object. The influence of fandom on the commercial versions has not been to expand or inspire possibilities, but to expose those professionals to the social and political trolling, the extreme defensiveness, that categorize much of fandom in the contemporary mainstream.

The 'fans who rail against any casting change to favoured products' are the minority but their influence is sizeable in terms of the individual (Bryan and Clark 2019, 157). The 'larger sea change taking place, with a growing acceptance to more diverse casting choices by the broader public and even fan communities themselves' (Bryan and Clark 2019, 157) is one that seems to inspire many of the more volatile anti-fans to worse behaviours. When looking at regendering it is tempting to imagine that it is the 'fanboys' whose abuse of Leslie Jones, or Jodie Whittaker, are examples of the misogynist audience rather than fandom. This not only ignores the racial aspect of Jones's experience, or that of other stars whose work was not regendered but similarly challenged or subverted the male default of existing works (*Star Wars* is an obvious example, but see also *Mad Max: Fury Road*, or *Shera*). This default may be the protagonists, or the audience, but it is also a white male default, not simply a function of gender but also of race. Meaning, of course, that there will be other instances of this subverted default with the negativity and abuse being enacted by the female audience.

Disruption, subversion and transgression are key to the way regendering is perceived by the audience. The practice relies on a default presentation and expectation that includes gender, but also race, ability, sexuality and other aspects of hierarchy in social environments. More specifically it relies on the existing work to have created that default and expectation, even if a specific character is not regendered. By basing themselves on the existing work the regendered version complicates the expectation of the original, which when approached with the deep sense of play common to transformational fans and fandom results in flow. Without that sense of play, regendering – or any other abruption to the default – is perceived as a fault, a weakness, or at worst something like violence. While play is common to some fannish counterpublics it is not always experienced by fans or audiences.

While much can be made of the similarities between the negative responses to *Answer the Call* and the Thirteenth Doctor, and other long-running franchises with new iterations that challenge the default, history shows that there is a change occurring. The presumption that this is a linear progressiveness in society is undermined by the qualitative differences between examples of regendering; *Battlestar Galactica* may have gotten furious letters from previous stars complaining about 'castrating' Starbuck, the public reaction is primarily one adoring the regendered Starbuck. Similarly, the letters and commentary about *Elementary* having a female Watson were greatly reduced once the series released and it is rarely signified in critique of the series now. Yet both *Answer the Call* and *Doctor Who* sustained not only significant criticism over the period of their release and after, but much higher levels of vitriol.

Leslie Jones's experience as a regendered character is one that makes clear the ways in which it can be dangerous for creators to engage in these kinds of subversions of the norm in contemporary culture. While Whittaker and the crew of *Doctor Who* also faced aggressive critique and continue to be the target of cultural critics and commentators, the abuse and harassment Jones suffered points to a significant element of regendering – it is not just about gender. Jones was targeted as a Black woman whose comedy does not pander to a white majority, and who became a scapegoat for the 'culture wars' based on white masculinity in America. While Lucy Liu also disrupted the assumed whiteness of Holmsean adaptations, *Elementary* was released before the destructive tendency towards abuse from online socio-political cultures that consider the shift from the white male default to be an attack on their values. The contemporary media environment is very much dominated by these voices even though they remain a minority – their methods of criticism and harassment are aggressive enough to create the illusion of majority.

Regendering as a fan practice is one that focuses on the playfulness inherent in fanworks; they may be serious topics with serious repercussions or examinations, but the deep play praxis allows fans to engage and disengage. In commercial adaptation though, the sense of play is often lost in the marketing drive for success, and in the way media objects have become synonymous with representation and identity. The way regendering makes the white male default the other subjects the audience to that othering even when they are not part of that demographic because the disruption to the expected norm identifies them as part of normative society. While fandom then finds some level of play or acceptance in the subversion – just as male homoerotic content is normalized within the counterpublic – the broader audience does not share the same reading or viewing practices. In addition to this the growing recognition of the ways media has been dominated by representations of masculinity, and attempts to balance that, have become signposts for cultural politics.

The issue of representation is one that demands a kind of fidelity and adherence to norms that preclude the more interesting ways of playing with gender and identity in media. The adherence to a specific set of cultural norms is one that denies some kinds of representation. What regendering offers is instead is a reflection – one that is distorted and piecemeal. Much like the shattered surface of womanhood, where women (and men, and non-binary people) are gendered according to that normative binary but identify themselves with the myriad and varied aspects of woman as a class, regendering pulls away from the presumed whole of a representation to instead reflect gender through the lens of an extant normative focal point.

Appendix 1: Survey questions

This research is being conducted to collect data on fans' perception of and participation in regendered fanworks (also known as genderbending, sexswap, Rule 63). Lucy is currently a PhD candidate and this research will form part of her thesis.

You may NOT participate in this survey if you are under eighteen years of age. By completing this survey you acknowledge that you are OVER eighteen years of age.

Thank you for clicking over to take this survey!

Participation is voluntary. You do not need to complete the survey. Participants should have some familiarity with fanworks (fanfic, fanart, fanmixes, fanvids) and regendered works (in fandom or mainstream media). You do not need to create works yourself, or participate in fan communities to participate in the survey (lurkers are welcome!).

This survey consists of between five and seventeen questions, depending on your decisions. You may quit at any time and save your answers if you wish to return, or clear the results if you no longer wish to participate.

The survey is being distributed online through fan-oriented communities; you may have received the link via a social network, a community you are involved in or via an email from someone you know. Completed surveys and the data collected will only be accessible by the research team.

You may NOT participate in this survey if you are under eighteen years of age. By completing this survey you acknowledge that you are OVER eighteen years of age.

Data collected in the survey will be anonymous. Participants will not be identifiable in publication. The data collected will be held in password-protected and/or key-locked environments.

Please see this information sheet for further information.

There are seventeen questions in this survey.

These are questions about who you are and how you identify.

How old are you?
(Please note that if you are under eighteen you will not be able to participate in this survey)

Please choose only one of the following:
18–25
26–30
31–35
36–45
45+

What gender do you identify as?
Please write your answer here:

What is your background?
Please write your answer(s) here:

What is your national, racial or tribal identity?

What is your primary family background language or languages?

What level of education have you achieved?

Please choose all that apply and provide a comment:
School
Technical/training institution
University/College
undergraduate
University/College postgraduate
Other

If employed or self-employed, what is your paid work?
Please write your answer here:

What fandoms are you most active in (creation, reading, lurking or any other activity)?
Please write your answer here:

These are questions about the fannish activities you engage in – this could be creation of, reading, viewing, reccing or beta-ing. You can answer for any and all fandoms.

What fannish activities do you engage in? This question must have at least one answer and you are able to elaborate on your answer in the text box provided if you wish.

Please choose all that apply and provide a comment:
Fanfic
Fanart
Fanvids
Cosplay
Fan-crafts
Meta
Conventions or conferences
Communities
Academia
Other

These are some questions about regendered fanworks (also known as genderbending, Rule 63, sexswap, starbucking, genderswap and a number of others – fanworks which change the gender of the original character in some way, including non-binary gender representations).

Do you specifically seek out media (including fanworks) that have women characters (regendered or original)?
(You can elaborate in the text box if you would like)
Yes
No
Haven't noticed
It makes no difference to me
Make a comment on your choice here:

Do you consume or create fanworks that change the gender of one or more characters? This includes meta (talking about the concept, or fandom's response, or mainstream adaptations).

Yes

No

If you would like to, could you please elaborate on why? You are welcome to provide links or recs to favourite works as well – please simply paste them into your comment.

(This question is optional)

Only answer this question if the following conditions are met: Answer was 'Yes' at question '9' (Do you consume or create fanworks that change the gender of one or more characters? This includes meta (talking about the concept, or fandom's response, or mainstream adaptations).)

Please write your answer here:

If you would like to, could you please elaborate on why not?

(This question is optional)

Only answer this question if the following conditions are met: Answer was 'No' at question '9' (Do you consume or create fanworks that change the gender of one or more characters? This includes meta (talking about the concept, or fandom's response, or mainstream adaptations).)

Please write your answer here:

Have you watched mainstream adaptations that change the gender of original characters (such as Elementary, BSG or Hannibal) or consumed any other mainstream media work that changes the gender of an original character (comics, TV shows, books)?

Yes

No

If you would like to, could you please elaborate on why? Have you enjoyed these works?

(This question is optional)

Only answer this question if the following conditions are met: Answer was 'Yes' at question '12' (Have you watched mainstream adaptations that change the gender of original characters (such as Elementary, BSG or Hannibal) or consumed any other mainstream media work that changes the gender of an original character (comics, TV shows, books)?)
Please write your answer here:

> If you would like to, could you please elaborate on why not?
> (This question is optional)

Only answer this question if the following conditions are met: Answer was 'No' at question '12' (Have you watched mainstream adaptations that change the gender of original characters (such as Elementary, BSG or Hannibal) or consumed any other mainstream media work that changes the gender of an original character (comics, TV shows, books)?)
Please write your answer here:

> Do you consume other adaptations or AUs?
> Yes
> No
>
> If you would like to, could you please elaborate on why? You are welcome to provide links or recs to favourite works as well – please simply paste them into your comment.
> (This question is optional)

Only answer this question if the following conditions are met: Answer was 'Yes' at question '15' (Do you consume other adaptations or AUs?)
Please write your answer here:

> If you would like to, could you please elaborate on why not?
> (This question is optional)

Only answer this question if the following conditions are met: Answer was 'No' at question '15' (Do you consume other adaptations or AUs?)
Please write your answer here:

Thank you for completing this survey. We hope that this research will provide a better understanding of why fans regender characters in their fanworks, and what that regendering means to audiences.

If you would like to participate in a series of interviews Lucy is undertaking with fans please click on the link below and fill out the form and she will contact you within a week. These interviews will primarily be an elaboration on the survey with the option of including your own regendered fanworks (if you create them) and discussing your creative/selective process, and about your perceptions of the representations of regendered characters (as either consumer or creator), and your reading (fannish or original) habits regarding the gender of characters. It is expected the interview will take approximately 30 minutes and may take place via written (IM or email) or audio/audio visual methods (Skype or in person, location permitting).

You may also contact Lucy with any questions or concerns, or to be put on a list of those wishing to obtain a copy of Lucy's completed thesis. Please contact her via email (lucy.baker@griffithuni.edu.au) or Skype (ms.lucybaker).

Thank you for completing this survey.

Appendix 2: Interview questions

- Do you seek out genderbent fanworks? (what kind/how often/why)
- Do you have favourite genderbent fanworks? Genderbent commercial works?
- Is there any genderbent fanwork meta that you wish to share?
- Do you create genderbent fanworks? (what kind/how often/why)
- What kind of feedback have you gotten?
- Has your creation of genderbent work changed your relationship to other fanworks or to canon?
- Do you think genderbent fanworks part of AU (Alternate Universe) works or are they something else? Why?
- What do you think makes a successful genderbent character?
- What are some ways you have seen genderbent characters be less successful?

References

Ackerman, Diane. (2011). *Deep Play*. United Kingdom: Knopf Doubleday Publishing Group.

Allen, Andrew. (2012). 'Has Hollywood Lost Its Way?' *Short of the Week*. 5 January 2012. http://www.shortoftheweek.com/2012/01/05/has-hollywood-lost-its-way/.

Ancelet, Barry Jean. (2001). 'Falling Apart to Stay Together: Deep Play in the Grand Marais Mardi Gras', *The Journal of American Folklore* 114 (452): 144–53. https://doi.org/10.2307/542093.

Arcy, Jacquelyn and Zhana Johnson. (2018). 'Intersectional Critique and Social Media Activism in *Sleepy Hollow* Fandom', *Transformative Works and Cultures* 26. https://doi.org/10.3983/twc.2018.1132.

Austin-Smith, Brenda. (2019). 'Cult Cinema and Gender', in *The Routledge Companion to Cult Cinema*, edited by Ernest Mathijs and Jamie Sexton, 1st ed., 143–51. London; New York: Routledge. https://doi.org/10.4324/9781315668819-19.

Bacon-Smith, Camille. (1992). *Enterprising Women: Television Fandom and the Creation of Popular Myth*. Philadelphia: University of Pennsylvania Press.

Baheri, Tia. (2013). 'Your Ability to Can Even: A Defense of Internet Linguistics', *The Toast*. 20 November 2013. http://the-toast.net/2013/11/20/yes-you-can-even/.

Baker, Lucy Irene. (2015). 'Joan Watson: Mascot, Companion and Investigator', in *Gender and the Modern Sherlock Holmes: Essays on Film and Television Adaptations Since 2009*, edited by Nadine Farghaly, 146–59. United States: McFarland.

Baker, Lucy Irene. (2016). 'Girl! Version: The Feminist Framework for Regendered Characters', *Journal of Fandom Studies* 4 (1): 23–36.

Baker, Lucy Irene. (2017). 'The Surface of Women', *Transformative Works and Cultures* 24. http://journal.transformativeworks.org/index.php/twc/article/view/879.

Barron, Lee. (2010). 'Intergalactic Girl Power: The Gender Politics of Companionship in 21st Century Doctor Who', in *Ruminations, Peregrinations, and Regenerations: A Critical Approach to Doctor Who*, edited by Chris Hansen, New ed., 130–49. Newcastle Upon Tyne: Cambridge Scholars Publishing.

Bartlett, Myke. (2009). 'Wizards, Fanboys and Geeks', *Screen Education* (55): 32–36.

Bartlett, Myke. (2017). 'Rose-Coloured Rear-View: "Stranger Things" and the Lure of a False Past', *Screen Education* (85) (June): 16.

Bay, Morten. (2018). 'Weaponizing the Haters: *The Last Jedi* and the Strategic Politicization of Pop Culture through Social Media Manipulation', *First Monday*. November. https://doi.org/10.5210/fm.v23i11.9388.

Beauvoir, Simone de. (2014). *The Second Sex*. United Kingdom: Random House.

Bennett, Alanna. (2012). '*Elementary* Creator Defends Decision to Make Watson a Woman', *The Mary Sue*. 13 July 2012. http://www.themarysue.com/elementary-on-gender-swap/.

Bennett, Lucy and Bertha Chin. (2014). 'Exploring Fandom, Social Media, and Producer/Fan Interactions: An Interview with *Sleepy Hollow*'s Orlando Jones', *Transformative Works and Cultures* 17. https://doi.org/10.3983/twc.v17i0.601.

Bennion-Nixon, Lee-Jane. (2010). 'We (Still) Need a Woman for the Job: The Warrior Woman, Feminism and Cinema in the Digital Age', *Senses of Cinema*. December 2010. http://sensesofcinema.com/2010/feature-articles/we-still-need-a-woman-for-the-job-the-warrior-woman-feminism-and-cinema-in-the-digital-age/.

Black, Holly. (2011). 'Ladies Ladies Ladies', *Holly Black*. 7 August 2011. http://blackholly.livejournal.com/157736.html.

Black, Suzanne. (2012). 'The Archontic Holmes: Understanding Adaptations of Arthur Conan Doyle's Sherlock Holmes Stories in the Context of Jacques Derrida's "Archive"', in *FORUM: University of Edinburgh Postgraduate Journal of Culture and the Arts*, edited by James Leveque and Lizzie Stewart. Vol. 15. http://www.forumjournal.org/site/sites/default/files/15_black.pdf.

Bowler, Alexia L. (2013). 'Towards a New Sexual Conservatism in Postfeminist Romantic Comedy', in *Postfeminism and Contemporary Hollywood Cinema*, edited by Joel Gwynne and Nadine Muller, 185–203. London: Palgrave Macmillan. https://doi.org/10.1057/9781137306845_12.

branwyn. (2011). 'The Skeleton Winter', Archive of Our Own. http://archiveofourown.org/works/279916/chapters/444847.

branwyn. (2012). 'Let Sense Be Dumb', Archive of Our Own. http://archiveofourown.org/works/279916/chapters/444847.

breathedout. (2013a). 'How the Mouth Changes Its Shape', Archive of Our Own. http://archiveofourown.org/works/704773?view_full_work=true.

breathedout. (2013b). 'Once Again I Was Sitting at the Porn …'. 13 November 2013. http://havingbeenbreathedout.tumblr.com/post/60776179293/pasiphile-once-again-i-was-sitting-at-the-porn.

breathedout. (2017). '… Having Been Breathed Out — Violsva Replied to Your Post: "fursasaida Replied …"'. 13 April 2017. http://havingbeenbreathedout.tumblr.com/post/158746955648/violsva-replied-to-your-post-fursasaida-replied.

Brennan, Sarah Rees. (2011). 'Ladies, Don't Let Anyone Tell You You're Not Awesome', *Into That World Inverted …* (blog). 4 August 2011. http://sarahtales.livejournal.com/188663.html.

Brough, Melissa M. and Sangita Shresthova. (2012). 'Fandom Meets Activism: Rethinking Civic and Political Participation', in *Transformative Works and Cultures* 10 (Transformative Works and Fan Activism), edited by Henry Jenkins and Sangita Shresthova. https://doi.org/doi:10.3983/twc.2012.0303.

Bryan, Peter Cullen and Brittany R. Clark. (2019). '#NotMyGhostbusters: Adaptation, Response, and Fan Entitlement in 2016's *Ghostbusters*', *The Journal of American Culture* 42 (2): 147–58. https://doi.org/10.1111/jacc.13067.

Bucher, Taina. (2018). *If … Then: Algorithmic Power and Politics*. United Kingdom: Oxford University Press.

Burgoon, Judee K., Michelle L. Johnson, and Pamela T. Koch. (1998). 'The Nature and Measurement of Interpersonal Dominance', *Communication Monographs* 65 (4): 308–35. https://doi.org/10.1080/03637759809376456.

Bury, Rhiannon. (2005). *Cyberspaces of Their Own: Female Fandoms Online*. Digital Formations. New York: Peter Lang.

Busse, Kristina and Alexis Lothian. (2009). 'Bending Gender: Feminist and (Trans) Gender Discourses in the Changing Bodies of Slash Fan Fiction', in *Internet Fiction(s)*, edited by Hotz-Davies, Sirpa Leppänen, and Anton Kirchhofer, 105–27. Newcastle Upon Tyne, UK: Cambridge Scholars Publishing. http://queergeektheory. org/docs/Lothian_BendingGender.pdf.

Busse, Kristina. (2010). 'Geek Hierarchies, Boundary Policing, and the Good Fan/ Bad Fan Dichotomy', *Antenna* (blog). 13 August 2010. http://blog.commarts.wisc. edu/2010/08/13/geek-hierarchies-boundary-policing-and-the-good-fanbad-fan-dichotomy/.

Busse, Kristina. (2013). 'Pon Farr, Mpreg, Bonds, and the Rise of the Omegaverse', in *Fic: Why Fanfiction Is Taking over the World*, edited by Anne Jamison and Lev Grossman, 562–73. Dallas, TX: Smart Pop.

Busse, Kristina. (2018). 'The Ethics of Studying Online Fandom', in *The Routledge Companion to Media Fandom*, edited by Melissa A. Click and Suzanne Scott. https:// search.ebscohost.com/login.aspx?direct=true&scope=site&db=nlebk&db=nlabk& AN=1625504.

Busse, Kristina and Shannon Farley. (2013). 'Remixing the Remix: Fannish Appropriation and the Limits of Unauthorised Use', *M/C Journal* 16 (4). http://journal.media-culture.org.au/index.php/mcjournal/article/ viewArticle/659/%22http://dx.doi.org/10.3983/%22http://voyagesoftheartemis. blogspot.com/2010/05/fan-fiction-and-moral-conundrums.html%22%20%5Ch.

Butler, Judith. (2011). *Bodies That Matter: On the Discursive Limits of 'Sex'*. New York: Routledge.

Cahn, Susan K. (1993). 'From the "Muscle Moll" to the "Butch" Ballplayer: Mannishness, Lesbianism, and Homophobia in U.S. Women's Sport', *Feminist Studies* 19 (2): 343–68. https://doi.org/10.2307/3178373.

Caines, Michael. (2018). 'The Regeneration Game', *The Times Literary Supplement*. Audio/ Visual, 6030 (October). https://www.the-tls.co.uk/articles/the-regeneration-game/.

Caldwell, Tracy L. and Paulina Wojtach. (2020). 'Men Are Funnier Than Women under a Condition of Low Self-Efficacy but Women Are Funnier Than Men under a

Condition of High Self-Efficacy', *Sex Roles* 83 (5–6): 338–52. https://doi.org/10.1007/
s11199-019-01109-w.

Castle, Terry. (1993). *The Apparitional Lesbian: Female Homosexuality and Modern
Culture*. New York: Columbia University Press.

Castle, Terry. (2013). *Boss Ladies, Watch Out!: Essays on Women, Sex and Writing*.
New York: Taylor and Francis.

Chamberlain, Shannon. (2020). 'Fan Fiction Was Just as Sexual in the 1700s as It
Is Today', *The Atlantic*. 14 February 2020. https://www.theatlantic.com/culture/
archive/2020/02/surprising-18th-century-origins-fan-fiction/606532/.

Chaney, Thyra. (2021). 'Age of Exploitation: Teen Sex Comedy Films of the 1980s', *The
Downtown Review* 8 (1). https://engagedscholarship.csuohio.edu/tdr/vol8/iss1/1.

Cho, Sumi, Crenshaw Kimberlé Williams, and Leslie McCall. (2013). 'Toward a Field
of Intersectionality Studies: Theory, Applications, and Praxis', *Signs* 38 (4): 785–810.
https://doi.org/10.1086/669608.

Clare, Ralph. (2017). 'Ghostbusters 2.0: An Equal Opportunity Franchise, edited
by Joseph Tabbi'. *American Book Review* 38 (2): 8,15. https://doi.org/10.1353/
abr.2017.0001.

Coccia, Emily. (2022). 'Femslash Fandom and the Cultivation of White Queer
Genealogies: Longing for Histories, Reading for Futures', *Transformative Works and
Cultures* 37 (March). https://doi.org/10.3983/twc.2022.2225.

Coppa, Francesca. (2017). *The Fanfiction Reader: Folk Tales for the Digital Age*.
Michigan: University of Michigan Press.

Coren, Victoria. (2012). 'Lucy Liu Playing Dr Watson: Put That in Your Pipe
and Smoke It', *The Guardian*. 14 October 2012. http://www.theguardian.com/
commentisfree/2012/oct/14/victoria-coren-lucy-liu-sherlock-holmes.

Cornell, Paul, ed. (1997). *License Denied: Writings from the Doctor Who Underground*.
1st ed. London: Virgin Books.

Crenshaw, Kimberle. (1991). 'Mapping the Margins: Intersectionality, Identity Politics,
and Violence against Women of Color', *Stanford Law Review* 43 (6): 1241–99. https://
doi.org/10.2307/1229039.

Cuelenaere, Eduard. (2021). 'The Remake Industry: The Practice of Remaking Films
from the Perspective of Industrial Actors', *Adaptation* 14 (1): 43–63. https://doi.
org/10.1093/adaptation/apaa016.

De Herder, William. (2021). 'So Bad It's Good: Articulations of Power in Ironic Film
Criticism', *The Journal of Popular Culture* 54 (2): 432–52. https://doi.org/10.1111/
jpcu.13009.

Derecho, Abigail. (2006). 'Archontic Literature: A Definition, a History, and Several
Theories of Fan Fiction', in *Fan Fiction and Fan Communities in the Age of the
Internet: New Essays*, edited by Karen Hellekson and Kristina Busse, 61–78. Jefferson,
NC: McFarland & Co.

Dill, Karen E., Brian P. Brown, and Michael A. Collins. (2008). 'Effects of Exposure to Sex-Stereotyped Video Game Characters on Tolerance of Sexual Harassment', *Journal of Experimental Social Psychology* 44 (5): 1402–8. https://doi.org/10.1016/j.jesp.2008.06.002.

Doctor Who. (2005–ongoing). UK: BBC.

Douglas, Edwards. (2017). '*Ghostbusters*: Paul Feig Talks Internet Backlash', *Den of Geek*. 27 April 2017. http://www.denofgeek.com/us/go/264279.

Doyle, Sir Arthur Conan. ([1892]1986). *The Complete Sherlock Holmes*. Deutschland: Openbook Publishing. online self-collection from https://sherlock-holm.es/.

Duffett, Mark, ed. (2017). 'Fan Practices', in *Fan Identities and Practices in Context: Dedicated to Music*, edited by Mark Duffett, 113–18. New York, NY: Routledge.

Duggan, Jennifer. (2022). 'Transformative Readings: Harry Potter Fan Fiction, Trans/Queer Reader Response, and J. K. Rowling', *Children's Literature in Education* 53 (2): 147–68. https://doi.org/10.1007/s10583-021-09446-9.

Dym, Brianna, Jed Brubaker, and Casey Fiesler. (2018). '"They're All Trans Sharon": Authoring Gender in Video Game Fan Fiction', *Game Studies* 18 (3). http://gamestudies.org/1803/articles/brubaker_dym_fiesler.

Ehrenrich, Barbara, Elizabeth Hess, and Gloria Jacobs. (1992). 'Beatlemania: Girls Just Want to Have Fun', in *The Adoring Audience*, edited by Lisa A. Lewis, 84–106. London: Routledge.

Elam, Diane. (1994). *Feminism and Deconstruction: Ms. En Abyme*. London; New York: Routledge.

Elementary. (2012–2019). California, USA: CBS.

Ellison, Hannah. (2013). 'Submissives, Nekos and Futanaris: A Quantitative and Qualitative Analysis of the Glee Kink Meme', http://participations.org/Volume%2010/Issue%201/8%20Ellison10%201.pdf.

etothepii. (2011). 'Seems So Easy for Everybody Else', Archive of Our Own. http://archiveofourown.org/works/198418.

Eyles, Allen. (1986). *Sherlock Holmes: A Centenary Celebration*. 1st U.S. ed. New York: Harper & Row.

Fang, Yijie. (2021). 'Blurring Boundaries: How Writing Slash Fanfiction Empowers Young Women in Mainland China', *Columbia Undergraduate Research Journal* 5 (1). https://doi.org/10.52214/curj.v5i1.7503.

Farghaly, Nadine. (2015). *Gender and the Modern Sherlock Holmes: Essays on Film and Television Adaptations since 2009*. North Carolina: McFarland.

Farley, Shannon K. (2013). 'Translation, Interpretation, Fan Fiction: A Continuum of Meaning Production', *Transformative Works and Cultures* 14. https://doi.org/10.3983/twc.2013.0517.

Fathallah, Judith. (2014). 'Moriarty's Ghost or the Queer Disruption of the BBC's *Sherlock*', *Television & New Media*. July. https://doi.org/10.1177/1527476414543528.

Feng, Peter X. (2002). *Screening Asian Americans*. United Kingdom: Rutgers University Press.

Ferber, Taylor. (2017). 'Paul Feig Regrets That His *Ghostbusters* Remake Became a "Cause"', *Vulture*. 20 November 2017. http://www.vulture.com/2017/11/paul-feig-regrets-that-ghostbusters-remake-became-a-cause.html.

Fey, Tina. (2011). *Bossypants*. United Kingdom: Hachette, UK.

Fiesler, Casey, Shannon Morrison, and Amy S. Bruckman. (2016). 'An Archive of Their Own: A Case Study of Feminist HCI and Values in Design', in *CHI '16: Proceedings of the 2016 CHI Conference on Human Factors in Computing Systems*, General Chairs: Jofish Kaye, Allison Druin, and Program Chairs: Cliff Lampe, Dan Morris, Juan Pablo Hourcade, 2574–85. New York, NY: ACM Press. https://doi.org/10.1145/2858036.2858409.

Flicker, Eva. (2003). 'Between Brains and Breasts—Women Scientists in Fiction Film: On the Marginalization and Sexualization of Scientific Competence', *Public Understanding of Science* 12 (3): 307–18. https://doi.org/10.1177/0963662503123009.

Foster, Guy Mark. (2015). 'What To Do If Your Inner Tomboy Is a Homo: Straight Women, Bisexuality, and Pleasure in M/M Gay Romance Fictions', *Journal of Bisexuality* 15 (4): 509–31. https://doi.org/10.1080/15299716.2015.1092910.

Frey, J. M. (2009). 'Water Logged Mona Lisa - Who Is Mary Sue, and Why Do We Need Her?' Masters thesis, Canada: Ryerson University and York University.

Gatens, Moira. (1996). *Imaginary Bodies Ethics, Power, and Corporeality*. London; New York: Routledge. http://search.ebscohost.com/login.aspx?direct=true&scope=site&db=nlebk&db=nlabk&AN=79949.

Genovese, Megan. (2019). 'Audience Reception of Intersectional Genderbent and Racebent Casting in *Elementary*', in *Pop Culture Matters: Proceedings of the 39th Conference of the Northeast Popular Culture Association*, edited by Martin F. Norden and Robert E. Weir, 148–58. United Kingdom: Cambridge Scholars Publishing.

Ghostbusters. (1984). Dir. Ivan Reitman. USA: Columbia-Delphi Productions.

Ghostbusters: Answer the Call. (2019). Dir. Paul Feig. USA: Columbia Roadshow.

Gilbert, Sarah Beth. (2017). '"Captain of the Innuendo Squad": Captain Jack Harkness' Sexuality, Addressing Homosocial Bonding, and Plot Use of Queer Characters in *Doctor Who*', *The Apollonian: A Journal of Interdisciplinary Studies* 4 (3): 106–113.

Gilbey, Ryan. (2014). 'Annie Proulx Regrets Writing *Brokeback Mountain*? She Needs to Let It Go', *The Guardian*. 29 December 2014, sec. Opinion. https://www.theguardian.com/commentisfree/2014/dec/29/annie-proulx-regrets-writing-brokeback-mountain.

Gray, Jonathan, Cornel Sandvoss, and C. Lee Harrington, eds. (2007). *Fandom: Identities and Communities in a Mediated World*. New York: New York University Press.

Gray, Jonathan, Cornel Sandvoss, C. Lee Harrington, and Kristina Busse, eds. (2017). 'Intimate Intertextuality and Performative Fragments in Media Fanfiction', in *Fandom, Second Edition: Identities and Communities in a Mediated World*, 45–59. New York: New York University Press.

Green, Shoshanna, Cynthia Jenkins, and Henry Jenkins. (1998). "'Normal Female Interest in Men Bonking": Selections from the "Terra Nostra Underground" and "Strange Bedfellows"', in *Theorizing Fandom: Fans, Subculture and Identity*, edited by Cheryl Harris and Alison Alexander, 9–38. Cresskill, NJ: Hampton Press.

Guerra, Cristela. (2017). 'Where'd the "Me Too" Initiative Really Come from? Activist Tarana Burke, Long before Hashtags – The Boston Globe', *BostonGlobe.Com*. 17 October 2017. https://www.bostonglobe.com/lifestyle/2017/10/17/alyssa-milano-credits-activist-tarana-burke-with-founding-metoo-movement-years-ago/o2Jv29v6ljObkKPTPB9KGP/story.html.

Guerrero-Pico, Mar and Carlos A. Scolari. (2016). 'Narrativas Transmedia y Contenidos Generados Por Los Usuarios: El Caso de Los Crossovers', *Cuadernos.Info* (38) (May): 183–200. https://doi.org/10.7764/cdi.38.760.

Gunnels, Jen, and Carrie J. Cole. (2010). 'Culturally Mapping Universes: Fan Production as Ethnographic Fragments', *Transformative Works and Cultures* 7. http://journal.transformativeworks.org/index.php/twc/article/view/241.

Hadas, Leora. (2014). 'Running the Asylum? *Doctor Who*'s Ascended Fan-Showrunners', *Deletion SciFi* 5 (June). https://www.deletionscifi.org/episodes/episode-5/running-asylum-doctor-whos-ascended-fan-showrunners/.

Halberstam, Jack. (1998). *Female Masculinity*. Durham: Duke University Press.

Halberstam, Jack. (2012). 'Global Female Masculinities', *Sexualities* 15 (3–4): 336–54. https://doi.org/10.1177/1363460712436480.

Hannell, Briony. (2020). 'Fan Girls', in *The International Encyclopedia of Gender, Media, and Communication*, edited by Ingrid Bachmann, Valentina Cardo, Sujata Moorti, and Marco Scarcelli, 1st ed. United Kingdom: Wiley. https://doi.org/10.1002/9781119429128.iegmc010.

Harmes, Marcus K. (2014). *Doctor Who and the Art of Adaptation: Fifty Years of Storytelling*. Washington, DC: Rowman & Littlefield.

Harmon, Amy. (1997). 'In TV's Dull Summer Days, Plots Take Wing on the Net', *The New York Times*. 18 August 1997, sec. Business Day. https://www.nytimes.com/1997/08/18/business/in-tv-s-dull-summer-days-plots-take-wing-on-the-net.html.

Harrington, C. Lee, Denise D. Bielby, and Anthony R. Bardo. (2011). 'Life Course Transitions and the Future of Fandom', *International Journal of Cultural Studies* 14 (6): 567–90. https://doi.org/10.1177/1367877911419158.

Haslett, M. (1994), 'Only the Ones We Love', *Skaro* (Winter): 10.

Haslop, Craig. (2016). 'Bringing *Doctor Who* Back for the Masses: Regenerating Cult, Commodifying Class', *Science Fiction Film & Television* 9 (2): 209–27. https://doi.org/10.3828/sfftv.2016.9.3.

Hellekson, Karen. (2010). 'History, the Trace, and Fandom Wank', in *Writing and the Digital Generation: Essays on New Media Rhetoric*, edited by Heather Urbanski, 58–69. Jefferson, NC: McFarland.

Hellekson, Karen and Kristina Busse, eds. (2006). *Fan Fiction and Fan Communities in the Age of the Internet: New Essays*. Jefferson, NC: McFarland & Co.

Hellekson, Karen and Kristina Busse, eds. (2014). *The Fan Fiction Studies Reader*. Iowa: University of Iowa Press.

Hermes, Joke, and Linda Kopitz. (2021). 'Casting for Change: Tracing Gender in Discussions of Casting through Feminist Media Ethnography', *Media and Communication* 9 (2): 72–85. https://doi.org/10.17645/mac.v9i2.3878.

Higgins, Michelle. (2014). 'Meet Our December Cover Star, Natalie Dormer', *Flare*. 4 November 2014.

Hills, Matt. (2013a). *Fan Cultures*. 1st ed. Hoboken: Taylor and Francis.

Hills, Matt. (2013b). 'From Chris Chibnall to Fox: *Torchwood's* Marginalized Authors and Counter-Discourses of TV Authorship', in *A Companion to Media Authorship*, edited by Jonathan Gray and Derek Johnson, 200–20. Oxford, UK: Wiley-Blackwell. https://doi.org/10.1002/9781118505526.ch10.

Hills, Matt. (2014). 'From Dalek Half Balls to Daft Punk Helmets: Mimetic Fandom and the Crafting of Replicas', *Transformative Works and Cultures* 16 (June). https://doi.org/10.3983/twc.2014.0531.

Hills, Matt. (2015a). 'Storyselling and Storykilling: Affirmational/Transformational Discourses of Television Narrative', in *Storytelling in the Media Convergence Age*, 151–73. London: Palgrave Macmillan. https://doi.org/10.1057/9781137388155_9.

Hills, Matt. (2015b). 'The Expertise of Digital Fandom as a "Community of Practice": Exploring the Narrative Universe of Doctor Who', *Convergence* 21 (3): 360–74. https://doi.org/10.1177/1354856515579844.

Hills, Matt. (2018). 'Peter Capaldi's "Enduring Fandom" and the Intersectionality of Ageing Male Fan-Celebrity: Becoming, Playing and Leaving the 12th Doctor in Doctor Who', *Celebrity Studies* 9 (2): 202–15. https://doi.org/10.1080/19392397.2018.1465297.

Hills, Matt. (2021). 'Toxic YouTubers "Hated" by Doctor Who? Animating Multiphrenic Incarnations of Not My Doctor Anti-Fandom', *Literatura Ludowa. Journal of Folklore and Popular Culture* 65 (2): 69–82.

Howell, Amanda and Lucy Baker. (2017). 'Mapping the Demimonde: Space, Place, and the Role of the Flaneur, Medium, Alienist and Explorer in *Penny Dreadful*', *Refractory* 28.

Hunting, Kyra. (2012). '*Queer as Folk* and the Trouble with Slash', *Transformative Works and Cultures* 11 (September). https://doi.org/10.3983/twc.2012.0415.

Ibarra, Herminia and Jennifer L. Petriglieri. (2010). 'Identity Work and Play', *Journal of Organizational Change Management* 23 (1): 10–25. https://doi.org/10.1108/09534811011017180.

Irigaray, Luce, ed. (1991). *The Irigaray Reader*. Blackwell: Oxford.

Jeffers Mcdonald, Tamar E. L. (2012). 'The View from the Man Cave: Comedy in the Contemporary "Homme-Com" Cycle', in *A Companion to Film Comedy*, edited by Andrew Horton and Joanne E. Rapf, 217–35. Chichester, West Sussex: John Wiley & Sons. https://kar.kent.ac.uk/31625/.

Jenkins, Henry. (2012). *Textual Poachers: Television Fans and Participatory Culture.* New York: Routledge.

Johns, Michelle Marie, Emily Pingel, Anna Eisenberg, Matthew Leslie Santana, and José Bauermeister. (2012). 'Butch Tops and Femme Bottoms? Sexual Positioning, Sexual Decision Making, and Gender Roles among Young Gay Men', *American Journal of Men's Health* 6 (6): 505–18. https://doi.org/10.1177/1557988312455214.

Johnson, Poe. (2019). 'Transformative Racism: The Black Body in Fan Works', *Transformative Works and Cultures* 29 (March). https://doi.org/10.3983/TWC.2019.1669.

Johnson, Poe. (2020). 'Playing with Lynching: Fandom Violence and the Black Athletic Body', *Television & New Media* 21 (2): 169–83. https://doi.org/10.1177/1527476419879913.

Jowett, Lorna. (2014). 'The Girls Who Waited? Female Companions and Gender in *Doctor Who*', *Critical Studies in Television: The International Journal of Television Studies* 9 (1): 77–94. https://doi.org/10.7227/CST.9.1.6.

Karlyn, Kathleen Rowe. (2011). *Unruly Girls, Unrepentant Mothers: Redefining Feminism on Screen.* 1st ed. Austin: University of Texas Press.

Kennedy-Karpat, Colleen. (2020). 'Adaptation and Nostalgia', *Adaptation* 13 (3): 283–94. https://doi.org/10.1093/adaptation/apaa025.

Kies, Bridget. (2017). 'Film Review', *Queer Studies in Media & Popular Culture* 2 (2): 265–8. https://doi.org/10.1386/qsmpc.2.2.265_5.

Kozinets, Robert V. (2009). *Netnography: Doing Ethnographic Research Online.* London: SAGE.

Kramer, Adam D. I., Jamie E. Guillory, and Jeffrey T. Hancock. (2014). 'Experimental Evidence of Massive-Scale Emotional Contagion through Social Networks', *Proceedings of the National Academy of Sciences* 111 (24): 8788–90. https://doi.org/10.1073/pnas.1320040111.

Kukka, Silja. (2021). 'Fandom's Pornographic Subset: Kink Meme Communities as Queer Female Practices', *Lambda Nordica* 26 (1): 53–79. https://doi.org/10.34041/ln.v26.721.

Lackner, Eden, Barbara Lynn Lucas, and Robin Anne Reid. (2006). 'Cunning Linguists: The Bisexual Erotics of Words/Silence/Flesh', in *Fan Fiction and Fan Communities in the Age of the Internet: New Essays*, edited by Karen Hellekson and Kristina Busse, 189–206. Jefferson, NC: McFarland & Co.

Lang, Nico. (2016). 'Free Jillian Holtzmann: It's Time for Sony to Let the Most Compelling Ghostbuster Be out and Proud', *Salon.* 19 July 2016. https://www.salon.com/2016/07/18/free_jillian_holtzmann_its_time_for_sony_to_let_the_best_character_from_ghostbusters_be_out_and_proud/.

Lawson, Caitlin E. (2018). 'Platform Vulnerabilities: Harassment and Misogynoir in the Digital Attack on Leslie Jones', *Information, Communication & Society* 21 (6): 818–33. https://doi.org/10.1080/1369118X.2018.1437203.

Leng, Rachel. (2013). 'Gender, Sexuality, and Cosplay: A Case Study of Male-to-Female Crossplay', *The Phoenix Papers* 1 (1): 89–110.

Levi, Antonia, Mark McHarry, and Dru Pagliassotti, eds. (2008). *Boys' Love Manga: Essays on the Sexual Ambiguity and Cross-Cultural Fandom of the Genre*. Jefferson, NC: McFarland & Co.

Lewis, Rebecca, Alice E. Marwick, and William Clyde Partin. (2021). '"We Dissect Stupidity and Respond to It": Response Videos and Networked Harassment on YouTube', *American Behavioral Scientist* 65 (5): 735–56. https://doi.org/10.1177/0002764221989781.

Lothian, Alexis, Kristina Busse, and Robin Anne Reid. (2007). '"Yearning Void and Infinite Potential": Online Slash Fandom as Queer Female Space', *English Language Notes* 45 (2): 103.

Loving, Olivia. (2012). 'Creativity (Or Lack Of It) in Hollywood: Adapted Scripts Take Over', *NYU Local*. 2 March 2012. http://nyulocal.com/entertainment/2012/03/02/creativity-or-lack-of-it-in-hollywood-adapted-scripts-take-over/.

Lowe, J. S. A. (2020). 'Toward a Queered and/as Affective Theory of Fandom', *Transformative Works and Cultures* 34 (September). https://doi.org/10.3983/twc.2020.1959.

MacCormack, Patricia. (2008). 'Perversion: Transgressive Sexuality and Becoming-Monster', *Thirdspace: A Journal of Feminist Theory & Culture* 3 (2). http://thirdspace.ca/index.php/journal/article/viewArticle/maccormack.

Mackay, Finn. (2019). 'Always Endangered, Never Extinct: Exploring Contemporary Butch Lesbian Identity in the UK', *Women's Studies International Forum* 75 (July): 102241. https://doi.org/10.1016/j.wsif.2019.102241.

Mar, Raymond A., Keith Oatley, and Jordan B. Peterson. (2009). 'Exploring the Link between Reading Fiction and Empathy: Ruling out Individual Differences and Examining Outcomes', *Communications* 34 (4): 407–28. https://doi.org/10.1515/COMM.2009.025.

Marriott, Zoë. (2011). 'The Zoë-Trope: You Can Stuff Your Mary Sue Where the Sun Don't Shine', *The Zoë-Trope* (blog). 1 August 2011. http://thezoe-trope.blogspot.com.au/2011/08/you-can-stuff-your-mary-sue-where-sun.html.

Martin, George R. R. (2010). 'Someone Is Angry on the Internet', Livejournal. *Not A Blog* (blog). 7 May 2010. https://grrm.livejournal.com/151914.html.

Marwick, Alice E. (2021). 'Morally Motivated Networked Harassment as Normative Reinforcement', *Social Media + Society* 7 (2). https://doi.org/10.1177/20563051211021378.

Massey, Erica Lyn. (2019). 'Borderland Literature, Female Pleasure, and the Slash Fic Phenomenon', *Transformative Works and Cultures* 30 (September). https://doi.org/10.3983/twc.2019.1390.

McClellan, Ann. (2014). 'Redefining Genderswap Fan Fiction: A *Sherlock* Case Study', *Transformative Works and Cultures* 17. https://doi.org/10.3983/twc.v17i0.553.

McDougall, Sophia. (2013). 'I Hate Strong Female Characters', *New Statesman*. 15 August 2013. http://www.newstatesman.com/culture/2013/08/i-hate-strong-female-characters.

McGuire, Seanan. (2011). 'I Know a Little Girl and Her Name Is Mary Mac: The Misuse of Mary Sue.' 11 October 2011. http://seanan-mcguire.livejournal.com/396047.html.

McNutt, Myles. (2017). '*The 100* and the Social Contract of Social TV [Symposium]', *Transformative Works and Cultures* 26 (October). https://doi.org/10.3983/TWC.2018.1297.

Miller, Laura. (2013). 'Fan Fiction: The Next Great Literature?' *Pacific Standard*. 26 November 2013. https://psmag.com/social-justice/fan-fiction-next-great-literature-67706.

Moi, T. (2008). '"I Am Not a Woman Writer": About Women, Literature and Feminist Theory Today', *Feminist Theory* 9 (3): 259–71. https://doi.org/10.1177/1464700108095850.

Monaco, Jeanette. (2010). 'Memory Work, Autoethnography and the Construction of a Fan-Ethnography', *Participations: Journal of Audience & Reception Studies* 7 (1): 102–42.

Morrison, Connie. (2016). 'Creating and Regulating Identity in Online Spaces: Girlhood, Social Networking, and Avatars', in *Girlhood and the Politics of Place*, edited by Claudia Mitchell and Carrie Rentschler, 244–58. United Kingdom: Berghahn Books.

Nagaike, Kazumi and Kaori Yoshida. (2011). 'Becoming and Performing the Self and the Other: Fetishism, Fantasy, and Sexuality of Cosplay in Japanese Girls'/Women's Manga', *Asia Pacific World* 2 (2): 22–43. https://doi.org/10.3167/apw.2011020204.

Narai, Ria. (2017). 'Female-Centered Fan Fiction as Homoaffection in Fan Communities', *Transformative Works and Cultures* 24 (June). https://doi.org/10.3983/twc.2017.01014.

Navar-Gill, Annemarie and Mel Stanfill. (2018). '"We Shouldn't Have to Trend to Make You Listen": Queer Fan Hashtag Campaigns as Production Interventions', *Journal of Film and Video* 70 (3): 85–100.

Nepveu, Kate. (2010). 'Diana Gabaldon & Fanfic Followup – Incidents and Accidents, Hints and Allegations – LiveJournal', *Livejournal*. 10 May 2010. https://kate-nepveu.livejournal.com/483239.html.

Nguyen, Giselle Au-Nhien. (2017). 'Tunesday – the Uncredited Lady behind the *Doctor Who* Theme Song', *Frankie Magazine*. 12 December 2017. https://www.frankie.com.au/article/tunesday-the-uncredited-lady-behind-the-doctor-who-theme-song-544250.

Noble, Jean Bobby. (2004). *Masculinities without Men?: Female Masculinity in Twentieth-Century Fictions*. Sexuality Studies Series. Vancouver: UBC Press.

Oak, Alan and Jenny Ashley. (2011). 'Review: Intro to Fanfiction and Slash', *Extrapolation* 52 (1): 128–30.

Oeming, Madita. (2021). 'Porn Poacher: Coming Out as an Aca Porn Fan', in *Porn and Its Uses (Special Issue Co-Edited for Synoptique: An Online Journal for Film and Moving Images)*, edited by Nikola Stepic, Rebecca Holt, and Darshana Sreedhar Mini, 245–52. Canada: Concordia University.

Ogas, Ogi and Sai Gaddam. (2012). *A Billion Wicked Thoughts: What the Internet Tells Us about Sexual Relationships*. Maryland: Penguin Publishing Group.

Pande, Rukmini. (2016). 'Squee from the Margins: Racial/Cultural/Ethnic Identity in Global Media Fandom', in *Seeing Fans: Representations of Fandom in Media and Popular Culture*, edited by Lucy Bennett and Paul Booth, 209–20. India: Bloomsbury Publishing USA.

Pande, Rukmini. (2018). *Squee from the Margins: Fandom and Race*. Fandom & Culture. Iowa City: University of Iowa Press.

Parry, Becky. (2013). 'Film Identities in Practice', in *Children, Film and Literacy*, edited by Becky Parry, 88–117. London: Palgrave Macmillan. https://doi.org/10.1057/9781137294333_6.

Pearson, Roberta. (2007). 'Bachies, Bardies, Trekkies, and Sherlockians', in *Fandom: Identities and Communities in a Mediated World*, edited by Jonathan Gray, Cornel Sandvoss, and C. Lee Harrington, 98–109. New York: New York University Press.

Pink, Sarah. (2008). 'An Urban Tour the Sensory Sociality of Ethnographic Place-Making', *Ethnography* 9 (2): 175–96. https://doi.org/10.1177/1466138108089467.

Popova, Milena. (2018). '"Dogfuck Rapeworld": Omegaverse Fanfiction as a Critical Tool in Analyzing the Impact of Social Power Structures on Intimate Relationships and Sexual Consent', *Porn Studies* 5 (2): 175–91. https://doi.org/10.1080/23268743.2017.1394215.

Primorac, Antonija. (2013). 'The Naked Truth: The Postfeminist Afterlives of Irene Adler', *Neo-Victorian Studies* 6 (2): 89–113.

Proctor, William. (2017). '"Bitches Ain't Gonna Hunt No Ghosts": Totemic Nostalgia, Toxic Fandom and the Ghostbusters Platonic', *Palabra Clave – Revista de Comunicación* 20 (4): 1105–41. https://doi.org/10.5294/pacla.2017.20.4.10.

Proctor, William and Will Brooker. (2019). 'Part Three and into the Future', *Critical Sudies in Television Online Blogs* (blog). 24 December 2019. https://cstonline.net/part-three-and-into-the-future-by-will-brooker-and-william-proctor/.

Proctor, William, Bridget Kies, Bertha Chin, Katherine Larsen, Richard McCulloch, Rukmini Pande, and Mel Stanfill. (2018). 'On Toxic Fan Practices: A Round-Table', *Participations* 15 (1): 24.

Raw, Adrienne E. (2020). 'Rhetorical Moves in Disclosing Fan Identity in Fandom Scholarship', *Transformative Works and Cultures* 33 (June). https://doi.org/10.3983/twc.2020.1731.

Reid, Robin Anne. (2009). 'Thrusts in the Dark: Slashers' Queer Practices', *Extrapolation* 50 (3): 463–83.

Reid, Robin Anne. (2016). 'Ethics, Fan Studies and Institutional Review Boards', *The Journal of Fandom Studies* 4 (3): 275–81. https://doi.org/10.1386/jfs.4.3.275_1.

RIP Doctor Who | *Jodie Whittaker's Doctor Was Destined to FAIL.* (2021). [YouTube]. Nerdrotic. https://www.youtube.com/watch?v=l6xHOz0UcQs&list=TLPQMjkwNTI wMjGGsVuGLgVvwA&index=2.

Rose, Jonathan A. (2020). "'My Male Skin": (Self-)Narratives of Transmasculinities in Fanfiction', *European Journal of English Studies* 24 (1): 25–36. https://doi.org/10.1080 /13825577.2020.1730044.

Ross, Iain. (2012). *Oscar Wilde and Ancient Greece.* United Kingdom: Cambridge University Press.

Rossiter, Hannah. (2016). 'She's Always a Woman: Butch Lesbian Trans Women in the Lesbian Community', *Journal of Lesbian Studies* 20 (1): 87–96. https://doi.org/10.108 0/10894160.2015.1076236.

Rothblum, Esther D., Kimberly F. Balsam, and Robert E. Wickham. (2018). 'Butch, Femme, and Androgynous Gender Identities within Female Same-Sex Couples: An Actor-Partner Analysis', *Psychology of Sexual Orientation and Gender Diversity* 5 (1): 72–81. https://doi.org/10.1037/sgd0000258.

Russ, Joanna. (1985). *Magic Mommas, Trembling Sisters, Puritans & Perverts: Feminist Essays.* The Crossing Press Feminist Series. Trumansburg, NY: Crossing Press.

Salmon, Catherine. (2015). 'The Impact of Prenatal Testosterone on Female Interest in Slash Fiction', *Evolutionary Behavioral Sciences* 9 (3): 161–9. https://doi.org/10.1037/ebs0000051.

Salmon, Catherine and Donald Symons. (2001). *Warrior Lovers: Erotic Fiction, Evolution and Female Sexuality.* New Haven, CT: Yale University Press.

Salmon, Catherine and Donald Symons. (2004). 'Slash Fiction and Human Mating Psychology', *The Journal of Sex Research, Evolutionary and Neurohormonal Perspectives on Human Sexuality* 41 (1): 94–100.

Sandvoss, Cornell. (2005). *Fans: The Mirror of Consumption.* Cambridge, MA: Polity Press.

Schur, Edwin M. (1984). *Labeling Women Deviant: Gender, Stigma, and Social Control.* New York: McGraw-Hill.

Scodari, Christine. (2003). 'Resistance Re-Examined: Gender, Fan Practices, and Science Fiction Television', *Popular Communication* 1 (2): 111–30. https://doi.org/10.1207/S15405710PC0102_3.

Sedgwick, Eve Kosofsky. (1985). *Between Men: English Literature and Male Homosocial Desire.* New York: Columbia University Press.

Shaw, David. (2016). 'Facebook's Flawed Emotion Experiment: Antisocial Research on Social Network Users', *Research Ethics* 12 (1): 29–34. https://doi.org/10.1177/1747016115579535.

'Sherlock (TV Series) – Fanlore'. (n.d.). Accessed 16 May 2017. https://fanlore.org/wiki/Sherlock_(TV_series).

Spender, Dale. (1985). *Man Made Language.* London; Boston: Routledge & Kegan Paul.

Stagg, Guy. (2012). 'Casting Lucy Liu as Dr "Joan" Watson Will Ruin One of the Great Bromances of All Time', *Culture – Telegraph Blogs* (blog). 29 February 2012. http://blogs.telegraph.co.uk/culture/guystagg/100061063/casting-lucy-liu-as-dr-joan-watson-will-ruin-one-of-the-great-bromances-of-all-time/.

Stanfill, Mel. (2013). 'Fandom, Public, Commons', *Transformative Works and Cultures* 14. https://doi.org/10.3983/twc.v14i0.530.

Stanfill, Mel. (2019). *Exploiting Fandom: How the Media Industry Seeks to Manipulate Fans*. Iowa City: University of Iowa Press.

Stanfill, Mel. (2020). 'Introduction: The Reactionary in the Fan and the Fan in the Reactionary', *Television & New Media* 21 (2): 123–34. https://doi.org/10.1177/1527476419879912.

Stein, Louisa Ellen, Kristina Busse, and Matt Hills, eds. (2014). 'Sherlock's Epistemological Economy and the Value of "Fan" Knowledge: How Producer-Fan's Play the (Great) Game of Fandom', in *Sherlock and Transmedia Fandom: Essays on the BBC Series*, 27–40. Jefferson, NC: McFarland.

Stella, Massimo, Emilio Ferrara, and Manlio De Domenico. (2018). 'Bots Increase Exposure to Negative and Inflammatory Content in Online Social Systems', *Proceedings of the National Academy of Sciences* 115 (49): 12435–40. https://doi.org/10.1073/pnas.1803470115.

Stout, Rex. (1941). 'Watson Was a Woman', *The Saturday Review of Literature* 23 (19): 3–4, 16.

Swann, Erik. (2021). 'Kevin Smith and the Russo Brothers Teamed Up for a New TV Show about Marvel and DC Comics', *Cinema Blend*. 16 December 2021. https://www.cinemablend.com/superheroes/kevin-smith-and-the-russo-brothers-teamed-up-for-a-new-tv-show-about-marvel-and-dc-comics.

Taylor, Noah. (2013). 'The Art of the Title: *Elementary*', *The Art of the Title*. 21 May 2013. http://www.artofthetitle.com/title/elementary/.

Throsby, Corin. (2010). *Flirting with Fame: Byron and His Female Readers*. United Kingdom: University of Oxford.

Tompkins, Jessica Ethel. (2019). 'Is Gender Just a Costume? An Exploratory Study of Crossplay', *Transformative Works and Cultures* 30 (September). https://doi.org/10.3983/twc.2019.1459.

Turner, Simon. (2016). 'Yaoi Online: The Queer and Affective Practices of a Yaoi Manga Fan Community', Ph.D., Birkbeck, University of London. http://bbktheses.da.ulcc.ac.uk/166/.

Valentine, Genevieve. (2013). '*Elementary* Demonstrates the Right Way to Update a Classic Hero', Io9. 21 May 2013. http://io9.com/elementary-demonstrates-the-right-way-to-update-a-class-509009246.

Van Steenhuyse, Veerle. (2011). 'The Writing and Reading of Fan Fiction and Transformation Theory', *CLCWeb: Comparative Literature and Culture* 13 (4). https://doi.org/10.7771/1481-4374.1691.

Walker, Tracy Deonn. (2019). 'Narrative Extraction, #BlackPantherSoLit, and Signifyin': *Black Panther* Fandom and Transformative Social Practices', *Transformative Works and Cultures* 29 (March). https://doi.org/10.3983/twc.2019.1643.

Wanzo, Rebecca. (2015). 'African American Acafandom and Other Strangers: New Genealogies of Fan Studies', *Transformative Works and Cultures* 20 (20). http://journal.transformativeworks.org/index.php/twc/article/view/699.

Warner, Helen. (2013). "'A New Feminist Revolution in Hollywood Comedy"?: Postfeminist Discourses and the Critical Reception of *Bridesmaids'*, in *Postfeminism and Contemporary Hollywood Cinema*, edited by Joel Gwynne and Nadine Muller, 222–37. London: Palgrave Macmillan. https://doi.org/10.1057/9781137306845_14.

Weisser, J. T. (2019). 'Transmasculinities and Pregnant Monstrosity: *Hannibal* Omegaverse Fan-Fiction', *Cultivate*. June. https://cultivatefeminism.com/transmasculinities-and-pregnant-monstrosity-hannibal-omegaverse-fan-fiction/.

Wilder, Billy. (1970). *The Private Life of Sherlock Holmes*. Film – Billy Wilder is the director. United Artists. https://en.wikipedia.org/wiki/The_Private_Life_of_Sherlock_Holmes.

Williams, Rebecca. (2015). *Post-Object Fandom: Television, Identity and Self-Narrative*. New York: Bloomsbury Academic.

Willis, Ika. (2006). 'Keeping Promises to Queer Children: Making Space (for Mary Sue) at Hogwarts', in *Fan Fiction and Fan Communities in the Age of the Internet: New Essays*, edited by Karen Hellekson and Kristina Busse, 153–70. Jefferson, NC: McFarland & Co.

Willis, Ika. (2012). 'Transgender Identification: Slash Fiction and the Erotics of Reception', Gender Studies seminar, University of Melbourne. March. http://ro.uow.edu.au/lhapapers/419/.

Willis, Ika. (2016). 'Amateur Mythographies', *Transformative Works and Cultures* 21. https://doi.org/10.3983/twc.2016.0692.

Wilson, Anna. (2016). 'The Role of Affect in Fan Fiction', *Transformative Works and Cultures* 21. https://doi.org/10.3983/twc.2016.0684.

Woolf, Virginia. (1996). *A Room of One's Own and Three Guineas*. United Kingdom: Random House.

Yamato, Jen. (2017). '*Ghostbusters* Director Paul Feig on the Film's Misogynistic Trolls: "It's Not for All These Guys!"' *Daily Beast*. 7 December 2017. https://www.thedailybeast.com/ghostbusters-director-paul-feig-on-the-films-misogynistic-trolls-its-not-for-all-these-guys.

Yi, Erika Junhui. (2012). 'Reflection on Chinese Boys' Love Fans: An Insider's View', *Transformative Works and Cultures* 12. https://doi.org/10.3983/twc.v12i0.424.

Yodovich, Neta. (2020). "'Finally, We Get to Play the Doctor": Feminist Female Fans' Reactions to the First Female *Doctor Who'*, *Feminist Media Studies* 20 (8): 1243–58. https://doi.org/10.1080/14680777.2020.1810733.

Zeisler, Andi. (2008). *Feminism and Pop Culture: Seal Studies*. New York: Basic Books.

Index

as activism 36–7
as artefact 153
consumption/production 21, 23, 52
and cosplay 23
as creators and consumers 35, 52–4
cross-dressing 87
as ethnodramaturgs 22
fannishness (*see* fannishness)
feminist media and cultural theory 8
illegitimacy 48
intense emotionality 5
interview questions 166
and ivory tower 43
and literary adaptation 72
literary ancestors of 17
as political praxis 41, 43
professional adaptations 3, 6–9, 25, 58,
    93, 105, 154–5
regendered adaptations and 6, 48
researcher analysis 4
social media 4
survey questions 160–5
of transformative works 30, 33, 48, 90,
    154
transgender 52, 101
turning mirror on themselves 61–2
Farley, Shannon K. 43
Fathallah, Judith 121
Feig, Paul 12, 124–5, 130, 135, 138
    Bridesmaids 125
    Ghostbusters: Answer the Call (*see*
        Ghostbusters: Answer the Call
        (2016, Feig))
female/feminine 15, 24, 39, 42, 49, 55, 62,
    66, 78–9, 105, 114, 120, 130–1, 146
    aesthetic 74 n.2
    audience 66, 148, 157
    binary construction/representation
        (gender) 27, 64
    characters (regendering) 41, 49, 66,
        72–4, 130
    cisfemale 36, 60, 64
    embodiment and essentialism 26
    fans 26, 33–4, 45 n.1, 50, 144–5, 147
    female-female relationship 85
    feminist activism 49
    intersectional demands 26
    oppression 26, 37, 42–3, 50, 100

performances 42, 49, 74 n.2, 80–1, 83,
    85, 88–9, 99, 107, 118, 131
    pornography 55, 78–9, 84
    transgressiveness 47, 50, 53, 75, 100
feminist theory 2, 55, 154
femmeslash 82–3, 86, 90
Fey, Tina 24
Fremedon, Ellen 32. *See also* Id Vortex

Gaddam, Sai 78
Gatens, Moira 26, 49, 67
The Gateways 74, 76, 78, 86–7, 89
gender 1, 3–4, 6, 9, 12, 21, 23, 27, 37, 42,
    64, 67, 69, 73–4, 88, 90, 93, 105,
    144, 154
    binary and representation 5, 27, 60,
        63–4, 101, 103, 146–7, 149
    and cosplay 8
    diversity 10, 103–4
    dysphoria 69, 103–4
    enlightenment 60
    genderbend 37, 60, 62, 162
    gender-blind casting 43
    gender-creative fanwork 23, 25, 52,
        153–4
    genderswap 8, 40, 42, 57, 60–1, 65, 82,
        162
    non-conformity/creativity 36, 46, 54–5,
        63–4, 73, 130
    non-normativity 94, 100, 147–8
    performance 60, 74 n.2, 77, 80–1, 87,
        103, 107, 111, 150
    play 57–8
    race and 47, 51, 112, 150, 157
    roles 15, 18, 25, 49, 61, 64, 78, 82, 85–6,
        90, 103, 116, 132, 148–9
    science and 130–1
    sexuality and (*see* sexuality, gender
        and)
    stereotypes 42, 57, 88
    theory 1, 45, 48
    transgression 75, 110, 118, 120, 154
    transition 68
gendered violence 27, 36, 77, 100, 109
genderfuck works 93
gender identity 1, 25, 30, 34, 46, 58, 65–6,
    158
    domestic violence 94